SACRED VIEWS

Before you start to read this book, take this moment to think about making a donation to punctum books, an independent non-profit press,

@ https://punctumbooks.com/support/

If you're reading the e-book, you can click on the image below to go directly to our donations site. Any amount, no matter the size, is appreciated and will help us to keep our ship of fools afloat. Contributions from dedicated readers will also help us to keep our commons open and to cultivate new work that can't find a welcoming port elsewhere. Our adventure is not possible without your support.

Vive la Open Access.

Fig. 1. Hieronymus Bosch, *Ship of Fools* (1490–1500)

Sacred Views of Saint Francis: The Sacro Monte di Orta. Copyright © 2020 by the authors. Unless mentioned otherwise, all photography © 2020 J. Ross Peters. This work carries a Creative Commons BY-NC-SA 4.0 International license, which means that you are free to copy and redistribute the material in any medium or format, and you may also remix, transform and build upon the material, as long as you clearly attribute the work to the authors (but not in a way that suggests the authors or punctum books endorses you and your work), you do not use this work for commercial gain in any form whatsoever, and that for any remixing and transformation, you distribute your rebuild under the same license. http://creativecommons.org/licenses/by-nc-sa/4.0/

First published in 2020 by punctum books, Earth, Milky Way.
https://punctumbooks.com

ISBN-13: 978-1-950192-77-9 (print)
ISBN-13: 978-1-950192-78-6 (ePDF)

DOI: 10.21983/P3.0283.1.00

LCCN: 2020935343
Library of Congress Cataloging Data is available from the Library of Congress

Book design: Vincent W.J. van Gerven Oei
Cover image: The Seraph appears to St. Francis. Ceiling fresco, Chapel XV, Sacro Monte di Orta. © 2020 J. Ross Peters.

HIC SVNT MONSTRA

Sacred Views of Saint Francis
The Sacro Monte di Orta

Cynthia O. Ho,
Kathleen Peters &
John McClain

To Cynthia Ho, our co-author and the originator of this project.
Her friendship and talent inspired its completion.

Pace e Bene

Cynthia Ho (1947–2014)

Table of Contents

Foreword · 13

Preface · 21

Chapter 1. The Sacro Monte di Orta within Franciscan Tradition · 25

Chapter 2. Catalogue of Chapels · 53
Chapel I. The Nativity of St. Francis · 55
Chapel II. The Speaking Crucifix of San Damiano · 58
Chapel III. St. Francis Renounces His Worldly Goods · 62
Chapel IV. St. Francis Listening to the Mass · 64
Chapel V. The First Followers of St. Francis Take the Habit · 68
Chapel VI. St. Francis Sends His First Disciples Out to Preach & Miracles Confirm the Preaching · 70
Chapel VII. Pope Innocent III Gives His Approval of the Order · 72
Chapel VIII. St. Francis on a Chariot of Fire · 75
Chapel IX. St. Clare Takes the Veil · 78
Chapel X. St. Francis Victorious over Temptation/Satan · 80
Chapel XI. The Indulgence of the Porziuncola · 84
Chapel XII. God Reveals the Rule to St. Francis · 87
Chapel XIII. The Humility of St. Francis · 90
Chapel XIV. St. Francis and the Sultan · 95
Chapel XV. St. Francis Receives the Stigmata · 98
Chapel XVI. St. Francis, Nearing Death, Returns to Assisi · 101
Chapel XVII. The Death of St. Francis · 104
Chapels XVIII, XIX, and XX: The Basilica of Assisi · 108
Chapel XVIII. The Vision of Francis in the Crypt · 110
Chapel XIX. The Miracles at the Saint's Tomb · 111
Chapel XX. The Canonization of St. Francis · 111
The New Chapel · 114

Chapter 3. The Birth of St. Francis · 125

Chapter 4. The Framework of St. Francis' Spiritual Journey · 133

Chapter 5. St. Francis' Triumph over Temptation · 151

Chapter 6. King Carnival in the Yoke of Humility · 161

Chapter 7. Advancing the Council of Trent · 171

Biographies of the Designers and Artists of the Sacro Monte di Orta · 181

Bibliography · 191

FOREWORD

Sacred Views of St. Francis: The Sacro Monte di Orta examines a Renaissance-era pilgrimage site, a sacred mountain that is a compelling essay placed in full relief against the visually stunning backdrop of the Northern Italian Alps. The ceiling of Chapel XX of the Sacro Monte stands as the powerful final paragraph of that essay, one in which priests, architects, artists, and craftsmen strove to create a case for St. Francis' powerful brand of *imitatio Christi*. On this ceiling Francis is ascending, while Christ, God, and the entire host of angels await him with crowns (see Fig. 1). There is music, too, a celestial symphony occasioned by the arrival of the man of Asissi in the realm beyond man. Created on a shaded hilltop on a small peninsula on the shore of Lake Orta, the Sacro Monte di Orta is made up of twenty chapels spread across the gentle hilltop topography dedicated to sharing the meaning and legacy of the life of St. Francis (see Fig. 2 and Chapter 1, Fig. 4). The ceiling of Chapel XX is not simply a conclusion to the essay, it is the powerful coda for the experience the pilgrims have as they traverse the chapels over the course of a day.

The ceiling of Chapel XX represents the end of an overwhelming *Life* of a Saint, a hagiography tracing Francis' nativity through the chapters of his life to his death and ascension. The case made above the picturesque setting of Lago di Orta, which sits like a thin blue teardrop at the mouth of the Ossola Valley, is more than a simple *Life*, however. It is an argument made to an exterior world beyond the Italian peninsula, up the Ossola Valley, and over the Semplon Pass, and it is a love letter to the population of the peninsula itself. The ideological landscape was changing at a speed seldom, if ever, matched in history, and this Sacred Mountain entered the fray both as part of a larger push against Protestantism, as well as a sort of theatrical homily imploring the body of the remnant church to have faith in its efficacy and continued centrality. Indeed, as opposed to the case regarding the preeminence of Francis that had to be made to the archbishops depicted in the terra-cotta diorama of Chapel XX, the Sacro Monte read as a whole is in large part a populist expression of the primacy of Francis' position in a post-Tridentine world. Francis is a local hero, an Italian, whose presence among them calls for their connection through him, through the Church, to God. His life, as presented on the verdant hilltop, is a reinterpretation of the gospel attributed to Christ: "I am the way."

Descending from the vision of Archbishop Carlo Borromeo, the design and execution of the chapels expresses the Church's desire to define, or perhaps better, redefine, itself for a transforming Christian diaspora. In the course of a few hours, pilgrims trace the text of Francis' life until in the end any ambiguity about Francis' centrality is finally erased as they see him rising to take possession of the crowns that await him. To see the ceiling

Fig. 1. St. Francis' Ascension into Heaven, Ceiling Chapel XX, Sacro Monte di Orta.

Fig. 2. View of Lago Orta and Isola San Giulio from the Sacro Monte di Orta.

of Chapel XX at all, however, requires turning one's eyes up, a task Chapel XX makes, and indeed to one degree or another each Chapel of the Sacro Monte di Orta makes, remarkably difficult, for the most immediate attractions in each chapel are the figures that populate them. They are a remarkable community of figures, representing all walks of life.

Francis had a vital role to play at this moment in the history of the Italian peninsula, and in no place is the case for his relevance made more beautifully, completely and comprehensively than the Sacro Monte di Orta. Riding a wave of enthusiasm created by the success of the Sacro Monte di Varallo, forty miles to the west, this Sacro Monte is both spectacle and hagiography, theme park and treatise. Its critical differences from the Sacro Monte di Varallo define and contextualize its importance.

There are a number of Sacri Monti in Northern Italy, the ones at Varallo and Orta being among the most fully realized and carefully preserved. Grouped together as World Heritage sites, it is all too easy to note their similarities and diminish their differences; however, when examining Varallo and Orta, the contrast is enlightening as it pertains to understanding the aesthetic and strategic vision of Orta. With over forty chapels, the Sacro Monte di Varallo leads the pilgrim on a far more rugged, exhausting and convoluted path than the Sacro Monte di Orta. It seems designed to challenge the pilgrim to exhaustion not only physically but spiritually. Perhaps the designers of Varallo were bent on shocking the pilgrim into submission to Christ and thus the Church. With chapels devoted to the Fall of Adam and Eve (Chapel I), Jesus' capture (Chapel XXIII), Jesus' trials (before Annas, Caiaphas, Pontius Pilate, and Herod, Chapels XXIV, XXV, XXVII, and XXIX respectively), and ten separate chapels devoted to stages of the Passion (see Fig. 3), perhaps most poignant example remains Chapel XI, "Slaughter of the Innocents" (see Fig. 4). It is grotesque, graphic, and leaves

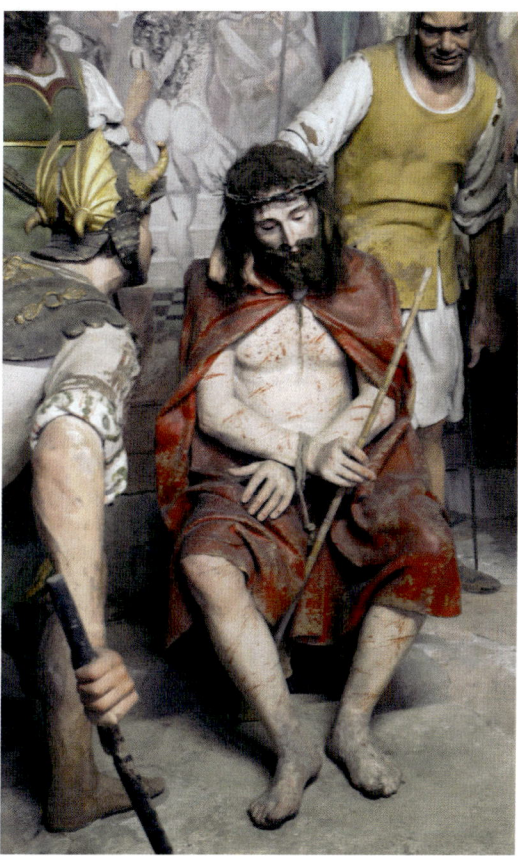

Fig. 3. Jesus Crowned with Thorns, Chapel XXXI, Sacro Monte di Varallo.

no doubt the designers were determined to demonstrate that the scene from Matthew's Gospel rivals the darkest moments of the Old Testament for horrors. Amidst such scenes of suffering, a pilgrim might lose sight of the Good News of Christ. The Sacro Monte di Orta on the other hand, constructed across a far softer landscape than Varallo, strives to use the life path of Francis to inspire the pilgrims to lead lives of Francis-like devotion.

While at times graphic, there is little to turn a pilgrim away at the Sacro Monte di Orta, certainly nothing as grotesque and graphic as some of the imagery in the chapels at Varallo. Even in Chapel X, "The Temptation," the pilgrim's gaze is pulled visually away from the deeply shadowed devils on the left (see Chapter 5, Fig. 1) and toward the radiant angels on the right (see Chapter 5, Fig. 2),

Fig. 4. Slaughter of the Innocents, Chapel XI, Sacro Monte di Varallo.

Fig. 5. The Franciscan Coat of Arms, Sacro Monte di Varallo.

compelling us to read the text of Francis' elevation from left to right. While the position of mankind is clearly precarious in Chapel X, a sentiment close to the heart of Borromeo's messaging, in this chapel the pilgrims' gaze moves quickly passed that dark prospect and beyond the chapel toward salvation—Francis' and perhaps their own.

The purposefulness of the site is strategically different as well. Telling the story of Christ was about translating verbal text to visual-theatrical text, yes, but it was not about proving that Jesus was Christ, while Sacro Monte di Orta is centered on making a nuanced case that Francis was something between a saint and a second Christ. Our authors point out later in this volume that Francis at Orta is presented as a *ne plus ultra* saint—something more than a saint and less than divine. So while Varallo is filled with episodes of Christ's life and particularly the extended narrative of his suffering and his death, Orta is an essay that elevates Francis not simply to sainthood but something just shy of the divinity occupied solely by the Father, Son, and Holy Spirit (see Fig. 5). Thus the Sacro Monte di Orta is a bold assertion of Francis' significance set bucolically above Orta San Giulio. Fascinatingly, this construct plays out in scenes where an observant pilgrim finds ample connections between Francis and numerous individuals and stories of the biblical tradition. Through its dioramas and its frescoes, the Sacro Monte di Orta conceives of Francis not only in the context of *imitatio Christi*, but also in the full panoply of biblical texts and its most sacred figures.

Often the Sacri Monti of the Piedmont have been described as spiritual barriers against frightening messages coming from Northern Europe as the engines of the Reformation generated more and more heat; however, the purposefulness of Orta is far more dynamic than the thesis of a spiritual barrier could fully explain. It is borne of a passion to bring a message of the Church's own strengthening position. By affirming the devotional role of art, the veneration of saints, the value of pilgrimage, and the power of the papacy, along with other doctrinal positions, the Sacro Monte di Orta is a stunning artifact of the Catholic Reformation; and its creation is not simply a defense against Protestantism but, even more, it is an offensive against it. It is righteous and purposeful propaganda standing both as a message to the outside world and importantly, as an epistle to the internal world of the Italian milieu. Demonstrating the intimacy of the message is the fact that Francis as represented in these chapels is deeply human—he is also a figure made more approachable by the proximity of the life he led to the lives of the pilgrims who made the trek to the Sacro Monte. The Holy Land must have seemed many worlds away. Its loss as a pilgrimage site also distanced Christ from the faithful. Francis, if made into viable conduit, allowed the faithful closer access to the divine than Christ could now provide. He was a local and somewhat contemporary hero compared to the more distant legendary status of Christ; thus the syllogism becomes: "He is one of us; he led a life that led to heaven; therefore, we will go to heaven as well if we follow his way"—a way that aligns with Catholicism.

The figures from the actual story of Francis—the nameable participants: Peter Bernadone, St. Clare, Lady Jacoba, Pope Innocent III, Pope Nicholas V, Pope Gregory IX, even Francis himself—are often the least interesting figures in any particular tableau. It is the extras that lend the chapels their lasting immediacy: an old woman, a multiple amputee, a dwarf, children, animals. In this way the most visually compelling chapels—XIII, XIV, XVI, XX—are more than simply theatre, they are operatic in their structure where each voice becomes present as a pilgrim scans through the momentum of each action-packed scene. These chapels tell a story that can only be told as a communal expression. The implicit message is that Francis and his story belong both to the terracotta figures in each chapel, as well as to the pilgrims viewing the scene. The poignancy of this idea intensifies when one recognizes that the kiln that heated and hardened the clay of the figures was located beside Chapel XIX, and evidence indicates that the models for many of the figures were likely people that lived in the area, perhaps as close as the ten-minute walk down to Orta San Giulio further narrowing the space between pilgrim, the figures in the chapels, and Francis. Thus, by the transitive property the Sacro Monte brings the catholic communion in short order from the world they inhabit, through Francis—a saint whose faith and action define his hagiography—to the divine. Notably, in Chapel XX representation of the Conclave that debated Francis' potential sainthood includes the explicit message that the path also goes through Rome. Francis' ascension as represented here reasserts the critical relevance of the *Roman Catholic Church*.

Here we come to the most crucial point: in the Sacro Monte we can see in physical representation the fine line, maybe an impossible line, the Church was attempting to walk after the Council of Trent—that is, the Church was seeking the narrow space between enfranchising a nascent kind of populism in the Piedmont, while re-cementing the hierarchical primacy of the Church. In virtually the same breath, the Church is giving Francis' story to the people and claiming it for Rome.

In Italy's post-Tridentine moment, we can see through to this tension in the presentation of contemporary figures who are dressed in period clothing. The figures in each chapel are remarkable for their clothes and the representations of fabric. The realistic presentation, intended to bring Francis to the pilgrim as much as to bring the pilgrim across time and space to Francis, embodies an idea not easily accepted in the Rome of the same period. The rigidity of the Catholic Church in Rome expressed itself through its religious art. Caravaggio, who spent much of his prime in Rome, grew up close enough to the Sacro Monte di Varallo to have borne the influence of the site throughout his career. If one looks at the cold reception of Caravaggio's style in Rome at this very moment in time, one can see evidence of the divisions in the peninsula. Caravaggio, whose chiaroscuro was influenced by the presentation of figures at Sacro Monte di Varallo, echoed the sort of theatrical presentation found at the Sacri Monti far more than the less dynamic presentations of the very artists who were quickest to dismiss his approach in Rome. They were in fact offended by his style due to the fact that it was realistic to an apparently blasphemous degree. In order to strengthen the tie of Rome to the piedmont, the Church needed something more than a one size fits all approach to proselytizing the primacy of the Catholic Church. They need a strategy that would work beyond Rome that Rome itself was not prepared for. What remained largely above reproach in Rome no longer could be a winning strategy beyond Rome. The Sacro Monte di Orta serves as an artifact of that recognition.

Caravaggio's volatile period in Rome is a harbinger the imminent arrival of change not only across Europe but in the seat of Catholicism itself. The eternal tensions between Rome and piedmont, between city and country, between educated and ignorant, between wealth and poverty, between high and low culture, and between desire to preserve a status quo and join a revolution sift to the surface through Caravaggio and the Sacro Monte di Orta, and sooner or later it was bound to leave a mark not simply beyond Rome on a hilltop beside a piedmont lake but within Rome as well.

Through the Sacro Monte di Orta, the peninsula of Orta San Giulio becomes a microcosm of the Italian peninsula itself, thus allowing the population of pilgrims who visited this Sacro Monte to see 'the way" as beginning from where they were rather than from an increasingly distant and abstract sense of Rome, much less the Holy Land. As a result, the Sacro Monte di Orta becomes the Rome of the Ortan Peninsula, a place where pilgrims could see their own faces close to the face of one as blessed as Francis. It was therefore vital to make Francis into more than a saint, one whose name might be lost in a quickly expanding catalogue of saints. In his role as a *ne plus ultra* saint, Francis provides a special link between humanity and the divine, a particular necessity in the face of the German Protestant threat.

After spending so much time photographing the chapels for *Sacred Views of Saint Francis: The Sacro Monte di Orta*, I began to wonder what we can know about these people who served as models for the terracotta figures. I also imagined their descendants visiting the chapels to see those clay faces echoed in their own. What were they trying to tell us through this fascinating place that they created on a bucolic hilltop? I now believe they have some relevant advice for us:

- **Live lives of civic engagement.** They were participants in, not simply observers of, their community. They helped create their world, as opposed to simply commenting on it.
- **Value the future, and believe in legacy.** The chapels were always intended for permanency. The commitment necessary to design them, build them, complete them was extraordinary. Our world often seems to value planned obsolescence over and above permanency.
- **See our lives among others as acts of devotion and as expressions of faith.** The chapels are filled with stunningly beautiful and ornate artwork: paintings, terracottas, ironwork, woodwork, stone carving. It seems clear that talented artisans spent years of their lives working in just this one site. Working on the Sacro Monte, which is completely focused on St. Francis, was in and of itself an expression of both faith and devotion. Their life of faith was inseparable from their professional lives.
- **Welcome the entire world community to share in important stories.** The figures in the chapels are not visions of ideal form nor do they represent one ethnicity or background. Many types of people are represented—African people, European people, Middle Eastern people, rich and poor, young, old and in between people, Christians, a Jew, Muslims, a Native American, as well as various individuals with physical impairments—a man with a goiter examines Francis' stigmata in one chapel, while a multiple amputee stares off wistfully in another. The scenes in the chapels seem to invite the world—not just the world at the beginning of the seventeenth century, but our world as well—to the story of St. Francis.

The authors of this volume believe we have much to learn from them.

J. Ross Peters
Caza Cinzia, 2019

PREFACE

Among Franciscan literature, the spiritual exercises, also known as meditations, have had perhaps the most lasting impact for Christians of all varieties. These meditations, such as the pseudo-Bonaventuran *Meditationes vitae Christi*, call on the reader to "seek," "hear," "touch," and "see" in their imagination the discrete moments in the Passion of Christ. Sarah McNamer describes the literature as "scripts"—an apt description of texts that direct the reader's mood and behavior. She identifies the texts as the mise-en-scène for the "production of emotion" that aspires to the "performance of feeling," and for the mediations, that feeling is compassion.[1] The hope of the believer is that through compassion for the suffering and death of Jesus, they will achieve a more intimate knowledge of God.

Like the meditations, pilgrimage too is performative but as both a spiritual and physical exercise. Also like the meditations, pilgrimage of the Late Medieval and Early Modern periods was orchestrated. No longer simple wandering, it was "goal centered, religious travel for an efficacious purpose,"[2] such as atonement, release, personal growth, new connections to a community of faith, or new connections to the divine. In sum, the pilgrim's goal was personal transformation. By the Early Modern period, pilgrimage and the use of images were two loci of Protestant contestation. The Council of Trent (1545–1563) affirmed the value of the practices, and various church agents, including the Archbishop of Milan, Cardinal Carlo Borromeo (active 1564–84), worked to assure the orthodox embrace of both.

The Sacri Monti, sacred mountain complexes developed over the 15th–18th centuries in the Lombard and Piedmont regions of northern Italy, are distinctive pilgrimage centers. They are cultural phenomena influenced by historical context: Ottoman control of the Holy Land; high costs of pilgrimage travel abroad; and, in the main, a desire to promote in plastic the decisions of the Council of Trent. They are centers where the traditions of spiritual exercises, pilgrimage, and imagery combined into a Church-approved multisensory, multimedia, multivalent theater for the penitential soul.

With an emphasis on affective devotion, mimesis allowed the pilgrim to a Sacro Monte to become a member of the Jerusalem crowd, to feel Christ's suffering, or to share in Mary's grief in a very tactile way: to seek, hear, see and touch as embodied witness within the simulacrum. At the Sacro Monte di Orta, which sims the spiritual life of St. Francis of Assisi, the pilgrim's goal is to conform to Francis the way the saint conformed to Jesus, to know Jesus through simming Francis.

The Sacri Monti offer important testimony not only to the Counter Reformation, but to popular religious practice and popular artistic forms as well. Yet as a focus of academic attention, their share has been concomitantly small, especially for English readers whose access to published material has been very limited. This is especially true in the case of the Sacro Monte di Orta, which has long stood in the shadow of its older and more well known counterpart, the Sacro Monte di Varallo.[3] In the following pages we hope to bring the richness of the Sacro Monte di Orta to a modern audience in the first English language large-scale treatment and as such we have used, whenever possible, scholarly articles and translations in the English language. *Sacred Views of Saint Francis: The Sacro Monte di Orta* is intended for an audience of both experts and lay readers. It contains analysis such as that found in scholarly works as well as the stunning photography of a picture book for which our photographer chose work in natural light in order to capture the daytime experience of the pilgrim.[4] With our publisher, punctum books, we affirm our commitment to open access and the free intellectual commons that benefits everyone. The grandeur of the site, in terms of both depth and breadth, extends beyond that of a single monograph and the open-access platform of punctum allows us to make ongoing additions with supplemental text and the development of a large photo index. This current edition includes introductory material, a catalogue of all the chapels, chapters devoted to particular chapels, a biographical list of the artists, and accompanying photographs.

Acknowledgment belongs first and foremost to Cynthia Ho. In the early 2000's Cindy, a well-regarded medieval scholar, bought a palazzo in Vogogna, Italy, after falling in love with its seventeenth-century frame and the neighborhood's storied association with Chaucer. As she explored the Piedmont, Cindy came across the Sacro Monte di Orta. Cindy found it compelling, so compelling in fact that she changed her research agenda and began an ambitious project to bring the richness of the Sacro Monte di Orta to English language readers and researchers. Sadly, by 2012 Cindy had been diagnosed with a rare, and terminal, cancer; yet, her dedication to the research project did not abate. Instead she enlisted the help of two colleagues, one with expertise in religious studies and material culture, the other a scholar of early modern Europe. She asked the husband of the first colleague, an educator, poet, and photographer, to take the photographs. This book is the product of Cindy's vision. Cin cin, Cinzia.

We are also indebted to Community of the Franciscan friars, the traditional Custodians of the Sacro Monte di Orta, whose centuries of service preserved the site into the postmodern era. The Italian National Park Service and Caesare, our indefatigable park ranger, were indispensable in facilitating our work. Lauren Crow, friend and tour guide, helped us secure the permissions we needed to get behind the scenes at the Sacro Monte di Orta, while friends Ken and Kali Marquart of the Associazione Canova, and Nicole Rose of Palazzo del Gabelliere, welcomed us into their homes over the years. Fr. Noel Muscat assisted with translation of the seventeenth-century Italian edition of Mark of Lisbon's *Croniche degli ordini istituiti dal P. San Francesco*, and we owe special thanks to Atlas Savini Kinzel for his mapmaking acumen. Our deepest gratitude is also due Dr. John Paul McDonald, omnipresent grammarian, linguist, and colleague in every sense; Eleanor Spencer Peters for her wry humor, patience, and willingness to "count the goiters"; the family of Cynthia Ho, especially Johnnie Ho, Amy Olson Chang, Elise Olson and Rebecca Geier, for their unerring encouragement; and Eileen Joy at punctum books for her steadfast belief in this project.

Endnotes

1   Sarah McNamer, *Affective Meditation and the Invention of Medieval Compassion* (Philadelphia: University of Pennsylvania Press, 2010), 11–14.

2   Maribel Deitz, *Wandering Monks, Virgins, and Pilgrims: Ascetic Travel in the Mediterranean World, AD 300–800* (University Park: The Pennsylvania State University Press, 2005), 7.

3   The following list is a sample of literature on the Sacri Monti: Luigi Zanzi, *Sacri Monti e Dintorni: Studi sulla cultura religiosa e artistica della Controriforma*, 2nd edn. (Milan: Jaca Book, 2005); Valère Novarina and Marc Bayard, *Sacri Monti Incandescence baroque en Italie du Nord* (Paris: L'Autre Monde, 2012); Loredana Racchelli, ed., *Antiche Guide del Sacro Monte di Orta* (Orta: Ente di Gestione delle Reserve Naturali Speciali del Sacro Monte di Orta, del Monte Mesma e del Colle della Torre di Buccione, 2008); the bilingual Italian–English Carola Benedetto, ed., *Donne e Madonne nei Sacri Monti del Piemonte e della Lombardia* (Savigliano: L'Artictica Savigliano, 2010); and two guides which have been translated from the Italian: E. de Filippis and F.M. Carcano, *Guide to the Sacro Monte of Orta* (Novara: Riserva Naturale Speciale del Sacro Monte di Orta, 1991), and Fr. Angel Maria Manzini, O.F.M. Cap., *Sacro Monte of Orta* (Orta: Community of the Franciscan Friars, Custodian of the Sacro Monte of Orta, 2006). For scholarly works in English, see, for example, Samuel Butler, *Ex Voto: An Account of the Sacro Monte or New Jerusalem at Varallo-Sesia* (London: Dodo Press, 1888); William Hood, "The Sacro Monte of Varallo: Renaissance Art and Popular Religion," in *Monasticism and the Arts*, eds. Timothy Verdon and John Dally (Syracuse: Syracuse University Press, 1984), 291–311; Alexander Nova, "'Popular' Art in Renaissance Italy: Early Response to the Holy Mountain at Varallo," in *Reframing the Renaissance: Visual Culture in Europe and Latin America, 1450–1650*, ed. Claire Farago (New Haven: Yale University Press, 1995), 113–26; D. Medina Lasansky, "Body Elision: Acting Out the Passion at the Italian Sacri Monti," in *The Body in Early Modern Italy*, eds. Julia L. Hairston and Walter Stephens (Baltimore: Johns Hopkins University Press, 2010), 249–23; Christine Göttler, "The Temptation of the Senses at the Sacro Monte di Varallo," in *Religion and the Senses in Early Modern Europe*, eds. Wietse de Boer and Christine Göttler (Leiden: Brill, 2013), 393–451; Geoffrey Symcox, "Varallo and Oropa: Two Sacri Monti and the House of Savoy," in *La Maison de Savoie et les Alpes: emprise, innovation, identifications XVe–XIXe siècle; Actes du 4e Colloque international des Sabaudian Studies 15–17 mai 2014, Grenoble*, eds. Stéphane Gal and Laurent Perrillat (Grenoble: Université de Savoie Mont Blanc, 2015), 151–66 and *Jerusalem in the Alps: The Sacro Monte of Varallo and the Sanctuaries on North-Western Italy* (Turnhout: Brepols, 2019).

4   Though uncommon, nighttime visits to the chapels were not unheard of, although they seem to have been reserved for special feast days and dignitaries. We know that Carlo Borromeo, Archbishop of Milan, for example, preferred to visit the chapels of Varallo at night (see Göttler, "The Temptation of the Senses," 403). For those occasions, the chapels would have been illuminated with candlelight. Wrought iron candleholders, albeit now without candles, are still present in several of the chapels of the Sacro Monte.

1

THE SACRO MONTE DI ORTA WITHIN FRANCISCAN TRADITION[1]

At the end of the fifteenth century, when the Ottoman Empire had made pilgrimages to the Holy Land increasingly difficult (both physically and financially), Franciscan Bernardino Caimi designed a "New Jerusalem" in the mountains of the Val Sesia of Northwest Italy, above the town of Varallo, to replicate, closer to home, a devotional experience for disenfranchised pilgrims.[2] It would become the first of a series of fifteen sacred mountain complexes constructed between the fifteenth and eighteenth centuries in the mountains of Italy's Piedmont and Lombardy regions. Each complex is based on a certain devotional theme, such as the life of Christ, the Rosary, or the Virgin Mary, and most, but not all, were founded and maintained by Franciscans. These Sacri Monti string a series of chapels, containing frescos and statuary, across the face of a mountain in a narrative sequence. As such, they are massive multi-media projects to provide a direct affective Christian experience. There are now nine Sacri Monti in northern Italy that have been designated as UNESCO World Heritage Sites (see Fig. 1), and the Sacro Monte di Orta, with its twenty chapels narrating the spiritual life of St. Francis of Assisi, is one of these nine.[3]

It is certainly not a coincidence that these sacred complexes were consistently established on remote mountain tops. Mountains are holy in almost all religions where they function as geologic mediators between the divine and the mundane. And in particular for Franciscans, the paradigm for all sacred mountains is La Verna where tradition holds that St. Francis was stigmatized in 1224. Mircea Eliade coined the term *hierophany* (something sacred shows itself to us) to explain this kind of "sacred center" which links earth to heaven, the human and the divine, where time stands still, where the transcendent can be touched.[4] And in particular for Franciscans, the paradigm for all sacred mountains is La Verna where tradition holds that St. Francis was stigmatized in 1224. The material setting also allows for a productive tension between the physical and metaphysical exertion that is at the heart of the pilgrimage experience. As in private devotional practices, the entire body is enlisted to make the experience as fulfilling as possible, for climbing the mountain is a physically strenuous activity that itself demands commitment.

Each of the Italian Sacri Monti is made up of a series of chapels; inside each chapel the pilgrim finds life-size sculptural depictions of a Station of the Cross, a point on the Rosary, an event in the life of Christ, Mary, or Francis (whatever the particular focus of the Sacred Mountian). The earlier figures were carved out of wood, and later ones molded out of terracotta or plaster, with color, real hair and

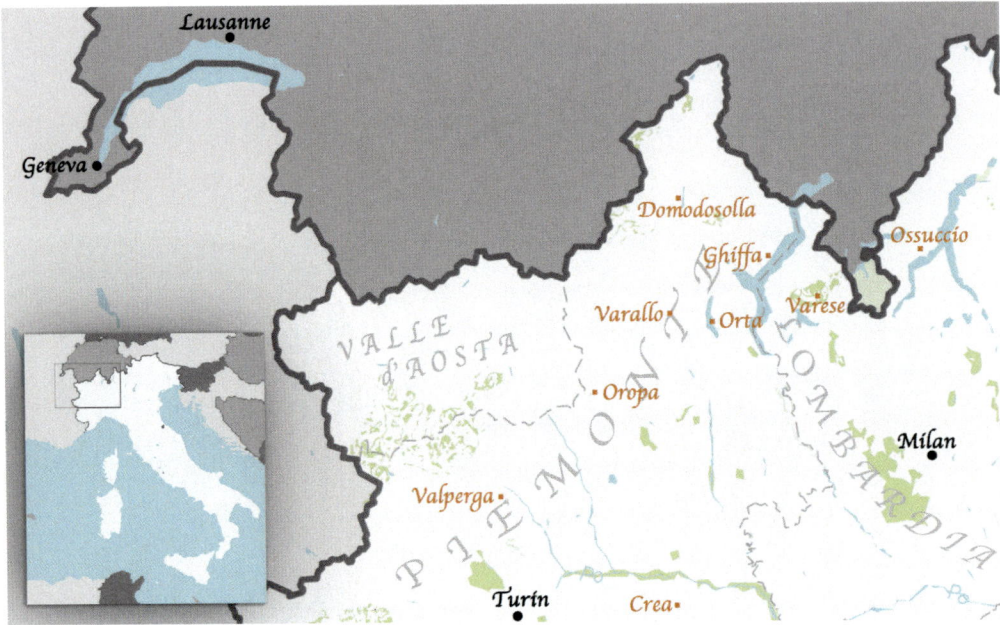

Fig. 1. Map of the Nine UNESCO World Heritage Sacri Monti in Italy. Copyright Atlas Kinzel.

glass eyes applied. The earliest chapels were simple, open, box-like rooms, in which the visitor could walk among the figures; later ones were larger and more complex, with more figures populating them. Since the mid-sixteenth century, the pilgrim has been kept at a distance behind iron or wooden screens often pierced with peepholes placed at ideal viewing points. In addition, the back and side walls are painted in illusionistic frescos that further reinforce the impression that one is beholding historical events being acted out. The artistic program creates levels of framing. The life-size statues are set as if on the depth of a stage; where the sculpture stops against the wall, painting takes up and uses its devices to continue the illusion of the staged event into a farther depth. These tableaux with their intense realism, or what Roberta Panzanelli calls "hyperreality,"[5] come very close in spirit to late medieval theatrical representations and to Francis' own teaching methods.

Popular culture

The Sacro Monte di Orta represents a particular moment of the intersection of high and popular religion in which the Catholic Church made use of images in its efforts to shape lay piety. This Sacred Mountain is thus powerful, public, popular art which has been an artistic, historical, and even literary witness to the aesthetics of northern Italian culture over more than four centuries.

Although many critics consider these spaces merely manifestations of outdated popular culture, they were and still are visited by tens and even hundreds of thousands every year.[6] At the height of its popularity, the site at Varallo had up to ten thousand pilgrims daily.[7] Even today in the summer, there are enough visitors to Orta that a tourist tram stays busy ferrying people up and down the mountain. Despite this sustained appetite for Sacri Monti, appreciation for them has languished in "art's outskirts."[8] Interrelated artistic objections to the sites are responsible for this disregard: a general disdain for their blunt didacticism, their "grotesque" or "vulgar" style, and their "popularity." Today, didacticism "has a strongly negative connotation; it designates works that are too close to propaganda to be artistically valid."[9] Modern readers, attuned to irony and ambiguity, are trained to assume that an artful story cannot be unambiguous. The agenda of these tableaux is to allow viewers to experience "Truth" concretely, so it is necessary for us to examine our prejudices about the place of didacticism in fictional representations in order to understand and appreciate the art of the Sacri Monti.

In addition, the distinctive heterogeneous aspects of the art of the Sacri Monti which fascinated early visitors have attracted later disdain. Real hair, glass eyes, and "readymades" such as clothing, toys, kitchen implements and furniture intensified the verisimilitude and turned, in Nevet Dolev's words, "a second-hand reality into a second reality."[10] However, situations in which "real" objects (re)presented themselves also have been condemned as a breach of artistic faith, overly dramatic, and garish.[11] Even the use of terracotta statuary at the Sacri Monti was cause for disdain. Terracotta, a perfectly acceptable medium for sculpture in fourteenth-century Italy and popular through the fifteenth century, became, by the sixteenth century, scorned as the base material of artisans rather than artists, at best suited to preliminary models rather than the finished work of art.[12] Indeed, Bruce Boucher describes the Sacri Monti as "the last great expression of the tradition of terracotta statuary," a concept that elsewhere had become "obsolete."[13] Thus, in many ways these works are a decidedly different kind of art from the classical works that populated elite private collections of Milan and Florence.

A third complaint about the Sacred Mountains is that they were created for a purely popular and unsophisticated audience. It is true that Borromeo explicitly tried to build upon the culture of the local audience. In 1573, at the Third Provincial Synod, Carlo Borromeo instructed bishops to "diligently collect together the names, character, and pastoral actions of their predecessors." Local antiquarians dedicated themselves to the recovery of historical precedents in order to support their local devotional practices, cults, and legends.[14] But the art of the Sacri Monti was not exclusively popular nor aimed solely at one particular group. The social background of visitors has in fact always been very mixed. While there is no doubt that most early pilgrims belonged to the lower strata, the early audiences also included members of aristocratic and humanistic circles.[15] Alessandro Nova has demonstrated the especially close rapport between the Milanese aristocracy and the Franciscan Observants (and subsequently the Capuchins) who oversaw many of the sites.[16] It seems, then, that the sites were able to speak simultaneously to audiences of differing critical backgrounds and had the capacity to address the well-educated few without ignoring the needs and experiences of both literate and illiterate lay viewers. Of course, scorn for the vernacular character, of either audience or medium, of the Sacri Monti did not faze the Franciscans; the goal was to reach as many people as possible, in the most effective way possible, to advance their message.

Catholic Reformation

The Catholic Reformation was promoted in its own time as a period of peace, prosperity, and cultural revival. But in the twentieth century it was often held responsible for "a closed, hierarchical, authoritarian conformism" which turned art "into a propagandistic base for the absoluteness of its doctrine."[17] The Sacri Monti can in fact be viewed both ways, as important works of art which also represent religious and political agendas. Reaffirming itself as the center of Christendom, the Catholic Church assertively tried to reclaim its margins.

Annabel Wharton points out that the nineteenth-century British traveller and author Samuel Butler advanced the idea that

Sacri Monti may have been built "as a Catholic bulwark against northern dissent."[18] In 1888, Butler wrote of Varallo:

> It was an attempt to stem the torrent of reformed doctrines already surging over many an Alpine pass, and threatening a moral invasion as fatal to the spiritual power of Rome as earlier physical invasions of Northmen had been to her material power.[19]

However, Wharton has argued that the Sacri Monti were begun too early to be a reaction to Luther (whose "Ninety-Five Theses" were publicized in 1517). Focusing her study on Varallo, the earliest of the Sacri Monti (built between 1491 and 1640), she argues that the flow of ideas went in the other direction, and that the Sacri Monti contributed to the northward flow of a Franciscan-inspired "theology of the cross."[20] Wharton is wise in emphasizing the importance of cross-fertilization of ideas during this voluble time. Nevertheless, by the time the Orta chapels were begun almost a hundred years later, Lutherans and Waldensians were powerful movements within a large group of Protestant agitators just across the border from Piedmont and Lombardy. There were clearly propagandistic salvos from both faith groups aimed at the other, and Sacro Monte di Orta was a key player.

The Protestant Reformation posed a number of challenges to Catholic belief and practice which are central to the didactic programs of Orta's chapels. For example, Francis' practice of *imitatio Christi* and subsequent Franciscan claims that he was *alter Christus* were the focus of Protestant critique. The work of Franciscan Bartholomew of Rinonico [sometimes called Bartholomew of Pisa, not to be confused with Bartholomew Albizzi (of Pisa)],'s *De Conformitate Vitae Beati Francisci ad Vitam Domini Jesu* (c. 1385), which contrived dozens of parallels between the life of Jesus and that of Francis, was ridiculed by reformers. Erasmus Alber's *Der barfusser Monche Eulenspiegel und Alcoran* (1542) was a compendium of extracts from *De Conformitate* glossed with satirical commentary and quickly translated into Latin,[21] French, Flemish, and English; the flow of Protestant "editions" continued to appear until the middle of the seventeenth century.[22] Alber's critique was aimed both at some of the ludicrous examples in the text, and at its theological assumptions. Its intent is made clear by the frontispiece of the English translation:

> The Alcoran of the Franciscans, or, A sink of lyes and blasphemies. Collected out of a blasphemous book belonging to that order, called the book of the conformites: with the epistles of Dr Martin Luther, and Erasmus Alberus, detecting the same: formerly printed in Latine, and now made English, for the discovery of the blasphemies of the Franciscans a considerable order of regulars amongst the papists.[23]

The Scottish humanist George Buchanan illustrated the international quality of the European Reformation. One of his first pieces was the *Somnium*, a satire on the Franciscans and monastic life. It was followed by *Franciscanus*, a critique of Bartholomew, which was made into a drama and presented before James V, his queen, and courtiers at Linlithgow Palace on Epiphany of 1539.[24]

The exaltation of Francis was emblematic of the veneration of the saints which was another important point of criticism directed at Roman Catholicism by the Protestant Reformation of the sixteenth century.[25] Early reformers Wycliffe and Hus first expressed doubts about the dogma of saints' veneration, but the issue became especially prominent with Luther, who reinterpreted the "communion of saints" in the *Apostle's Creed* to mean the body of believers.[26] In response to these criticisms the Council of Trent enacted restraints on indulgences, though the Catholic response centered on the problem of abuse and not the essential soundness of the doctrine. Veneration of saints, pilgrimage, indulgences, the sacraments, and the power of the pope were all upheld. The very issue of indulgences presented the faithful with a conundrum: if Christ died for all mankind, and the benefits of his passion have already been applied, why do they need to be accessed once again? The didactic agendas of the chapels at Orta are an answer to these and other critiques.

The Council of Trent and the Borromeos

The religious climate which sustained the production of the Sacri Monti of Northern Italy began with the Council of Trent (1545–63) and subsequent efforts to enforce its proclamations. The Council, which met with the aim of purifying the Catholic faith, considered the correct use of religious art an important tool of internal revitalization. The question of icons and figures has been a contentious one in Christianity, and the Second Council of Nicaea (787 CE) took the official position that images of "the figure of our Lord God and Savior Jesus Christ, of our spotless Lady, the Mother of God, of the Honorable Angels, of all the saints and of all pious people" are essential to Christian worship.[27] In 1563, the Twenty-fifth Session of the Council of Trent issued a statement reiterating these ideals in "On the Invocation, Veneration, and Relics of Saints, and on Sacred Images." Specifics on the production and use of the art were laid out, insisting that all religious art programs should stay focused on the official Truth. The bishop had the role of approving sacred works of art and making sure that art left no room for accidentally errant readings and potential heresy.[28] As a result of the Council of Trent, the desire to revitalize sacred space and its decorations for devotional practice created a flowering of visual piety.

As a cardinal and Archbishop of Milan (1564–1584), Carlo Borromeo was the most influential reformer in the Catholic Reformation drive to implement the Tridentine reforms. In 1565, soon after the close of the Council of Trent and upon the death of his maternal uncle, Pope Pius IV, twenty-seven-year-old Carlo returned from Rome to Milan prepared to give full attention to his ecclesiastical responsibilities.[29] Before returning to the north of Italy, Borromeo had worked on various architectural projects including explorations of the newly discovered Christian catacombs, which helped to develop his sense of a prototype for sacred architecture.[30] Wietse de Boer describes Borromeo's intention to overhaul completely the teaching and practice in the Milanese region as an "extraordinary social experiment" that sought "to transform the social order by reaching into the consciences of its subjects" through "a system of discipline that was comprehensive, consistent, and unswerving."[31] Reformation of the arts became one of his special concerns. His series of written pronouncements demonstrate that the central reality for the Borromean reform is a consistency between the word preached, the art viewed, and the pastoral ministries of baptism, confession, and Eucharist.[32]

Despite the decisions of the Council of Trent, quarrels over the use of religious imagery continued to surface, culminating in intense attacks by iconoclastic Protestant reformers in the sixteenth century. In Italy's Piedmont, efforts to thwart the Protestants were especially vigorous. In 1532 the Waldensians voted to unite with the Calvinists in Geneva, and Catholics and Protestants killed each other across the Alpine borders.[33] Later, in response, a Vatican decree ruled that architecture and art were to be used "to draw the line against Protestantism."[34]

In 1573 and again in 1576 Borromeo warned that those who did not conform to his reform measures regarding painting and sculpture would be heavily fined, clergy as well as artists. He ordered that, "in order that bishops might more easily execute these and other prescriptions of the Council of Trent, let them call together the painters and sculptors of their diocese and inform all equally about things to be observed in produced sacred images."[35] Soon after, in 1577, he published the first full treatise regarding sacred art and architecture, including a summary of Catholic traditions regarding church design, in *Instructiones Fabricae et Supellectilis Ecclesiasticae*. This became the central document that applied the decrees of the Council of Trent to the design and furnishing of Catholic churches. Two chapters and portions of others identify directives regarding the use of decoration, religious images, relics, and graphic inscriptions. Part 17, bearing the lengthy name

> Sacred images and pictures
> what is to be avoided and observed in sacred images
> the dignity of sacred images
> the symbols of the saints
> places unsuitable for sacred pictures
> the ceremony of blessing images
> occasional inscription of saints' names
> accessories and additions for ornamentation
> votive tables ...

has been called "a veritable manifesto against artistic license."[36] Borromeo prescribed the content (historical truth or valid theological teaching) and the viewer response (evocation of piety) for sacred works of art.[37] In this way, the cardinal was a decidedly hands-on micromanager, and surely a surprise to his diocese after decades, even centuries in some cases, of absentee benefice holders. Acting as apostolic visitor, appointed by the pope, he imposed his vision on multiple churches and institutions which had previously been left to follow their own desires.[38]

Carlo Borromeo died in 1584, and in 1589 he was succeeded in Milan by his cousin Federico Borromeo. The lengthy program of renovating and constructing churches begun in Carlo's administration necessarily continued in later years. Coming a generation later, Federico nuanced, but did not change, his sainted cousin's didactic program. What has been called Federico's "Christian Optimism" was the second wave of Catholic Reformation thought and appealed to a sensory appreciation of nature in order to attract contemplative minds to Catholic truth.[39] With this vision, Federico founded what would eventually become the famous Biblioteca Ambrosiana of Milan. In the academy's rules of 1620 he explained that he created the gallery and library in order to teach aspiring artists how to reform sacred art in accordance with the decrees of the Council of Trent. Federico's conception of sacred art's efficacy demanded that it be "natural" in order to reflect Christian truth while appealing to the senses.[40]

The lakeside towns ringing northern Italy's Lake Maggiore all bear the imprint of the noble Borromeo family: land, water, islands, gardens, architecture, castles, churches, even grand hotels. At the southern end of the lake in the port of Arona stands the thirty-five-meter (115 feet) copper statue of San Carlo. Erected in 1624, this huge hollow statue has interior stairs which lead the visitor to the top. From there, one can look out through the saint's eyes at a panorama of the countryside. This literal imposition of Borromeo's gaze upon his domain reifies the power of his reforming vision, which transformed the religious life of northern Italy following the Council of Trent.[41]

It is in this time that a second generation of Sacri Monti flourished in the region, inspired by Varallo and spurred on by "the militant Counter-Reformation values propagated in the archdiocese of Milan" under the auspices of the Borromean cousins.[42] While the idea of the Sacri Monti dates prior to the Council of Trent, and, indeed, the Sacro Monte di Varallo was well established by that time, the imagery and didactic effect that they project was in fact perfectly matched with the programmatic intentions developing from Tridentine and Borromean ideals. Carlo was both patron and pilgrim to the Sacro Monte di Varallo, which represents the life of Christ. Federico was especially interested in two other Sacri Monti, one at Arona devoted to the life of San Carlo and the other, based on the Mysteries of the Rosary, at Varese.[43]

The Borromean cousins demonstrated interest in the Sacri Monti both for their theological implications and for their real presence as pilgrimage destinations. Carlo had a passion for making pilgrimages to Italy's sacred shrines; one of his biographers has written that "he considered pilgrimage a valuable element in that grand design of counter-reform which was the real program of all his pastoral activity."[44] Carlo wrote, "even though in our unhappy times, when the religious exercise of making pilgrimages has diminished to so great an extent, you must not become tepid, my dearest brethren, but you must become more enkindled because this is precisely the time when real Catholics and obedient sons of the church show the zeal of their faith and piety."[45] For the pilgrim, the experience of the Sacri Monti evokes the multivalent aspects of pilgrimage and makes an ideal model for Tridentine visual piety. As Dee Dyas has noted, from the fourth century, the term "pilgrimage" came to refer to a journey with a particular religious goal; the pilgrim is someone who is taking either a literal, physical trip to a place which grants special access to God, a "vortex" of power, or the pilgrim is experiencing one piece of a lifelong spiritual practice.[46] At the Sacri Monti, the tensions between these two kinds of pilgrimage are mediated in one space. Here the pilgrim takes a symbolic journey and worships at a symbolic relic, but they can nevertheless replicate the benefits of the real concrete experience. All Sacri Monti are a facsimile of something else which provides the opportunity for an interior journey, undertaken in common with others.

St. Francis and the Capuchin Reform

Many of the Sacri Monti were built under the aegis of and managed by Franciscans during a period of great Franciscan popularity, led by the Capuchin reform and concomitant with the general renewal of the Catholic Church. As such the shrines may be seen as a visual manifestation of religious revitalization and reaffirmation. The Capuchins were reformers, rigorously pursuing a "perfect imitation of St. Francis and complete fidelity to his every intention."[47] The Order of the Friars Minor Capuchin was established in 1520 by Matteo da Bascio. This new movement was an outgrowth of the Observant tradition that, in turn, developed from the Spirituals. Though the three movements are distinguishable from each other, they all claimed to recapture and emulate the lifestyle first established by their founder, St. Francis of Assisi (1181–1226). To this end, the Capuchin's adopted robes with a capuche (an elongated pointed hood or cowl from which they derive their name) following early sources that depict Francis in robes of that style.[48] For Francis the robe was not mere fashion; it represented the Tau, the Greek form of the last letter of the Hebrew alphabet (Tav), a cruciform symbol of penance inspired by Ezekiel 9:4: "And Yahweh said to him, 'Go through the city, through Jerusalem, and put a mark [tav] on the foreheads of the men who sigh and cry over all the abominations that are done within it.'" As expressed in his *Testament*, doing penance was the foundation of Francis' spiritual life, part of his *raison d'être*, and the Tau was his standard.[49] The Capuchins were further inspired by the physicality of discipline, devotion, and suffering found in 1 Corinthians 9:27, 2 Corinthians 4:10, and Colossians 1:24. They earned a reputation for their dedication to spiritual growth through bodily mortification and, through bodily mortification, an internal mortification of the self in pursuit of union with God:[50]

> Their sufferings were a balm for their consciences. Being pilgrims and strangers on earth, without even a cup of water, they relished their sufferings with delight. They found in them the occasion for acts of penitence for the love of God, and for the observance of holy poverty

and the Rule they had promised to follow.[51]

But in addition to severe austerity, the Capuchins also embraced Francis' missionary work among the general population and importantly, particularly for their long-term success, his recognition of papal authority. And their adaptation of the primitive life to allow for ecclesiastical studies followed along the lines of those established at the Council of Trent (as reflected in the intellectual depth of the artistic program at the Sacro Monte di Orta). Thus the Capuchin Reform worked within the traditional orthodox parameters of the Catholic Church—with its permission and blessing.[52]

In a sense the Sacri Monti may be understood as a Franciscan institution, like the Third Order, whose purpose was to popularize, in the best sense of the word, the great tradition of monastic spirituality. The Franciscans were especially adept at what we would now call "outreach," having been founded as a mendicant order working and living among hoi polloi, particularly the impoverished. St. Francis of Assisi was a teacher of great renown, famous for the humble simplicity of his preaching and pastoral care. He is still revered today, by both Catholics and non-Catholics, for his love of all creation—from lepers to Brother Sun to the lowly wolf.

Some preconceptions we have about St. Francis and his teaching might be colored by our knowledge of the friar's legendary reputation as emulated by the great Franciscan missionary and preacher Bernadino of Siena (1380–1444) as well as by Chaucer's rather infamous friar in the *Canterbury Tales*. But in recounting Francis' life, Thomas of Celano (1185–1265), Francis' first biographer, demonstrates that the great teacher did not in fact teach in the conventional sense of just lecturing or preaching, while the Brothers Leo, Angelo, and Rufino, compliers of the thirteenth-century *Legend of the Three Companions* state: "Everything that he said to them in word, however, he would show them in deed with eagerness and affection."[53] Numerous observers confirm the power of Francis' actions more than his words. Celano, in *The Remembrance of the Desire of a Soul* (also known as *Second Life of St. Francis*), reports that "A physician and learned and eloquent man once said 'I remember the sermons of other preachers word for word, only what the saint Francis says eludes me. Even if I memorize some of his words, they don't seem to me like those that originally poured from his lips."[54] From Celano's two accounts of Francis' ministry, we see that Francis, in speaking with his followers, did use a number of genres that we recognize: framed tales, dream visions, metaphors and of course sermons. The content of his sermons, however, are major gaps, lacunas in the text, for the content is never reported, only that he always spoke "simply."

The most typical of Francis' devices was the teaching tableau. By this we mean that Francis mindfully created scenes calculated to teach by their stunning visual impact. He made himself a concretely accessible example to others, who were then expected to interact with him in a great variety of ways. Francis was a dramatist, the king of drama. This form of teaching extends itself to the representational in a number of ways, including artistic reproduction. His carefully crafted teaching moments are impressive, graphic, and indeed scenic, although some might strike us today as over the top. We are told that, celebrating Christmas in the stable at Greccio, he pronounced the word Bethlehem in imitation of a bleating lamb.[55] This was, in fact, in the context of creating the first crèche; not content to simply read or preach the nativity of Jesus, Francis orchestrated a reenactment. In this emphasis on the deed, Francis is both an innovator and participant in his age.

Caroline Walker Bynum has illustrated the theoretical centrality of teaching by examples in the twelfth century. The idea that a preacher should corroborate in his own life the moral teaching he gives to his flock came down to the twelfth century through the Church Fathers from the New Testament itself and thus in eleventh- and twelfth-century literature, the prevalence of "imitation of example" was significant.[56] "To evangelize was to offer a pattern [of behavior] to others,"[57] and while it was a universally accepted ideal, few religious make themselves an example as enthusiastically and as inventively as Francis. According to Bynum, Francis "sums up not only the twelfth-century emphasis on emotion and inner change in his mystical ravishment, but also the stress on imitation in that ultimate imitation, the reception of the stigmata."[58] What he was (his example) and what he did (his word) coincided. In Francis, as Celano saw him, the individual who rebels against the world becomes the pattern for the world. Francis embodied, according to Erich Auerbach, "in exemplary fashion, the mixture...of *sublimitas* and *humilitas*, of ecstatically sublime immersion in God and humbly concrete everydayness—with the resulting irresolvable fusion of action and expression, of content and form."[59]

This "exemplarism" is uniquely active—for "to be exemplary is to be exemplary to others; it is to perform for an audience expected to interact with the exemplary."[60] With this type of teaching, as Andrew Ladis notes, there was an aesthetic element, one that in turn gave impetus to Italian Franciscan painting.[61] And as Bradly Franco describes, the visual arts were vital to the Franciscans, "as depictions of the life and miracles of Francis were, together with vernacular preaching, the primary method through which the friars propagated their message and explained the order's mission to the laity."[62] In Giotto's thirteenth-century Francis cycle of the Upper Basilica of Assisi, for example, the *Miracle of the Spring*, *Preaching to the Birds*, *St. Francis Renouncing his Father*, and *Francis' Trial by Fire* are, among others, uniquely discrete, dramatic episodes easily captured in single panels in which word, deed, and meaning could be simply conveyed. In the same way, dossals of Francis' life, such as the Bardi and Pescia dossals, draw on the exempla of his teaching.[63] Both the narrative cycles and dossals establish a dramatic tradition of representing Francis that continues hundreds of years later in the Sacri Monti of Italy. Sacri Monti are dossals transferred from the canvas to the face of mountainous landscape. In doing so, they create a pilgrimage experience for worshippers who seek a model that simultaneously shapes both "outer person" (behavior) and "inner person" (soul).

Franciscan Devotion

Affective devotion as performed at Orta has a strong affinity with longstanding Franciscan practice. Simulacra are devotional objects or sites that depend for their effect on the viewer's controlled access to a highly illusionistic, even literalistic, representation of a sacred story. Francis' own didactic methods laid the foundation for the characteristic Franciscan interest in such concrete devotion. As mentioned previously, the most typical of Francis' devices was to create teaching moments with stunning visual impact and to craft himself as a concretely accessible example. Stephen Jaeger argues that the twelfth century was an age whose mentality derived its values from charismatic presences. Francis is clearly such a person: "The living presence of the teacher is the curriculum. The personal aura is the locus of pedagogy, and the language of the body is its medium. The charismatic teacher ushers the student into the charged field of his personality and transforms him, demiurge-like, into a little copy of himself."[64] Under this influence, then, Michael Carroll argues that the Christocentric Catholicism of the reforming church, through the preaching orders, used dynamic images associated with particular narratives, rather than the static miraculous images, that is images "not associated with a commonly known story," popularly venerated in Italy.[65]

Four texts, written at nearly hundred year intervals, show the continuity found in Franciscan exemplary devotion. St. Bonaventure's *The Soliloquium: A Dialogue on the Four Spiritual Exercises* (c. 1260) was written for a general audience and, in the form of a dialogue between the soul and the *homo interior*, leads the reader through various paths of reflection with the goal of using contemplation as a means know and experience God's love.[66] Bonaventure invokes the sense of sight repeatedly, as he calls the reader to vividly see Mary "reclining with her little one in the manger," "worriedly fleeing with him from the face of Herod into Egypt," "wailing, crying out and complaining," and "lamenting tearfully," in an emotionally wrought description crafted to bring about an affective response through contemplation.[67] *Meditatione Vitae Christi*, generally attributed to the Italian Franciscan John of Caulibus and written sometime between 1346 and 1364, became immediately influential.[68] The overall structure of the text divides meditation on the life of Christ over the seven days of the week, apportioned at canonical hours of the day, and relies on sensory perception to heighten the overall experience and secure success of the mediation. Caulibus urges his reader, an unnamed Poor Clare, that "if you truly desire to bear fruit from all this, you are to make yourself as present to whatever is related as said or done were by the Lord Jesus as if you were hearing it with your own ears, were seeing it with your own eyes, with a total mental response."[69] Nicholas Love's *Mirror of the Blessed Life of Jesus Christ* is the 1410 translation of Caulibus' work into Middle English. On a meditation for Friday, for example, the text urges readers to imagine that they are comforting the Virgin and apostles, urging them to eat and sleep after the burial of Christ.[70] A fourth text, *Zardino de Oratione Fructuoso*, appears in Venice at the end of the fifteenth century and encourages its readers to project biblical persona, places, and events on real people. The author, Nicolaus of Ausmo, urges his audience "to move slowly from episode to episode, meditating on each one, dwelling on each single stage and step of the story" by choosing someone well known to them to represent people involved in the passion.[71]

By the 16th century, Jesuit Ignatius of Loyola's *Spiritual Exercises* (1548) is the outstanding example of what came to be called *devotio moderna*. While it is different from some older forms of mystical contemplation, it clearly has roots in traditional Franciscan practice. Loyola encourages the creation of vivid and concrete imagery; he constantly stresses the importance of "seeing the place"—and this seeing amounts to a sort of mental exercise that enabled the imagination to clothe an idea with visible form. The success of the meditation depended upon the penitent's ability to produce a clear and distinct image of the subject so that the image could be studied, retained, and used in the future as a guide to conduct. Every "composition" had two parts: the image and its place. If the subject was the crucifixion of Christ, then the image would be the suffering body on the cross and the place would be the hill outside Jerusalem.[72] Sacri Monti artwork functions as a manifestation of all these devotional practices, and especially of Loyola's Spiritual Exercises. As pilgrims approach each chapel, they focus meditation on the scene inside, and thus it assumes a reality. Each chapel of the Sacro Monte becomes one of Loyola's "compositions of place," activated when a visitor looks through the grilles.

Imitatio Christi

Imitatio Christi, or following in Christ's example, has been a significant theological tenet since the earliest centuries of Christianity. One can find it as early as the book of Acts, which depicts Stephen's death as an imitation of Christ's. It is also apparent in the hermetic ideal of the Desert Fathers, who chose a life of simplicity and poverty of possessions. It was the inspiration behind the sixth-century Benedictine prohibition against personal ownership of property by the monastic brothers.[73] By the High and Late Middle Ages, *imitatio Christi* had become a central spiritual theme for lay and religious both.[74] And Francis was, in the words of the medievalist Ivan Gobry, "a most fervent imitator."[75] In Francis' "A Letter to the Entire Order", he appeals to God, "that...we may follow in the footsteps of your dearly beloved Son, our Lord Jesus Christ, and by your grace alone may arrive at our destination in you, O Most High."[76] In the *Earlier Rule*, Francis states: "The rule and life of these brothers is this, namely: 'to live in obedience, in chastity, and without anything of their own, consists of living in obedience, in chastity and without owning anything,' and to follow the teaching and footprints of our Lord Jesus Christ."[77] Gobry writes, "To follow Christ is not only to serve him, it is not enough to do his will; it also means becoming like him."[78] And for Francis, the key to becoming like Christ and living the life of the Gospel was to embrace poverty. Jesus was in essence a permanent wanderer; he had no home, and "nowhere to lay his head" (Matt 8:20; Luke 9:58). He ordered his disciples to leave behind all possessions, their careers and even family, to follow him (Matt 4:18–22, 9:9//Mark 2:14//Luke 5:27–28). When a rich man asked about acquiring eternal life, Jesus replied that he should follow the ten commandments, but additionally, Jesus told him: "Sell all that you own and distribute the money to the poor, and you will have treasure in heaven; then come, follow me." (Luke 18: 18–22//Matt 19:16–21)

Francis took such injunctions to poverty literally. In his *Earlier Rule* (c. 1221), Francis evoked the words of 1 Timothy 6:8–9 when he enjoined:

> Let all the brothers strive to follow the humility and poverty of our Lord Jesus Christ and let them remember that we should have nothing else in the whole world except as the Apostle says: "having food and clothing, we are content with these." They must rejoice when they live among people considered of little value and looked down upon, among the poor and powerless, the sick and the lepers, and the beggars by the wayside.[79]

Francis' medieval biographers highlight his likeness to Jesus —his charity, poverty and suffering—from Thomas of Celano (d. 1265), who wrote that Francis transformed "into the very image of Christ,"[80] to St. Bonaventure (d. 1274), who described Francis as "fixed with Christ to the cross, in both body and spirit,"[81] and Bartholomew of Pisa (d. 1361), who argued that Francis conformed to Jesus in totality.[82]

Celano, a Franciscan, published his *Life of St. Francis* in 1228–29. A second biography followed, originally entitled *The Remembrance of the Desire of a Soul*, but sometimes known as the *Second Life of St. Francis* (1246–47). Celano first developed the theme of the similarity of Francis to Christ that gave his sainthood a special significance. In the latter work, Celano characterized Francis' commitment to the Gospel:

> His highest aim, foremost desire, and
>   greatest intention was
> to pay heed to the holy gospel in all
>   things and through all things,
> to follow the teaching of our Lord Jesus
>   Christ
> and to retrace His footsteps completely
>   with all vigilance and all zeal,
> all the desire of his soul
> and all the fervor of his heart.[83]

This commitment to the Gospel life (*imitatio Christi*) was linked inextricably with a life of poverty (both his own and others). Kenneth B. Wolf notes that Francis' initial response to his spiritual awakening was to undertake penance "by responding to his [Jesus'] call to relieve the sufferings of the poor and downtrodden."[84] Celano, in his *Life of Saint Francis*, records: "Then the holy lover of profound humility moved to the lepers and stayed with them...he was also a helper of the poor. He extended a hand of mercy to those who had nothing and he poured out compassion for the afflicted."[85] In *The Remembrance of the Desire of a Soul*, Celano says of the young Francis:

Already he was a lover of the poor
And his sacred beginning gave a glimpse
Of what would be fulfilled in the future.
He often stripped himself to clothe the poor.
Although he had not yet made himself one of them
He strove to be like them with his whole heart.[86]

Not only did Francis aspire to imitate Christ-like poverty and charity, he aspired to be like Christ in His suffering. According to tradition, Francis denied the needs of his body, "Because of the suffering and bitter experiences of Christ, which He endured for us, he grieved and afflicted himself daily in body and soul to such a degree that he did not treat his own illnesses."[87] Francis desired to suffer persecution and death like Christ:

In the fervent fire of his charity
He strove to emulate
The glorious triumph of the holy martyrs in whom
the flame of love could not be extinguished,
nor the courage weakened.
Set on fire, therefore,
By the perfect charity which drives out fear,
He desired to offer to the Lord
His own life as a living sacrifice in the flames of martyrdom
So that he might repay Christ, who dies for us,
And inspire others to divine love.[88]

And Francis so identified with the pain of the crucifixion that, according to tradition, he received the stigmata as a grace-filled gift of compassionate love:

And although his body was already weakened
By the great austerity of his past life
And his continual carrying of the Lord's cross,

He was in no way terrified,
But was inspired even more vigorously
To endure martyrdom.
The unconquerable enkindling of love in him
For the good Jesus
Had grown into lamps and flames of fire,
That many waters could not quench so powerful a love.
With the seraphic ardor of desires, Therefore,
He was being borne aloft into God;
And by compassionate sweetness
He was being transformed into Him
Who chose to be crucified out of
The excess of His love.[89]

Francis' conversion came at a time when artistic depictions of the crucified Christ became increasingly popular, and a new spirit of naturalism dominated those depictions. Gone was the robust and youthful body of Christ enthroned. Phyllis Justice observes, "it is difficult for modern Christians to imagine a time when Jesus was not perceived as a figure for emulation, yet prior to the High Middle Ages, this was so; Jesus was simply too far above the human condition to be imitated."[90] Now, the weakened, bloody and painfully suffering body of the Christ engaged believers in an affective devotional experience encouraging them to partake not only of the Passion but also of the life of Christ.[91] Artistic depictions of saints changed as well: "Gone is the early medieval conventional portrait of a saint as miracle worker."[92] Instead we see portraits of saints, particularly Saint Francis, as an imitation of Christ. This convention was carried through in Renaissance art.

Alter Christus

The Christ-like Francis is an established Franciscan theme beginning with Thomas of Celano, in *The Life of Saint Francis*, who says that at the death of the saint, he was "conformed to the death of Christ Jesus by sharing in His sufferings."[93] While every believer could attempt *imitatio Christi* (the endeavour on the part of humans to follow Christ), Francis had actually achieved *conformitas Christi* (a gift conferred by God of likeness to Christ). For the Friars Minor, Francis was not just another saint, but an exceptional being—a *ne plus ultra* saint—to whom God had granted the stigmata at La Verna, which made him a new Christ: *alter Christus*. Bonaventure, in the *Major Legend of Saint Francis* (1260), developed for the first time in unequivocal fashion the theme of the similarity of Francis to Christ which gave his sainthood a special significance. Later texts in the Franciscan hagiographical tradition emphasized even more strongly the fact that the life of Francis was indeed a copy of that of the Savior and that, in the words of the author of the *Miracula sancti Francisci*, composed in the second half of the fourteenth century, "God renewed his Passion in the person of St. Francis."[94] The Sacro Monte of Orta is the most explicitly Franciscan of the Sacri Monti, for it portrays the life of the saint, saturated with the powerful image of Francis as the *alter Christus*. The site encourages the pilgrim's communion with the Christ via the mediation of Francis.

Sacro Monte di Orta

The decision to build a pilgrimage site on the heavily forested mountaintop above the colorful lake town of Orta was made by the city in 1583 (see Fig. 3). Abbot Amico Canobio oversaw the design and initial construction of the chapels, supported by his own commission of Chapels XVIII, XIX, and XX.[95] By 1593, Carlo Bascàpe, bishop of Novara, was given supreme authority over the construction, and funding came from guilds, organizations, and local families. Brother Cleto di Castelletto Ticino became the chief architect and designed the layout for the entire park. Bascape's frequent site visits and precise instructions about the content of each chapel illustrate his meticulous concern about the ways the chapels were to be read.[96] The selection of particular scenes from the

Fig. 2. The pilgrim's gaze is engaged with that of a terracotta statue through a peephole in the iron screen of Chapel XX, Sacro Monte di Orta.

life of Francis and the details within those scenes are crafted to deliver a pointedly orthodox message to the viewers, as the subsequent chapters of this book will address.

The pilgrim's journey begins at the base of the mountain, in the small lakeside town of Orta san Giulio (see Fig. 4). The path to the top is winding and fairly steep—it is intended to be physically taxing. Toward the summit, trees line the path to provide a respite of shade for the weary pilgrims. A seventeenth-century archway welcomes visitors with an inscription: "Here, in various chapels (we relate) the life of Francis. Visitor, if you want to know who is the author, the author is love,"[97] (see Fig. 5). As the pilgrim crosses the threshold into sacred space, a fountain (c. 1666) and a wall shrine (c. 1770?) offer the pilgrim the opportunity to purify both body and spirit (see Figs. 6 & 7). From the entrance, then, the pilgrim proceeds along a well-marked devotional path; the paths are lined with

Fig. 3. Panoramic view of the Sacro Monte di Orta National Park (largely shielded by the dense foliage) with Isola San Giulio and the comune of Orta San Giulio in the foreground.

Sacro Monte di Orta

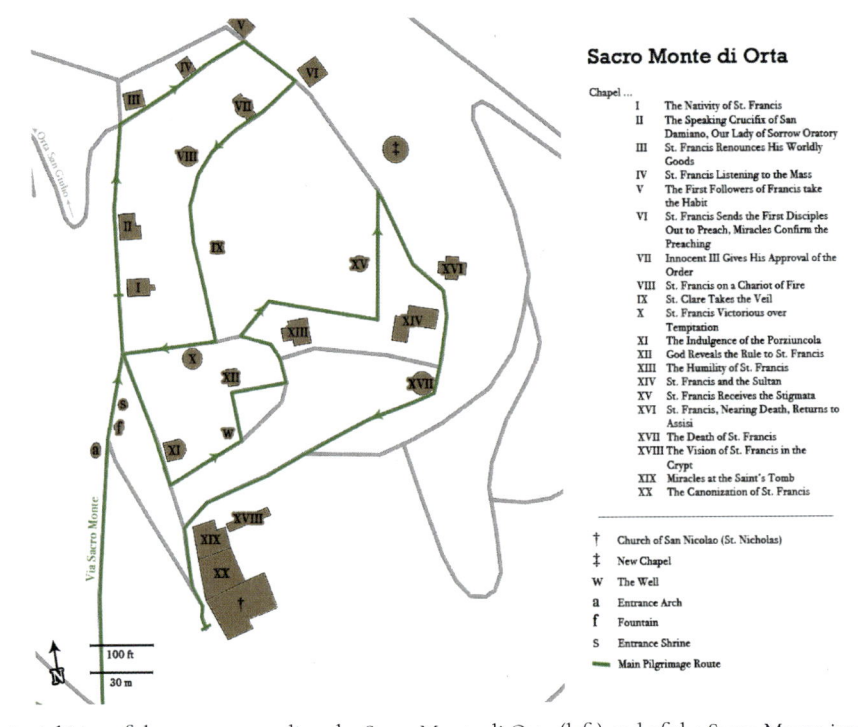

Chapel …
I	The Nativity of St. Francis
II	The Speaking Crucifix of San Damiano, Our Lady of Sorrow Oratory
III	St. Francis Renounces His Worldly Goods
IV	St. Francis Listening to the Mass
V	The First Followers of Francis take the Habit
VI	St. Francis Sends the First Disciples Out to Preach, Miracles Confirm the Preaching
VII	Innocent III Gives His Approval of the Order
VIII	St. Francis on a Chariot of Fire
IX	St. Clare Takes the Veil
X	St. Francis Victorious over Temptation
XI	The Indulgence of the Porziuncola
XII	God Reveals the Rule to St. Francis
XIII	The Humility of St. Francis
XIV	St. Francis and the Sultan
XV	St. Francis Receives the Stigmata
XVI	St. Francis, Nearing Death, Returns to Assisi
XVII	The Death of St. Francis
XVIII	The Vision of St. Francis in the Crypt
XIX	Miracles at the Saint's Tomb
XX	The Canonization of St. Francis

†	Church of San Nicolao (St. Nicholas)
‡	New Chapel
W	The Well
a	Entrance Arch
f	Fountain
s	Entrance Shrine
—	Main Pilgrimage Route

Fig. 4. Aerial Map of the area surrounding the Sacro Monte di Orta (left) and of the Sacro Monte itself, with walkways and chapels delineated (right). © Atlas Kinzel.

Fig. 5. The pilgrim's approach to the Sacro Monte di Orta and the Entrance Arch along the Via del Sacro Monte.

Fig. 6. Back side of the Entrance Arch (right) and purification Fountain (left). Sacro Monte di Orta.

Fig. 7. Shrine at the entrance to the park with a statue of St. Francis of Assisi. Sacro Monte di Orta.

ing tromp l'oeil wall fresco in a sort of faux terrain that creates the illusion of blending fresco and foreground. In other chapels the artists painted illustrative scenes of biblical or hagiographic stories. These interior walls further reinforce the impression of historical events being acted out. Decorative ceilings, often composed of religious symbols and inscribed within cartouches, complete the didactic program.

The chapels as they look today reflect changes in style and content through the long years of construction. The early chapels from the sixteenth century were executed with small, intimate groups of terracotta figures, but towards the middle of the seventeenth century a colorful and dramatic baroque style was introduced. Later, the Lombard painter Stefano Maria Legnani introduced early examples of the rococo style, which typified the additions of the eighteenth century. Later still, the earlier chapels were extensively remodelled, such as Chapel XV "Francis Receives the Stigmata" (1580), which was remade in a much newer style in 1783. Thus it happens that any one chapel, because of centuries of ongoing renovation, can display numerous artistic styles.

Several chapels emphasize the Christocentric function of Francis' life, in keeping with the thematic tradition begun by Thomas of Celano. Most notably, Chapel I illustrates the way Francis was born in a stable like Jesus; Chapel X shows him dealing with lustful temptation that recalls the temptations of Christ in Matthew Ch. 4, and Chapel XIV shows the reception of stigmata. But fully half of the twenty chapels could be called "Franciscan chapels" because their primary focus is to glorify Francis and the Order itself. They affirm the orthodoxy of Francis, his clear allegiance to the Church's teachings and hierarchy, and argue for the legitimate authority of the Order. These Franciscan scenes are not unusual—they appear in all the main biographies of Francis. Some of the most interesting in this regard are Chapel IV, "Francis listens attentively to the Mass,"

vegetation, the lanes are named after natural elements mentioned in the *Canticle of the Sun* (such as the wind and sun; see Chapter 2, Catalogue of the Chapels, Figs. 81 & 82), and the chapels are numbered sequentially. An early seventeenth-century well, an oratory, a small convent, and the medieval Church of St. Nicolao (rededicated in the seventeenth century to both St. Nicolao and St. Francis) are also located within the sacred park (see Figs. 8 & 9).

Although the original plan at Orta called for thirty-six chapels, the complex now contains twenty completed and one partially completed chapel.[98] Each individual chapel houses life-size, painted terracotta figures (nearly 400 in all) set as if on a stage and depicts a particular event in the life of St. Francis of Assisi. In some chapels the artists fused the action of the dioramas with surround-

Fig. 8. The Well at the Sacro Monte di Orta.

Chapel V, "Francis gives the habit to his followers," and Chapel XVI, "Francis returns to Assisi to the acclaim of many." It is striking, however, that many of Francis' important and famous teaching moments concerning the essential Christian teachings on faith and works are missing; preaching to the birds and the wolf of Gubbio are among the most notable absences.

Literary and Ideological Sources

The exact textual sources used for planning the didactic program of Orta are difficult to identify. The large number of medieval texts written about St. Francis bear witness to how well his life is documented in comparison to those of other medieval individuals. So much so that we know more about him than almost any other medieval person. Thomas of Celano's *Life of Saint Francis* (1228) was the earliest biography, followed by his revised and expanded version, *The Remembrance of the Desire of a Soul* (1245). Bonaventure's *Major Legend of Saint Francis* (1260) superseded these to become the official orthodox account. But many other compilations and versions exist as witnessed by the three-volume *Francis of Assisi: The Early Documents*.[99] The ideological framework for the subject of each chapel comes from Bartholomew of Pisa's *De Conformitate Vitae Beati Francisci ad Vitam Domini Jesū*.[100] This is the fullest expression of the long Franciscan tradition that Francis was in all respects conformable to Christ, but Bartholomew goes further with his systematic defence that Francis "conformed" himself to Jesus in every aspect of his life. Every feature of the life and passion of Christ, he says, was duplicated in Francis. Like his master, Francis was subject to sale, betrayal, the agony in the garden, the binding, mockery, scourging, crowning with thorns, stripping of raiment, crucifixion, piercing with a lance and the offer of vinegar.[101] Authorial choices for narratives are made to increase the piety of the reader rather than to remain faithful to biographical historicity, and important

Fig. 9. Main altar of the Church of St. Nicolao. Sacro Monte di Orta.

events in the lives of both Jesus and Francis are omitted when a correlation cannot be found or contrived.[102] Thus the apparent reliance at Orta on Bartholomew's agenda, which privileges these pious correlations, seems to have dictated specific scene selections from the many available episodes of Francis' life.[103] Bartholomew's *alter Christus* reading remained popular in literature and art two hundred years later, partly because of the efforts of dynamic and well-regarded Franciscan preachers such as Bernardino of Siena (d. 1444).

It appears, however, that the biographical sources and ideological framework of the Sacro Monte di Orta were probably accessed through a secondary source. Abbot Amico Canobio asks, in a letter dated 1589, for a text he calls *Croniche di San Francesco*. This is probably *Delle Croniche de gli Ordini Instituiti dal P.S. Francesco*, written originally in Portuguese by Mark of Lisbon (also called Marcos da Silva, Bishop of Porto) and eventually edited and printed in Italian in 1582—just as the plans for Orta were being made.[104] A copy now resides in the library of the local convent of Orta, called Monte Mesma. The importance of the *Croniche* is evident from the direct quotations from the text found in many cartouches attached to the frescos. Mark's text was based on the classic sources of the Franciscans including Celano, Bonaventure, and Bartholomew of Pisa among other lesser known Franciscan sources. Above all, Mark relied on Bartholomew's *De Conformitate Vitae Beati Francisci ad Vitam Domini Jesu*, using it "without the slightest reticence."[105] Thus in addition to its archival function, this lengthy text also proposes ideological correlations which exalt Francis, through biographical comparisons with Jesus, to a level of suprahuman similarity to him.

Pilgrims to the Sacri Monti

Phenomenologically speaking, most world religions envision a universe bifurcated into conditioned and unconditioned reality. Various rites and practices attempt to bridge the gap between the realms. Pilgrimage is one avenue commonly used by the faithful to facilitate that communion. To be sure, and as the saying goes, "Not all who travel to Rome are pilgrims": some travelers are tourists; some look for economic advantage; and, particularly in the medieval period, some simply travel as a way of imitating Christ, as a form of exile and detachment from earthly ties akin to the exile of the monastic Desert Fathers.[106] Building on Dyas' earlier definition of pilgrimage, Maribel Deitz asserts that pilgrimage is not mere religious wandering: it is rather "goal centered, religious travel for an efficacious purpose."[107] The motivations of a pilgrim vary. The pilgrimage can be an act of personal devotion or can be a voluntary obligation (as in Judaism, Islam, and Hinduism). It can be fulfillment of a vow or mandatory as punishment; it can be voluntary or involuntary penance. Motivation notwithstanding, all pilgrims seek a transformative experience: atonement, release, personal growth, new connections to a community of faith, or new connections to the divine.

Art often plays a significant role in a pilgrim's journey. In his clarion call to acknowledge the "visionariness of purpose," Paul Barolsky admonishes art historians to keep in mind:

> The ultimately apparitional character of devotional art...one rooted in the understanding that illusionism, not developed for its own sake, was the beginning of the journey of the soul from mere sight to vision. Whether calmly contemplative or ecstatically rapturous, all such devotional images were intended, in their very exemplariness, to elevate the spirit, to absorb the worshiper's mind in God, to direct the devout beholder's gaze toward a realm ultimately beyond what can be seen corporeally in nature, to the divine truth, which can only be apprehended (as the church fathers taught) with spiritual eyes.[108]

As pilgrimage centers, the Sacri Monti provide a direct affective experience at its Renaissance best, as the pilgrim is guided through prayer and contemplation toward a spiritual awakening.

The Pilgrim's Gaze

Of medieval art, Martina Bagnoli observes:

> Knowledge was gained chiefly through sensation. Medieval images and objects were made to speak to all the senses.... They operated in a rich sensory world that was often integral to their appreciation. They were not only seen, but also and at the same time, touched, tasted, smelled, and heard. The sensory language they employed appealed to the body, and it was through the body that they helped construct a reality in which empirical knowledge overlapped with spiritual imagination.[109]

Pre-modern art was immersive, and individuals were invited to experience art with mind and body, as well as the soul. The same may be said equally of art in most eras, with the possible exception of the modern day. Bagnoli argues, for example, that the contemporary museum experience takes "the body out of the equation" in favour of an emotionless, "'appetiteless' looking."[110] It is perhaps reflective of a broader social trend in which one finds that even sociopsychological analysts failed to recognize the importance of non-verbal communication, particularly sensory perception, until the second half of the twentieth century.[111]

Within the context of visual culture, art criticism and media theory from the mid-twentieth century onward, *gaze* is understood as a mode of communication though which information is transmitted and refers to psychological and power relations through the act of looking intently. In an era described, not hyperbolically, as one "based upon a hegemony of vision," a study of *gaze* reveals its role among visual practices in everything from identity construction to interpersonal power structures.[112] It can be analyzed from various perspectives such as the *male gaze, female gaze, spectator gaze, tourist gaze,* and *photographer's gaze*. The gaze can be hegemonic, mutual, or reversed. David Morgan writes extensively on the *sacred gaze*, which he defines as

> a term that designates the particular configuration of ideas, attitudes, and customs that informs a religious act of seeing as it occurs within a given cultural and historical setting. A sacred gaze is the manner in which a way of seeing invests an image, a viewer, or an act of viewing with spiritual significance.[113]

Furthermore, for Morgan such visual piety consists of a gaze that fixes on the divine as present. Two specific forms may be distinguished: a yearning to escape the bounds of the ego and mingle with the object of the gaze, and a *be-holding* or gripping of the Other in the gaze to derive a favor from it. The second, more common and less spectacular form of beholding is an active beseeching, an act of seeing that invites the sacred into mundane existence in order to achieve a particular end such as a healing.[114]

In *Sacred Views of Saint Francis: The Sacro Monte di Orta*, our use of the term *pilgrim's gaze* encapsulates both the notions of *be-holding* and beseeching located in the particular religious experiences, expectations, and goals related to the visual aspects of pilgrimage.

Amidst the growth of this still relatively new field of study among social psychologists, we should note that the writers, artists, philosophers, and theologians of pre-modernity long recognized the sociopsycological power of sight.[115] Georgia Frank has studied the role of sight in the accounts of Late Antique Christian pilgrims to the Holy Land, and written extensively on sight (and touch) as a way of knowing divine presence. It is akin to the Hindu concept of *darśan*, where to see is to touch is to know.[116] But even beyond knowledge of the divine, for the early Christian pilgrim sight is a mode of participation and presence unbounded by time. Through the eye, particularly the "eye of faith," Christian pilgrims were able to "witness" events of the biblical past and actually participate in their dramatic unfolding. Frank refers to this phenomenon as "biblical realism,"[117] in which the suggestive power of vision facilitates contact and engagement, and "sight manifest[s] the reality."[118]

In their prayer treatises, Tertullian, Origen, and Cassian argued that prayer demanded postures of attentiveness to facilitate dialogue, communion, and reciprocity with the divine. Attentiveness was essential to prayer's efficacy.[119] In the medieval period, the "attention-in-prayer topos" of prayer theory may be seen at play in devotional images such as Byzantine icons, wherein

the gazes of sacred figures out of the picture, toward the observer, could surely elicit in the devout...decorous attentive behavior...[and] may have represented the attentiveness of the living God and his celestial servants to the devotee, and, more particularly, the reassurance that the attentive prayer directed in like manner to the prototype would be more efficacious.[120]

As with early Christian pilgrims, by the late medieval period such visual attentiveness, or what Stuart Clark calls "sacramental seeing," elicited a spiritual communion that was tactile, where "seeing the elevated host, the crucifix, or sacred images meant touching them with one's own visual rays or being touched by them."[121] This is paradigmatically expressed in the Franciscan meditations on Christ's Passion,[122] that, in turn, contributed to an increasing naturalism in late medieval Italian art. Jaś Elsner states that naturalistic verisimilitude encouraged the devout "to suspend his or her disbelief that the image is just pigment or stone."[123] Paul Barolsky goes further:

Naturalistic, devotional art brings the beholder closer to the Holy Spirit by rendering its manifestation to the corporeal eye through appearances and, that confrontation made, the worshipper is encouraged by the image to rise beyond mere appearances to the contemplation of pure spirit. Naturalism is thus not an end in itself, but a stylistic means of rendering spiritual meaning.[124]

Though with the Protestant Reformation, the widely accepted efficacy of "sacramental seeing" became fiercely contested, indeed the source of "unprecedented confessional dispute,"[125] Catholics held fast to the important devotional role of images and vision. We have previously noted Carlo and Federico Borromeo's leadership in implementing the decisions of the Council of Trent on Church art, and Frederico's special concern for naturalism in Tridentine art. Their influence is felt just as, during the Renaissance, Göttler describes "a new religious culture of emotion… explored and tested the effects of various visual media on the mind and the senses of the devout." Gottler describes the Sacro Monte of Varallo as "a laboratory where controversial theories of visual and sensual perception were developed, introduced, changed, and changed again."[126] As with the affective experience of the early Christians in the Holy Land, Rudolf Wittkower notes that the realism in the art of the Sacri Monti "evoked in the beholder the sensation of participating in the actual event."[127] At Orta, aural sensations are manipulated in the crowded street scenes of Chapel XIII and Chapel XVI, for instance, with representations of neighing horses, barking dogs, laughing children, and gossiping adults. The herald angels, cherubic musicians, and musical score in the ceiling fresco of Chapel XX also promote a sympathetic auditory experience. Of course, prior to electrification, there would have been the very real olfactory stimuli of candles and smoke (and presumably incense—not to mention body odor—as well) as the pilgrim made their way into each chapel. Visually, and through the use of what Medina Lasansky terms "stereoscopic viewing,"[128] the beholder is immersed in each tableau via illusionistic frescos and life-sized figures modeled after the local inhabitants[129] and decorated in contemporary Renaissance-era attire. The oculocentrism of the dioramas is made even more explicit through what Susan Stanbury calls the "ocular plot," wherein gaze directs the "linear drama."[130] At the Sacri Monti, as each scene reenacts a discrete moment in history, the pilgrim's gaze is controlled by peepholes in the screens, doors and windows (see Fig. 2 and Chapter 2, Catalogue of Chapels, Fig. 75). There are, typically, multiple sightlines in each chapel, and each sightline is in turn guided by architectural cues (such as lighting and framing), by the narrative trajectory of the depicted event, and most especially by the mediating gestures and "eye contact" of the statues themselves. The fixed and perpetually sustained gaze of certain figures arrest, engage, and beckon the pilgrim into the scene.

In the interactive space between the diorama's plastic society and living society of the pilgrim, gazes are exchanged. Power is transferred from the terracotta figures serving as conduits of enhanced communion within the affective devotional experience, to the pilgrim who "makes real" and becomes a participant in the events before them. The pilgrim is thus positioned kinetically—attentively—by the architecture (as with kneelers and grilles)[131] and repositioned psychologically—also attentively—by the gaze. The controlled gaze of the pilgrim does not serve to alienate but to enhance both a physical and spiritual journey towards an experientially-based, transformative divine communion: the pilgrim's goal.

Endnotes

1 Portions of this chapter were previously published as "The Visual Piety of the Sacro Monte di Orta," in *Finding Saint Francis in Literature and Art*, eds. Cynthia Ho, Beth Mulvaney, and John K. Downey (New York: Palgrave, 2009), 109–28. Used with permission of Palgrave Macmillan.

2 Guido Vannini and Riccardo Pacciani, *La Gerusalemme di S. Vivaldo in Valdelsa* (Montaione: Comune di Montaione, 1998), 59. Caimi's "New Jerusalem" was created as a topomimetic experience, a *luogo santo*, a sacred site simulating in detail the important places of events in Jesus' life. The distances between the chapels were reproduced proportionally to the original space between locations in and around Jerusalem, such as Bethlehem and the Holy Sepulchre, and the topographical location of each chapel was matched to the topography of Holy Land. This notion of "substitutive sacrality" allowed the pilgrim to (affectively) follow in the footsteps of Christ. This meant, however, that a pilgrim might encounter the events in Christ's life out of chronological sequence. Thus, as the site developed the focus shifted from topomimesis, with priority to the geospatial locations of events in Christ's life, to prioritizing a chronological framework of Christ's life according to the Gospel narratives. In this way, the topography of Jerusalem did not determine the order of the chapels, rather the pilgrim could easily walk through a chronological progression of the Christ-centered Gospel accounts. This rerouting eliminated a great deal of confusion. On the concept of substitutive sacrality, see Allie Terry-Fritsch, "Performing the Renaissance Body and Mind: Somaesthetic Style and Devotional Practice at the Sacro Monte di Varallo," *Open Arts Journal* 4 (Winter 2014–15): 113. For more on the redevelopment of Varallo, see Rebecca Gill, "Galeazzo Alessi and the Redevelopment of the Sacro Monte di Varallo," in *AID Monuments. Conoscere, progettare, ricostruire: Galeazzo Alessi Architect-Engineer*, eds. Caludia Conforti and Vittorio Gusella (Rome: ARACHE, 2013), 101–13.

3 The nine Sacri Monti, with the year their construction began, are: Sacro Monte di Varallo (1486), Sacro Monte di Crea (1589), Sacro Monte di Orta (1583), Sacro Monte di Varese (1604), Sacro Monte di Oropa (1617), Sacro Monte di Ossuccio (1635), Sacro Monte di Ghiffa (1591), Sacro Monte Calvario di Domodossola (1657), and Sacro Monte di Belmonte (1712). See http://www.whc.unesco.org for more information about the contribution of the Sacri Monti to World Heritage.

4 Mircea Eliade, *The Sacred and the Profane*, trans. Willard Trask (New York: Harcourt, Brace, and World, Inc., 1959). See also Mircea Eliade, *Patterns in Comparative Religion*, trans. Rosemary Sheed (Lincoln: University of Nebraska, 1996), 367–87.

5 Roberta Panzanelli, *Pilgrimage in Hyperreality: Images and Imagination in the Early Phase of the "New Jerusalem" at Varallo (1486–1530)*, PhD Diss., UCLA, 1999.

6 See Alessandro Nova, "'Popular' Art in Renaissance Italy: Early Response to the Holy Mountain at Varallo," in *Reframing the Renaissance: Visual Culture in Europe and Latin America, 1450–1650*, ed. Claire Farago (New Haven: Yale University Press, 1995), 113–26.

7 Ibid., esp. 123.

8 Dolev Nevet, "The Observant Believer as Participant Observer: 'Ready-Mades' avant la lettre at the Sacro Monte, Varallo, Sesia," *Assaph: Studies in Art History* 2 (1996): 189. D. Medina Lasansky echoes this conclusion in "Body Elision: Acting Out the Passion at the Italian Sacri Monti," in *The Body in Early Modern Italy*, eds. Julia L. Hairston and Walter Stephens (Baltimore: Johns Hopkins University Press, 2010), 253–54.

9 Susan Rubin Suleiman, *Authoritarian Fictions: The Ideological Novel as a Literary Genre* (New York: Columbia University Press, 1983), 2–4.

10 Nevet, "The Observant Believer as Participant Observer," 178.

11 S.J. Freedberg, *Painting in Italy, 1500–1600*, Pelican History of Art, 3rd edn. (New Haven: Yale University Press, 1993), 393.

12 See Bruce Boucher, "Italian Renaissance Terracotta: Artistic Revival or Technological Innovation?" in *Earth and Fire: Italian Terracotta Sculpture from Donatello to Canova*, ed. Bruce Boucher (New Haven: Yale University Press,

12 2001), 1–31, and Maria Giulia Barberini, "Base or Noble Material? Clay Sculpture in Seventeenth- and Eighteenth-Century Italy," in ibid., 43–59.

13 Boucher, "Italian Renaissance Terracotta: Artistic Revival or Technological Innovation?" 27–28.

14 Simon Ditchfield, *Liturgy, Sanctity and History in Tridentine Italy* (Cambridge: Cambridge University Press, 2002), 7.

15 See Nova, "'Popular' Art in Renaissance Italy."

16 Ibid., 114. See also D. Medina Lasansky, "Body Elision," 254–55.

17 Eric Cochrane, "Counter Reformation or Tridentine Reformation? Italy in the Age of Carlo Borromeo," in *San Carlo Borromeo: Catholic Reform and Ecclesiastical Politics in the Second Half of the Sixteenth Century*, eds. John M. Headley and John B. Tomaro (Washington, DC: The Folger Shakespeare Library, 1988), 31–46.

18 Annabel Wharton, *Selling Jerusalem: Relics, Replicas, Theme Parks* (Chicago: Chicago University Press, 2006), 119.

19 Samuel Butler, *Ex Voto: An Account of the Sacro Monte or New Jerusalem at Varallo-Sesia* (London: Dodo Press, 1888), 43.

20 Wharton, *Selling Jerusalem*, 119–20. More recently, Geoffrey Symcox has argued persuasively that the Sacri Monti "did not serve so much as a barrier against the inroads of heresy, but rather as instruments through which the Counter-Reformation clergy sought to canalize and discipline popular devotion." Geoffrey Symcox, *Jerusalem in the Alps: The Sacro Monte of Varallo and the Sanctuaries of North-Western Italy* (Turnhout: Brepols, 2019), 206.

21 The Latin translation, *Alcoranus Franciscanus*, is probably the most widely known edition of Alber's work.

22 Carolly Erickson, "Bartholomew of Pisa, Francis Exalted: De conformitate," *Mediaeval Studies* 34 (1972): 255. Also see Paschal Robinson, *The Catholic Encyclopedia* (New York: Robert Appleton Company, 1907), 2:221, s.v. "Bartholomew of Pisa."

23 Erasmus Alber, *The Alcoran of the Franciscans* (London: L. Curtise, 1679).

24 George Buchanan and George Neilson, *George Buchanan: Glasgow Quatercentenary Studies 1906* (Glasgow: James MacLehose and Sons, 1907), 297–301.

25 See, for example, Marina Miladinov, "Usage of Sainthood in the Reformation Controversy: Saints and Witnesses of Truth in Mathaias Flacius Illyricus," *New Europe College Yearbook* 10 (2002–3): 15–61.

26 John Wycliffe, *Johannes Wyclif Tractatus de ecclesia*, ed. Johann Loserth (London: Wyclif Society, 1886). See Robert Swanson, "Passion and Practice: The Social and Ecclesiastical Implications of Passion Devotion in the Late Middle Ages," in *The Broken Body: Passion Devotion in Late-Medieval Culture*, eds. A. MacDonald et al. (Groningen: Egbert Forsten, 1998), 11–12.

27 "The Decree of the Holy, Great, Ecumenical Synod, the Second of Nicea," *Medieval Sourcebook: Decree of the Second Council of Nicea, 787*, ed. Paul Halsall, Fall 1996, http://sourcebooks.fordham.edu/halsall/source/nicea2-dec.asp.

28 See E. Cecilia Voelker, "Borromeo's Influence on Sacred Art and Architecture," in *San Carlo Borromeo: Catholic Reform and Ecclesiastical Politics in the Second Half of the Sixteenth Century*, eds. John Headley and John Tomaro (Washington, DC: Folger Books, 1988), 172–87. See also Benjamin Westervelt, "The Prodigal Son at Santa Justina: The Homily in the Borromean Reform of Pastoral Preaching," *The Sixteenth Century Journal* 32, no. 1 (2001): 109–26.

29 R. Mols, S.J., "Borromeo, Charles, St," in *New Catholic Encyclopedia*, 15 vols., eds. Thomas Carson and Joann Cerrito (Detroit: Thompson Gale, 2003), 2:539–41.

30 Golda Balass, "Taddeo Zuccaro's Fresco in the Apse-Conch in S. Sabina, Rome," *Assaph: Studies in Art History* 4 (1999): 107.

31 Wietse de Boer, *The Conquest of the Soul: Confession, Discipline, and Public Order in Counter-Reformation Milan* (Leiden: Brill, 2001), ix.

32 Westervelt, "The Prodigal Son at Santa Justina," 126. Also see Matthew Gallegos, "Carlo Borromeo and Catholic Tradition Regarding the Design of Catholic Churches," *The Institute for Sacred Architecture* 9 (2004): 14–18, and E. Cecilia

Voelker, "Borromeo's Influence on Sacred Art and Architecture," 172–87.

33   For example, in July 1618 the Protestant party in the Valtellina murdered their Catholic opponents and cut the strategic communications between Milan and the Tyrol, but in another coup engineered by the Spanish governor in Milan, the Catholic Party there, in turn, rose and massacred Protestants in the so-called Sacro Macello of 1620. For an account of the conflict and the Valtellina Massacre, see Randolf Head, *Jenatasch's Axe: Social Boundaries, Identity, and Myth in the Era of the Thirty Year's War* (Rochester: University of Rochester Press, 2008), 22–24. See also Peter Cannon-Brookes, *Lombard Paintings c1595–c1630: The Age of Federico Borromeo* (Birmingham: City Museums and Art Gallery, 1974), 12.

34   Michael P. Carroll, *Veiled Threats: The Logic of Popular Catholicism in Italy* (Baltimore: Johns Hopkins University Press, 1996), 186. See also Roger Aubert, *The Church in the Industrial Age* (London: Crossroad, 1981), 288–306, and Sean O'Reilly, "Roman versus Romantic: Classical Roots in the Origins of a Roman Catholic Ecclesiology," *Architectural History* 40 (1997): 223.

35   Voelker, "Borromeo's Influence on Sacred Art and Architecture," 177.

36   Ibid.

37   Gallegos, "Carlo Borromeo and Catholic Tradition Regarding the Design of Catholic Churches," 14–15.

38   Sean O'Reilly, "Roman versus Romantic: Classical Roots in the Origins of a Roman Catholic Ecclesiology," *Architectural History* 40 (1997): 222–40, and Giles Knox, "The Unified Church Interior in Baroque Italy: S. Maria Maggiore in Bergamo," *The Art Bulletin* 82, no. 4 (2000): 683–84.

39   Pamela Jones, "Federico Borromeo as a Patron of Landscapes and Still Lifes: Christian Optimism in Italy ca. 1600," *The Art Bulletin* 70, no. 2 (1988): 268.

40   Ibid.

41   For a discussion of the Borromean influence on art, see de Boer, *The Conquest of the Soul*, and Voelker, "Borromeo's Influence on Sacred Art and Architecture," 172–87.

42   Symcox, *Jerusalem in the Alps*, 205.

43   See Piero Bianconi et al., *Il Sacro Monte sopra Varese* (Milan: Paolo Zanzi, Gruppo Editoriale Electa, 1981).

44   Cesare Orsenigo, *Life of St. Charles Borromeo*, trans. Rudolph Kraus (St. Louis: B. Herder, 1943), 302–3.

45   David Leatherbarrow, *Topographical Stories: Studies in Landscape and Architecture* (Philadelphia: University of Pennsylvania Press, 2004), 211.

46   Dee Dyas, *Pilgrimage in Medieval English Literature, 700–1500* (Suffolk: D.S. Brewer, 2001), 2.

47   Thaddeus MacVicar, O.F.M Cap., *The Franciscan Spirituals and the Capuchin Reform*, ed. Charles McCarron, O.F.M. Cap. (St. Bonaventure: The Franciscan Institute, 1986), 57.

48   See the multiple attestations of such early depictions in William Cook's *Images of St. Francis of Assisi in Painting, Stone and Glass from the Earliest Images to ca. 1320 in Italy: A Catalogue*, ed. L.S. Olschki (Florence: Olschki, 1999). The artists of the Sacro Monte di Orta always depict Francis and his companions in Capuchin robes.

49   Francis of Assisi, *The Testament*, in *Francis of Assisi: Early Documents*, 3 vols., eds. Regis Armstrong, O.F.M. Cap., et al. (New York: New City Press, 1999–2001), 1:124. This three-volume collection by Armstrong et al. contains translations of all the texts from the first one hundred plus years of the Franciscan tradition.

50   We see evidence of this ascetic devotion in the numerous visual references to penance and discipline in the chapels at Orta. See, for example, the ceiling frescos of Chapel III.

51   Paul Hanbridge, O.F.M. Cap., trans., *The Capuchin Reform, A Franciscan Renaissance: A Portrait of Sixteenth- Century Capuchin Life, An English Translation of La bella e santa riforma by Melchiorre da Pobladura, O.F.M. Cap.* (Delhi: Media House, 2003), 39.

52   Thaddeus MacVicar, O.F.M Cap., *The Franciscan Spirituals and the Capuchin Reform*, ed. Charles McCarron, O.F.M. Cap. (St. Bonaventure: The Franciscan Institute, 1986), 66–68, 79, 88–89, 98–99, for example.

53   *Legend of the Three Companions*, in *Francis of Assisi: Early Documents*, 2:101.

54 Thomas of Celano, *The Remembrance of the Desire of a Soul*, in *Francis of Assisi: Early Documents* 2:318.

55 Thomas of Celano, *The Life of Saint Francis*, in *Francis of Assisi: Early Documents*, 1:256.

56 Caroline Walker Bynum, *Jesus as Mother: Studies in Spirituality of the High Middle Ages* (Berkeley: University of California Press, 1982), 95–106.

57 Ibid., 90.

58 Ibid., 105–6.

59 Erich Auerbach, *Mimesis: The Representation of Reality in Western Literature*, trans. Willard Trask (Princeton: Princeton University Press, 2013), 163.

60 Hester Goodenough Gelber, "A Theater of Virtue: The Exemplary World of St. Francis of Assisi," in *Saints and Virtues*, ed. John Stratton Hawley (Berkeley: University of California Press, 1987), 15.

61 Andrew Ladis, Introduction to *Giotto and the World of Early Italian Art: An Anthology of Literature*, vol. 4: *Franciscanism: The Papacy, and Art in the Age of Giotto: Assisi and Rome*, ed. Andrew Ladis (New York: Garland Publishing, Inc. 1998), 88.

62 Bradley R. Franco, "The Functions of Early Franciscan Art," in *The World of St. Francis of Assisi: Essays in Honor of William R. Cook*, eds. Bradley R. Franco and Beth Mulvaney (Leiden: Brill, 2015), 19.

63 See Franco, "The Functions of Early Franciscan Art," 19–44.

64 Stephen Jaeger, "Charismatic Body–Charismatic Text," *Exemplaria* 9, no. 1 (1997): 122.

65 Carroll, *Veiled Threats*, 80.

66 Bonaventure of Bagnoregio, "The Soliloquium: A Dialogue on the Four Spiritual Exercises," in *Works of St. Bonaventure: Writings on the Spiritual Life*, vol. 10: *Writings on the Spiritual Life*, ed. Edward Coughlin, O.F.M. (St. Bonaventure: Franciscan Institute Publications, 2006), 214–15. See also Bonaventure's *On the Reduction of the Arts to Theology*, where he argues that all knowledge is, at its essence, theological wisdom which in turn leads the origin of all things—God's love—and to union with God: *Works of St. Bonaventure*, vol. 1: *On the Reduction of the Arts to Theology*, trans. Zachary Hayes, O.F.M. (St. Bonaventure: Franciscan Institute Publications, 1996), esp. 1–2, 45–47, 49–53.

67 Bonaventure of Bagnoregio, "The Soliloquium," 338–39.

68 C. Mary Stallings-Taney, "The Pseudo-Bonaventure 'Meditaciones vite Christi': Opus Integrum," *Franciscan Studies* 55 (1998): 253–80. For a recent discussion on the authorship of the text, see Sarah McNamer, "The Debate on the Origins of the Meditationes vitae Christi: Recent Arguments and Prospects for Future Research," *Archivum Franciscanum Historicum* 111, nos. 1–2 (July 2018): 65–112.

69 Stallings-Taney, "The Pseudo-Bonaventure 'Meditaciones vite Christi'," 272.

70 *Meditations on the Life of Christ: An Illustrated Manuscript of the Fourteenth Century*, trans. Isa Ragusa and Rosalie B. Green (Princeton: Princeton University Press, 1961); Nicholas Love, *Mirror of the Blessed Life of Jesus Christ: A Critical Edition*, ed. Michael G. Sargent (New York: Garland, 1992).

71 Nevet, "The Observant Believer as Participant Observer," 180.

72 Ignatius of Loyola, *Ignatius of Loyola: Spiritual Exercises and Selected Works*, Classics of Western Spirituality, ed. George E. Ganss, S.J. (New York: Paulist Press, 1991). Also see Leatherbarrow, *Topographical Stories*, 213.

73 Lee Palmer Wandel, "The Poverty of Christ," in *The Reformation of Charity: The Secular and Religious in Early Modern Poor Relief*, ed. Thomas M. Safley (Leiden: Brill, 2003), 15–29, at 16.

74 Catherine Mooney, "Imitatio Christi or Imitatio Mariae? Clare of Assisi and her Interpreters," in *Gendered Voices: Medieval Saints and Their Interpreters*, ed. Catherine Mooney (Philadelphia: University of Pennsylvania Press, 1999), 53.

75 Ivan Gobry, *Saint Francis of Assisi: A Biography* (San Francisco: Ignatius Press, 2006), 217.

76 Francis of Assisi, "Letter to the Entire Order," in *Francis of Assisi: Early Documents*, 1:121.

77 Francis of Assisi, *Earlier Rule*, in *Francis of Assisi: Early Documents*, 1:63–64.

78 Gobry, *Saint Francis of Assisi*, 217.

79 Francis of Assisi, *Earlier Rule*, in *Francis of Assisi: Early Documents*, 1:70; I Timothy 6:8–9.

80 Thomas of Celano, *The Remembrance of the Desire of a Soul*, in *Francis of Assisi: Early Documents*, 2:334.

81 Bonaventure of Bagnoregio, *The Major Legend of Saint Francis*, in *Francis of Assisi: Early Documents*, 2:640.

82 In *De Conformitate Vitae Beati Francisci ad Vitam Domini Jesu Redemptoris nostri*, Bartholomew outlines forty life events that correlate between Francis and Jesus. The reprint of 1510 (Milan: Gotardus Ponticus) is commonly available under the title *Liber conformitatum*.

83 Thomas of Celano, *The Remembrance of the Desire of a Soul*, in *Francis of Assisi: Early Documents*, 2:254.

84 Kenneth Baxter Wolf, *Poverty of Riches* (Oxford: Oxford University Press, 2003), 45.

85 Thomas of Celano, *The Life of Saint Francis*, in *Francis of Assisi: Early Documents*, 1:195.

86 Thomas of Celano, *The Remembrance of the Desire of a Soul*, in *Francis of Assisi: Early Documents*, 2:247.

87 *The Assisi Compilation*, in *Francis of Assisi: Early Documents*, 2:180.

88 Bonaventure of Bagnoregio, *The Major Legend of Saint Francis*, in *Francis of Assisi: Early Documents*, 2:600.

89 Ibid., 2:631–32.

90 Phyllis Justice, "A New Fashion in Imitating Christ," in *The Year 1000: Religious and Social Responses to the Turning of the First Millennium*, 3rd edn., ed. Michael Frassetto (New York: Palgrave Macmillan, 2002), 166.

91 See also Bynum, *Jesus as Mother*, 16–17.

92 Patricia Ranft, *How the Doctrine of Incarnation Shaped Western Culture* (Lanham: Rowman and Littlefield, 2012), 223.

93 Thomas of Celano, *The Life of Saint Francis*, in *Francis of Assisi: Early Documents*, 1:119. See also one of the first systematic studies of the *Franciscus alter Christus* theme in Stanislao da Campagnola, *L'angelo del sesto sigillo e l'alter Christus Genesi e sviluppo di due temi francescani nei secoli XII–XIV*, Studi e ricerche 1 (Rome: Antonianum, 1971).

94 André Vauchez, *Sainthood in the Later Middle Ages*, trans. Jean Birrell (Cambridge: Cambridge University Press, 1997), 114.

95 Symcox, *Jerusalem in the Alps*, 208–9.

96 Ibid., 210–12.

97 Angelo Maria Manzini, O.F.M. Cap., *Sacro Monte of Orta* (Orta: Community of the Franciscan Friars, Custodian of the Sacro Monte of Orta, 2006), 11.

98 The completed chapels of Orta are: I. *The Nativity of St. Francis*; II. The Cross Speaks to Saint Francis; III. Francis Renounces His Clothing; IV. Francis Hears Mass; V. Francis' First Followers Take the Habit; VI. Francis and His Followers Hear the Mass; VII. Pope Innocent III Approves the Order; VIII. Francis on the Chariot of Fire; IX. St. Clare Takes the Veil; X. Victory Over Temptation; XI. Indulgence of Portiuncula; XII. Christ Approves the Franciscan Order; XIII. Francis Led Naked through the Streets; XIV. Francis before the Sultan; XV. Francis Receives the Stigmata; XVI. Francis Returns to Verna; XVII. Death of Francis; XVIII. Nicholas III at the Tomb; XIX. Miracles at the Tomb; XX. Canonization. Chapel XXI was intended to celebrate the "Canticle of the Sun." For background on Orta, see Elena De Filippis and Fiorella Mattioli Carcano, *Guide to the Sacro Monte of Orta* (Novara: Riserva Naturale Speciale del Sacro Monte di Orta, 1991), and Manzini, *Sacro Monte of Orta*.

99 Regis Armstrong, O.F.M. Cap. et al., eds. and trans., *Francis of Assisi: Early Documents*, 3 vols. (New York: New City Press, 1999–2001).

100 Bartholomew of Pisa, *De Conformitate*, in *Analecta Franciscana* 4, ed. Fathers of the College of Saint Bonaventure (Quaracchi: Collegium S. Bonaventurae, 1906).

101 Roland Bainton, "Durer and Luther as the Man of Sorrows," *The Art Bulletin* 29, no. 4 (1947): 269–72.

102 See Erickson, "Bartholomew of Pisa, Francis Exalted."

103 Artistic representation of *Franciscus alter Christus* had become popular in the early fifteenth century. See H.W. Van Os, "St. Francis of Assisi as a Second Christ in Early Italian Painting," *Simiolus* 7, no. 3 (1974): 115–32. In the last decades

of the sixteenth and early seventeenth century, St. Francis became the most paradigmatic of saints. The attention bestowed upon him in Italian painting of this period rivals that which he received from painters of the thirteenth and fourteenth centuries. See Pamela Askew, "The Angelic Consolation of St. Francis of Assisi in Post-Tridentine Italian Painting," *Journal of the Warburg and Courtauld Institutes* 32 (1969): 280–306.

104 Mark of Lisbon, *Croniche degli ordini instituiti dal P. San Francesco. Prima parte divisa in dieci libri che contiente la sua vita, la sua morte e i suoi miracoli, composta dal R.P. Fra Marco da Lisbona, traduz. dal portoghese* (Naples, 1680). See Pier Giorgo Longo, "Immagini e immaginario di San Francesco al Sacro Monte di Orta," in *Antiche Guide del Sacro Monte di Orta*, ed. Loredana Racchelli (Orta: Ente di Gestione delle Reserve Naturali Speciali del Sacro Monte di Orta, del Monte Mesma e del Colle della Torre di Buccione, 2008), 63.

105 John Tolan, *Saint Francis and the Sultan: The Curious History of a Christian–Muslim Encounter* (Oxford: Oxford University Press, 2009), 221.

106 See Maribel Deitz's careful analysis and discussion of the various categories of Christian travelers, as well as the types of and motivations for pilgrimage, in *Wandering Monks, Virgins, and Pilgrims: Ascetic Travel in the Mediterranean World, AD 300–800* (University Park: The Pennsylvania State University Press, 2005), esp. 1–42.

107 Ibid., 7.

108 Paul Barolsky, "Naturalism and the Visionary Art of the Early Renaissance," in *Giotto and the World of Early Italian Art: An Anthology of Literature*, vol. 4: *Franciscanism: The Papacy, and Art in the Age of Giotto: Assisi and Rome*, ed. Andrew Ladis (Abingdon-on-Thames: Routledge, 1998), 323.

109 Martina Bagnoli, ed., *A Feast for the Senses: Art and Experience in Medieval Europe* (New Haven: Yale University Press, 2017), 13.

110 Ibid., 14.

111 Mark Cook, "Gaze and Mutual Gaze in Social Encounters," *American Scientist* 65, no. 3 (May–June 1977): 328.

112 Alex Gillespie, "Tourist Photography and the Reverse Gaze," *Ethos* 34, no. 3 (Jan. 2008): 360. Cf. David Levin, *Modernity and the Hegemony of Vision* (Berkeley: University of California Press, 1993), and also Michael Foucault, *Discipline and Punish: The Birth of the Prison*, trans. Alan Sheridan (New York: Vintage Books, 1977), 171ff.

113 David Morgan, *The Sacred Gaze, Religious Visual Culture in Theory and Practice* (Berkeley: University of California Press, 2005), 3.

114 David Morgan, *Visual Piety: A History and Theory of Popular Religious Images* (Berkeley: University of California Press, 1998), 31.

115 Georgia Frank has catalogued a list of pre-modern commentators on the polyvalence of sight from Plato and Aristotle to Jerome, Paula, Egeria, Cyril of Jerusalem, Gregory of Nyssa, John Chrysostom, and Giotto. See Georgia Frank, "The Pilgrim's Gaze in the Age Before Icons," in *Visuality Before and Beyond the Renaissance: Seeing as Others Saw*, ed. Robert Nelson (Cambridge: Cambridge University Press, 2000), 98–115; "'Taste and See': The Eucharist and the Eyes of Faith in the Fourth Century," *Church History* 70, no. 4 (Dec. 2001): 619–43; and *The Memory of the Eyes: Pilgrims to Living Saints in Christian Late Antiquity* (Berkeley: University of California Press, 2000), particularly the final three chapters. To the list of pre-modern commentators, Christine Göttler would add Ignatius of Loyola; see Christine Göttler, "The Temptation of the Senses at the Sacro Monte di Varallo" in *Religion and the Senses in Early Modern Europe*, eds. Wietse de Boer and Christine Göttler (Leiden: Brill, 2013), 423.

116 Diana Eck, *Darśan: Seeing the Divine Image in India*, 3rd edn. (New York: Columbia University Press, 1998), 9.

117 Frank, *The Memory of the Eyes*, 29.

118 Ibid., 173.

119 Robert W. Gaston, "Attention in Court: Visual Decorum in Medieval Prayer Theory and Early Italian Art," in *Visions of Holiness: Art and Devotion in Renaissance Italy*, eds. Andrew Ladis and Shelley E. Zuraw (Athens: Georgia Museum of Art, 2001), 140–43.

120 Ibid., 144.

121   Stuart Clark, *Vanities of the Eye: Vision in Early Modern European Culture* (Oxford: Oxford University Press, 2007), 161.

122   Ibid., Gaston, "Attention in Court," 154.

123   Jaś Elsner, "Between Mimesis and Divine Power: Visuality in the Greco-Roman World," in *Visuality Before and Beyond the Renaissance: Seeing as Others Saw*, ed. Robert Nelson (Cambridge: Cambridge University Press, 2000), 45.

124   Barolsky, "Naturalism and the Visionary Art of the Early Renaissance," 317.

125   Clark, *Vanities of the Eye*, 161.

126   Göttler, "The Temptation of the Senses at the Sacro Monte di Varallo," 413. See also comments pertaining to the relationship between the Catholic Reformation and the emphasis on exploitation of the senses by baroque artists in Gallegos, "Carlo Borromeo and Catholic Tradition," 14.

127   Rudolf Wittkower, *Idea and Image: Studies in the Italian Renaissance* (London: Thames and Hudson, 1978), 177.

128   Lasansky, "Body Elision," 259.

129   For more on the practice of modeling terracotta statuary individually, see Boucher, "Italian Renaissance Terracotta," 7, 12, 18–19.

130   Sarah Stanbury, "The Virgin's Gaze: Spectacle and Transgression in Middle English Lyrics of the Passion," *PMLA* 106, no. 5 (Oct. 1991): 1087–88.

131   See Lasansky's comments to this effect, in "Body Elision," 252, 260.

2

Catalogue of Chapels

This section contains short essays describing each chapel and providing the raison d'être for each. There are twenty chapels in the park-like setting of the Sacro Monte di Orta. The architecture, style, and setting are uneven from chapel to chapel, and can vary in emphasis and attention to ornamentation. The essays reflect these disparities: for some chapels, more space is devoted to a description of the exterior than the interior; for others, the frescos receive attention equal to or greater than the dioramas. Photos of both the exterior and interior accompany each essay.

Content of the Artistic Program

Despite the distinctiveness of each chapel, the reader will find unity in the artistic program. The chapels teach visually what the Franciscans so adeptly preach, while simultaneously explaining the identity of the Order in the program. Each chapel, in its own way, asserts: (1) the unique status of Francis, who, according to Franciscan tradition, conformed to Christ; (2) the distinctiveness of the Franciscans and their special, penitential mission in following the gospel life; (3) the orthodoxy of the Franciscan order and its close ties with the institutional church; (4) the program of the Tridentine reform; and (5) Francis' role in revitalizing the church of the thirteenth century and the parallel role of the Franciscans in revitalizing the church of the post-Tridentine era. The emphasis on the legitimacy of Francis and the Franciscan order is one that played out in Franciscan art over centuries. Bradley Franco observes that the repeated selection of certain events in the saint's life, events in which the presence of church authorities is notably highlighted, underscored the orthodoxy of the movement.[1] This is certainly the case at Orta, where we see church authority on display in Francis' penitential renunciation before the bishop (Chapel III), his attendance at Mass (Chapel IV), the papal approval of the Order (Chapel VII), the administration of Last Rites at Francis' deathbed (Chapel XVII), the papal visit to Francis' tomb (Chapel XVIII), and the gathering of cardinals, bishops, abbots and the pope at the saint's canonization (Chapel XX). Authorities appear in multiple frescos, such as the gathering of bishops before whom Francis announces the Porziuncola Indulgence (Chapel XI) and that of Innocent III's dream in which Francis holds up the Lateran church (Chapel VII and Chapel XI). The depiction of numerous Old Testament and New Testament personalities, as well as that of saints such as Dominic, Basil, Benedict, Augustine, Rocco and John Nepomuk, are also found throughout the chapels.

Design and Execution of the Artistic Program

The Sacro Monte di Orta was developed over a period of almost two hundred years. During that time, a number of artistic styles came in and out of vogue: classicism, mannerism, baroque, and rococo. The chapels reflect that great diversity of tastes and it is not unusual to find the elements of a single chapel exhibiting differing styles: an exterior in one style and the frescos in another. Several chapels underwent repairs or "updating" with a facelift to the façade, the addition of statues, or new interior painting.

Our records of the construction are incomplete, particularly owing to the destruction of archives when Napoleon closed religious houses in 1810.[2] Typically, Franciscan building projects had two governing bodies, called *fabbriciere* (pl. *fabbricieri*). They functioned much like a modern day vestry might, except that, because of the Franciscan prohibition against handling money, a secular *fabbriciere* handled all the financial matters of the project, while a *fabbriciere* of friars directed the design and its execution.[3] We have some records of the secular *fabbriciere* at Orta, and though we have found no reference to a religious *fabbriciere* there, Father Cleto da Castelletto Ticino, the main designer and architect of the site from 1594–1619, had experience serving on several *fabbricieri* for projects at other locales. Already at work on the site, Father Cleto was appointed supervisor by Carlo Bascapè, who became Bishop of Novara in 1593. The Sacro Monte di Orta belonged in the Bishop's diocese, and we know that he took an avid interest in selecting artists and designing the artistic program of the pilgrimage site. He funded Chapel III, Francis Renounces his Worldly Goods, and it is widely considered that the statue of the Bishop of Assisi in this same chapel is in Bascapè's likeness.[4]

As discussed in Chapter 1, the Sacro Monte di Orta is a precinct, surrounded by a *temenos* of hedgerows, trees, and walls. Pilgrims approach the sacred site via a fairly difficult walking path, the physical exertion intended to prepare both the body and mind of the faithful for kinesthetic, sensory, and mental participation at the shrine. The builders designed the park as an immersive experience with entrance arch, purification font, wall shrine, well, green spaces, and chapels, all amplified by the naming of lanes and piazzas after elements in *Canticle of the Sun*, such that the pilgrim physically moves through the song as part of the devotional performance. In keeping with the Borromean emphasis on discipline,[5] the pilgrim's visit is controlled by a set itinerary along a clear-cut path leading from chapel to chapel, with the chapel numbers painted on each structure and a frescoed hand pointing the pilgrim in the correct direction. The pilgrim is further controlled by the prescribed viewing opportunities relative to each chapel. The interior of some chapels may be viewed only from the exterior through screened windows that direct one's line of vision. Even in those chapels that allow entry, the pilgrim's gaze is controlled by iron, wood, and/or glass screens that serve to intentionally frustrate the viewer's access to the devotional images. Despite such restraints, the transformative experience that is the pilgrim's goal may actually be enhanced by these viewing controls. The screens frame the tableau and concentrate the viewer's attention. As frames, the screens serve to revere and celebrate, to create desire and awe, much the same way, Margaret Bell argues, that reliquaries serve to enhance the relic.[6] The pilgrim's body is manipulated into a devotional posture, to bend and to kneel in order to look through the viewing holes that punctuate the screens. In some chapels this manipulation allows the pilgrim to positionally identify with the terracotta figures, such as in Chapel II where the kneeling pilgrim is positioned alongside the young Francis as he, too, kneels before the feet of Christ on the San Damiano Cross.[7] Apertures (both windows and screens) as well as candles controlled lighting for effect that, in addition to creating a sense of sanctity, could create mood and unleash the pilgrim's imagination. Play between lightness and darkness inside the chapels, an environmental chiaroscuro, might animate the images in the pilgrim's gaze.[8] The architects of the Sacro Monte di Orta designed the physical fabric of the shrine be to simultaneously, and orthodoxly, kinesthetic, tactile, and spiritual so that the pilgrim could fully experience, and bear witness to, what they believed was the miraculously transformative nature of pilgrimage to this Franciscan shrine.

We know something of the manufacturing techniques that would have been used by the artists of the Sacro Monte di Orta. The terracotta figures were crafted *in situ*. The artists might mold the clay and then hollow out the figures, using various interior and exterior structural support systems so that the clay shell did not collapse during the firing process. Alternately, the clay could be coiled into place, again with the assistance of supports for strength. At this point the figures were cut into sections (so as to fit into the oven and bake evenly) and fired. The oven at the Sacro Monte di Orta adjoins Chapels XIX and XX. The figures were then reassembled using clasps and brackets (see Fig. 1). Plaster could be used to conceal cracks, joins, and breaks.[9] Painters were employed at Orta to work on the narrative frescos, ornamental and architectural motifs, and painted sculptures. The terracotta statues might be glazed (which would require a second firing) and/or painted. Oil and tempera in the full range of colors were painted onto figures over an egg-based sealant, or they could be applied to an undercoating of gesso and glue.[10] As opposed to marble or bronze statues, the naturalistically painted figures of Orta and the other Sacri Monti further enhanced the mimesis and immediacy desired for an affective devotional experience.

As indicated in the artist's biographies (see Appendix), some very well-known artists of the period worked at Orta. For a few, painting or sculpting was a multigenera-

Fig. 1. A behind the scenes view of terracotta figures showing construction techniques. Nave, Chapel VI. Sacro Monte di Orta.

tional family occupation. Artists such as the d'Enricos, the Nuvolones, and Mazzucchelli had established workshops; they employed assistants and trained apprentices. Several of the artists at Orta also worked on the Duomo in Milan or taught in the prestigious academies of that city. Most of the artists focused their employment in Lombardy and Piedmont and thus shared a sphere of influence.

Chapel I. The Nativity of St. Francis

Chapel I is devoted to the stories surrounding Francis' birth, particularly the tradition that Francis, like Christ, was born in a stable.[11] The chapel was designed by the Capuchin Father Cleto da Castelletto Ticino and built between 1592–1604, though the façade one sees today was added in 1848 by Novaran

Fig. 2. Exterior of Chapel I, The Nativity of Francis. Sacro Monte di Orta.

architect Paolo Gaudenzio Rivolta. For the interior decoration, the frescos by Bernardo and Giacomo Filippo Monti were completed in 1615, and the terracotta statues of sculptor Christoforo Prestinari were installed by 1617. Funding for the chapel is variously attributed to the citizens of Orta, a local tinsmiths guild, and terracotta artists from France and Spain.[12]

The nineteenth-century façade of the chapel is scored with faux marble blocks (see Fig. 2). Engaged Ionic columns flank the central double door, where each column sits on a tall plinth. Note that all the chapels at the Sacro Monte di Orta follow the Renaissance-era preference for smooth (non-fluted) columns. A shallow stylobate forms the base of the chapel. Two steps lead to the front door, which is topped by a cornice and crest. The eye follows the rectilinear lines of the columns upwards, to a demilune window, corbel, architrave, and pediment. The chapel itself is rectilinear, though attached to the left are a two additional, smaller buildings that originally served as a meetinghouse and caretakers quarters but currently house a bookshop, vending, and souvenirs.

The square chapel is divided into two equal parts: a vestibule with frescoed walls and the nativity scene behind an arched wooden screen (see Fig. 3). The archway is filled on the lower course by a solid wooden screen topped with a perforated wooden screen. A kneeler lies at the base of the screen. On either side of the arched screen, frescoed faux-niches depict Francis (to the left) and Dominic (to the right). Above the niches are single panels representing, respectively, Francis and Dominic giving alms. The decoration of the vault is largely ornamental, painted in garish hues that emphasize the intricate plaster modeling.

On the right and left interior walls of the vestibule are large frescos, each with a single scene. Two smaller panels flank the interior of the front entrance. Each scene foreshadows certain aspects about the life of Francis: that he will be born in a stable, that he will be a reformer and rebuild the church, that he is blessed by God, and that he will be an inspiration to his fellows. One scene, in particular, recalls the story in Luke 2:25–35 of Simeon who, upon meeting the holy family on the steps of the Jerusalem Temple, took the Christ-child in his arms and foretold the crucifixion. Here on the steps of the Porziuncola, Lady Pica hands Francis into the arms of an angel, a reinterpretation of the account in both Arnald of Sarrant's *Kingship of St. Francis* (1365) and Bartholomew of Pisa's *De Conformitate* in which a pilgrim (for Bartholomew, and as depicted here, the pilgrim is an angel in disguise) appears to Francis' mother and predicts that he will be a blessing (see Fig. 4).[13]

In the tableau behind the screen are almost a dozen terracotta figures—both hu-

CATALOGUE OF CHAPELS

Fig. 3. Vestibule of Chapel I. Sacro Monte di Orta.

Fig. 4. Lady Pica presents her newborn to the Angel. Chapel I, Sacro Monte di Orta.

57

Fig. 5. Lady Pica, attendants, stable animals, and the newborn Francis. Chapel I, Sacro Monte di Orta.

Fig. 6. Exterior of Chapel II, The Speaking Crucifix of San Damiano, and of the Oratory, Our Lady of Sorrow. Sacro Monte di Orta.

man and animal. Lady Pica, Francis' mother, with her rose dress and bluish-green cloak, appears *imitatio Mariae* (see Fig. 5). Both servants and well-dressed women attend her needs. The newborn Francis holds his hands in benediction. The walls of the nave are painted to imitate stone, the ceiling is painted to imitate wood, and a hayloft hangs on the wall. Additional attendants grace the background frescos.

Though the early biographers of Francis provide scant details of his birth, the tradition becomes amplified to the point that by the fourteenth century, legends aggressively portray Francis as a saint who lived in perfect conformity with Christ, even in his birth. As the first chapel of the pilgrimage, it explicitly identifies the connection between Christ and Francis. It establishes the message that at the Sacro Monte de Orta a pilgrim is able to directly encounter Christ through Francis.

Chapel II. The Speaking Crucifix of San Damiano

The iconographic program of Chapel II focuses on the mystical encounter between Francis and the crucified Christ in the San Damiano Church, an encounter long con-

CATALOGUE OF CHAPELS

Fig. 7. The Speaking Crucifix of San Damiano. Chapel II, Sacro Monte di Orta.

Fig. 8. A stableman and horse. Chapel II, Sacro Monte di Orta.

sidered a decisive moment in Francis' conversion.[14] The chapel was built in three years, between 1606 and 1609, with Father Cleto da Castelletto Ticino as the architect. It is a rectilinear building fronted by a foreshortened portico supported by a Romanesque colonnade (see Fig. 6). The portico is adorned with now faded landscape and architectural frescos. The niche-flanked doorway of the portico leads into a large vestibule. The frescos of the vestibule walls, painted by the Fiamminghini (Giovanni Battista and Giovanni Mauro Di Roberio, c. 1608) depict scenes of Francis' youth (below), the virtues (in four lunettes, above), and angels in various poses, some holding instruments of penance (above). Two cherubs in heavenly glory grace the vault. A demilune window above the outer entrance and a rectangular window on a sidewall provide natural light. Opposite the vestibule entrance is an arched window cut into the interior stonewall that separates the vestibule from the nave. The lower portion of the opening is fitted with a wooden divider and kneeler for pilgrims, while the upper portion is of leaded glass. An iron screen protects the lower half of the glass window. Just beyond is the central vignette of St. Francis before the San Damiano Cross. Cristoforo Prestinari created the original statues (c. 1606), which included Francis, crucified Christ, and four angels, though the sculpture of Francis seen in the chapel today is by Dionigi Bussola. Bussola also added a stableman, a horse, three dogs and a hare (c. 1609), all reflecting a distinctive baroque influence. The walls of the diorama show a verdant landscape below and the heavenly host above and surrounding Christ crucified.

In the dimly lighted nave of Chapel II, the statue of Francis kneels before the crucified Christ, his right arm outstretched in supplication, his left arm clutched to his chest (see Chapter 3, Fig. 1). The pilgrim sees, and can even feel, Francis' penitence. Meanwhile, Christ, surrounded by four terracotta angels, looks down upon Francis (see Fig. 7). His sorrow-filled figure is imposing in its authority. Blood drips from his wounds; blood from his hands and feet stain the cross. Christ and Francis lock eyes in intimate communion. Meanwhile the stableman to the left of Francis tries to attend to a horse, as well as to three dogs chasing a hare along the back wall of the nave (see Fig. 8). The concentrated focus between Francis and Christ is reinforced by the flurry of activity to the side and between them. That fact that the dress is not representative of the thirteenth century but rather that of seventeenth-century couture encouraged the pilgrim to see the event in their own contemporary context. Within that context, the viewer could project themself into the mystical scene, becoming a participant in the action imitating Francis in both his penitence and devotion to the Crucified Christ. In a similar vein, the depiction of angels on the vaulted ceiling, some with instruments of penance such as the fasces, discipline and cilice, call the pilgrim to repentance.

Though the focus of the chapel is on the purported miraculous encounter between Francis and Christ, other episodes in Francis' spiritual evolution are addressed in the wall frescos of the vestibule. The fresco cycle tells a story of divine intervention, and of the Holy Spirit at work within Francis. To the immediate right of the chapel entrance, and flanking the exterior door, is a panel depicting Francis on his sickbed. According to his biographers, it was at this time that Francis became disillusioned with the world around him. The central panel on the right-hand wall shows Francis giving his fine clothes to a noble but bedraggled knight (see Fig. 9). The panel just to the right of the archway, leading from the vestibule into the nave, shows the dream of Francis in which Jesus points to his future as a mighty leader. Armor and weaponry indicate Francis' misconception of the message as a prediction of knightly success. The panel to the left of the archway depicts the second dream, in which Jesus corrects that misconception, telling him to abandon knightly aspirations and to go home to Assisi. The panel on the left wall portrays the

Fig. 9. Francis exchanges clothes with a poor knight. Chapel II, Sacro Monte di Orta.

Fig. 10. Francis kisses a leper. Chapel II, Sacro Monte di Orta.

story of Francis, who despite his revulsion, kisses a leper (see Fig. 10), thus marking the moment Francis "began doing penance."[15] On the panel on the back wall to the left of the vestibule entrance, the fresco repeats Francis' ecstatic vision of Christ crucified. These hagiographical portraits, arranged according to content and sequence following Bonaventure's *Major Legend of Saint Francis*,[16] underscore the special relationship that they assert Francis had with the divine long before donning a friar's robe. Their accounts of his many dreams and visions of Christ (and his later reputation for prophecy) call to mind the biblical text of Numbers 12:6: "He said, 'Now listen to the words of the Lord: Should there be a prophet among you, in visions will I reveal Myself to him, in dreams will I speak to him.'" These visions, so vividly portrayed for the pilgrim, were used by the artists "as a tool for demonstrating the saint's eminence and the divine legitimization of his actions."[17] The scenes also remind the pilgrim that the Gospel life was not easy; even Francis had many missteps and struggles.

Though not every chapel at Orta carried special sacramental blessings, a pilgrim guide from the seventeenth century noted that Chapel II earned the pilgrim an "indulgence of 100 days" for a once weekly recitation of the late sixteenth-century Litany of the Blessed Virgin Mary.[18] The incorporation of this prayer into the program of Chapel II underscores the emphasis on Marian devotion by both the Capuchins and by the post-Tridentine Church.

"Our Lady of Sorrow" Oratory

Some seventy years after the construction of Chapel II, an oratory dedicated to Our Lady of Sorrow was added to the left side of the chapel (c. 1681, see Fig. 11). It was sponsored by noted fabric merchant, Giovanni Righetti of Orta, and his bust is located in a niche just inside and above the front window of the oratory.[19] The wall frescos are by Francesco Gianoli (c. 1681), including three putti, one of whom carries a banner that reads in Latin "Virgo Mater Dolorosa," or Our Lady of Sorrow. Angels and various witnesses (including, presumably, portraits of Joseph of Aramathea, Nicodemus, and John the Evangelist) appear against a backdrop of clouds and rocks as they adorn the walls of the small chapel. The focus of the oratory is a *pietà*, a terracotta statue of Mary grieving her son; the lifeless body of Christ, carved in marble by Rossi of Novara, lies atop a sarcophagus which is in effect the upper portion of an altar designed by Monti di Borgomanero and added in 1846. Mary is flanked on either side by a terracotta angel, both of whom are looking down in the direction of Christ's face. The angels hold a white cloth with which to cover his body. The maker of the terracotta statues is unknown, but they were placed in the oratory after the altar, so sometime after 1846. In post-Tridentine Italy, this chapel underscores the importance of Mary in the devotional life of Church.

The chapel and the oratory, side by side, indelibly link the beginning of Francis' spiritual journey with the death of Jesus. Here Franciscan devotion is firmly situated within the spiritual exercises of Passion devotion. The crucifixion (Chapel II) and *pietà* (Oratory) are signposts incorporated into a shrine dedicated to St. Francis, instructing the pilgrim to meditate on the stations of Francis' spiritual journey, housed within the chapels of the Sacro Monte di Orta, just as a penitent would meditate at the Stations of the Cross.

Chapel III. St. Francis Renounces His Worldly Goods

Designed by Father Cleto da Castelletto Ticino and funded by Carlo Bascapé, the Bishop of Novara, Chapel III was constructed between 1596 and 1599. The rectilinear, classically styled chapel sits on a three-foot stylobate that is articulated along the façade and interrupted by five steps that lead up to the entrance (see Fig. 12). Two engaged, Doric columns, sitting upon tall rectilinear plinths, flank each side of the double door. Each door is pierced with a small screen-covered oval window that allows in little light. Above the doorway is a leaded-glass demilune window. Atop the columns, a plain architrave forms the

Fig. 11. The tomb of Christ. Our Lady of Sorrow Oratory, attached to Chapel II, Sacro Monte di Orta.

base of the entablature with its cornice and pediment. Toward the front end of the slate rooftop perch three crosses. The effect of the tall and linear but proportionally narrow façade compels the viewer's gaze upward and gives the chapel a sense of majesty.

Chapel III has both a nave and a vestibule. As with most chapels at Orta, the diorama occupies the nave. The theme of the chapel is renunciation, and the setting is a hearing before the church court of Assisi, the bishop presiding, where Francis breaks ties with his family:

> Within earshot of many who had gathered about, he declared: "From now on I will say freely: 'Our Father who are in heaven,' and not 'My father, Pietro di Bernardone.' Look, not only do I return his money; I give him back all my clothes. I will go to the Lord naked."[20]

There are seven terracotta statues, including the Bishop of Assisi (thought to be modeled after Bishop Bascapè), Francis, Francis' father Pietro Bernardone, three members of the council and one attendant. The action is dynamic: Francis, clothed only in a hairshirt, has just renounced his name and inheritance, and in so doing has stripped down (see Fig. 13).[21] As Francis kneels before the bishop, the prelate bends forward to wrap his mantle (a symbol of his legal and spiritual protection) around the young man. Francis has become the penitential Prodigal. Indeed, the posture of Francis and the Bishop emulates the composition of paintings, sculpture and illustrations of medieval and Renaissance depictions of The Prodigal Son. It is distinctive, however, in extending the reading of the Prodigal to the story of Francis' renunciation. Meanwhile Francis' father steps forward in irritation while the council looks on. The background frescos portray several additional onlookers both of the community and the council. Meanwhile an attendant brings Francis a "new" cloak that he cuts it into a cruciform

Fig. 12. Exterior of Chapel III, St. Francis Renounces his Worldly Goods. Sacro Monte di Orta.

shape, thus turning the garment into a statement of his faith.

In the vestibule, along the lower portion of the three exterior walls runs a course of faux marble slabs. Above that are a series of panels depicting various events relevant to Francis' spiritual evolution just prior to and after his renunciation, though the series does not run in the narrative sequence provided by the hagiographers. To the pilgrim's immediate right upon entering the chapel is the scene of Francis praying before the San Damiano cross. Moving to the left along the wall, the next scene is Francis selling his father's cloth and horse at market, followed by Francis being mocked and bullied by local children and, lastly along this wall, a depiction of Francis being captured and escorted home by his father. Along the opposite wall, the scenes depict Francis giving money to the priest of San Damiano, Francis ministering to the lepers, Francis being beaten by thieves, and Francis, after having been given a tunic by the bishop, tailoring it into the shape of a cross.

As the eye travels upward from the wall panels, the viewer takes in lunettes decorated with the personification of virtues such as perseverance, vigilance, patience, solitude, simplicity, humility, victory over oneself, compunction, suffering, and penance (see Fig. 14). For didactic purposes Franciscans used depictions of personified virtues (as well as vices, though not in this program) to promote an emotional response during meditation.[22] Such artistic images complimented the mental images friars used to aid memory in preaching and meditation.[23]

The ceiling is adorned with eight roughly triangular frescos of angels, each carrying a penitential instrument such as the Bible, fasces, hairshirt, rope, scourge and flail. The Capuchin Franciscans were particularly well known for their strict observance of discipline, including bodily mortification. In this they imitated the practices of their revered founder whose goal was to embrace and imitate the sufferings of Christ.[24]

The message of this chapel urges pilgrims to follow in Francis' footsteps by detaching themselves from worldly possessions. But it does more than that. As the fresco cycles make clear, for the Capuchins renunciation comprises more than goods—money and clothes; renunciation extends to all things of this world, including the flesh and, through that, the self and self-will. An image above the central section of the vestibule screen underscores this message; there stands an armored knight, a warrior for Christ, holding the palm of victory. It is inscribed, "*Dispregio del Mundo*" or "Contempt of the World."

Chapel IV. St. Francis Listening to the Mass

The chapel, another designed by Father Cleto da Castelletto Ticino, was constructed between 1609 and 1610, and replicates the occasion when Francis experienced his calling as a mendicant:

Fig. 13. Francis renounces his family, his name and his inheritance before the Bishop of Assisi. Chapel III, Sacro Monte di Orta.

Fig. 14. Personification of virtues. Ceiling frescos, Chapel III, Sacro Monte di Orta.

Fig. 15. The exterior of Chapel IV, St. Francis Listening to the Mass. Sacro Monte di Orta.

The Prestinari statues were crafted over the period from 1610 to 1616. Giovanni Battista and Giovanni Mauro Di Roberio (the Fiammenghini) painted the interior and exterior chapel frescos in 1614–15, though this attribution is contested.[26] Funds for construction of the chapel, in keeping with the populist nature of the Franciscans, their art and its purpose, were raised through begging.

Chapel IV, which a pilgrim can view only through two iron-screened exterior windows, is small in comparison to the chapels that allow entry (see Fig. 15). The building is rectilinear with a portico along the length of the front exterior. The portico's dual-arched façade and vaulted roof are richly frescoed with faded scenes of various Christian symbols—all underscoring the orthodoxy of the Franciscan tradition (the bishop's miter, the crucifix, the instruments of penance, a chalice and monstrance, and the mandylion) as well as cherubs, angels, and faux marble panels.

The interior is intended to replicate the church of St. Mary of the Angels, or the Porziuncola (see Fig. 16). Looking inside, to the pilgrims' left is an altar upon which stand a metal crucifix and four tall candlesticks. On the left wall, serving as a backdrop to the altar, is a fresco of a suffering Christ crucified that echoes Francis' encounter with the crucifix of San Damiano. Before the altar and with his back to the congregation stands the Benedictine priest from the Abbey of Monte Subasio, whose once colorful vestment, now faded with time, contrasts sharply with the tattered garment of Francis, who stands to the viewers' right and just behind the priest. Though Francis' tunic is humble, he wears both shoes and a belt that in terms of the narrative chronology indicate a moment prior to his revelatory understanding of scripture (the Gospel reading Matthew 10:9–10) and, in turn, his new vocation (see Fig. 17). The priest stands on the raised dais of the altar. Francis and one other religious stand on a elevated floor just below the dais. All three hold their hands clasped in supplication. Their elevated

One day while he was devoutly hearing a Mass of the Apostles, the Gospel was read in which Christ sends out his disciples to preach and give them the Gospel form of life, that they may not keep gold or silver or money in their belts, nor have a wallet for their journey, nor may they have two tunics, nor shoes, nor staff. Hearing, understanding, and committing this to memory, the friend of the apostolic poverty was then overwhelmed with an indescribable joy. "This is what I want," he said, "this is what I desire with all my heart!" Immediately, he took off the shoes from his feet, put down his staff, denounced his wallet and money, and, satisfied with one tunic, threw away his leather belt and put on a piece of rope for a belt. He directed all his heart's desire to carry out what he had heard and to conform in every way to the rule of right living given to the apostles.[25]

Fig. 16. An interior view of Chapel IV, St. Francis Listening to the Mass. Sacro Monte di Orta.

Fig. 17. St. Francis and the Priest, Chapel IV, Sacro Monte di Orta.

Fig. 18. Exterior of Chapel V, The First Followers of Francis take the Habit. Sacro Monte di Orta.

status, both literally and figuratively, sets them apart from the other figures in the diorama that cluster to the right side of the chapel and are placed on a lower elevation. In the mix are children and adults, men and women, the impoverished and the burghers—even a dog is welcome in the sanctuary. The frescos surrounding the diorama in the lower register of the walls are a continuation of the scene, depicting more of the faithful with the same demographic diversity.

The frescos of the upper walls, lunettes, and vault depict Francis abandoning his shoes, bag, and stick; Francis in his new garb (tunic with cowl and rope belt); Francis before Mary enthroned; angelic personifications of the gifts of the Holy Spirit; and angelic illustrations of Desire for God, Obedience to God, and Diligence. A fourth angelic illustration, whose inscription has been lost, depicts a delightful scene of a semi-nude angel holding a squirrel in the palm of her hand. The representation of the resourceful and tenacious squirrel could well represent strength in the face of adversity,[27] an important message for each pilgrim on his or her own path to spiritual growth.

Sometime during the year 1208 or 1209 at the little chapel of the Porziuncola, Francis heard the Gospel of Matthew 10:9–10. It was at this juncture that Francis changed garments by altering his hermit's tunic into a symbol of his own making: that of apostolic missionary. The identity of Francis, and thus of the Franciscan mission, was firmly established. With the significance of this moment in mind, the message of Chapel IV is threefold. In the first place the composition identifies an important juncture in Francis' calling, an event that foreshadows the founding of the Franciscan Order. Secondly, Francis' epiphany, mediated at it was by a priest, illustrates the important and close relationship between the Franciscans and Catholic orthodoxy. Lastly, the artistic program of the chapel emphasizes the Franciscan message of inclusion. For the pilgrim this is implicit; Francis is a saint for all believers and all are welcomed in the congregation of the church.

Chapel V. The First Followers of St. Francis Take the Habit

Father Cleto drew the blueprints for Chapel V in 1609 and construction began in 1610. The building was completed in 1613. The style of the exterior façade is classical, with a single arch and a wide architrave capped by cornice and pediment (see Fig. 18). Two freestanding, smooth-sided Doric columns on either side of the arch and two engaged Doric columns flanking a center rectilinear window support the portico. Traces of faded and damaged frescos decorate the façade. Like Chapel IV, this chapel can only be viewed from outside. Both Christoforo Prestinari's statues and Giovanni Battista Fiammenghino's frescos were completed by the end of 1615. The financiers of the chapel were the residents of Orta.

The thematic content of the chapel follows the narrative trajectory of Francis'

Fig. 19. The ordination of the first brothers. Chapel V, Sacro Monte di Orta.

newfound vocation, depicted in Chapel IV. By 1209, Francis was devoted to a life of poverty. Shortly thereafter, according to his biographers, like-minded men began to follow Francis

> as the truth of the man of God's simple teaching and life became known to many, and men began to be moved to penance and, abandoning all things, joined him in habit and life. The first among these was Bernard, a venerable man, who was made a sharer in the divine vocation and merited to be the firstborn son of the blessed Father, both in priority of time and in the gift of holiness.[28]

A statue of Francis stands at the center of the sanctuary (see Fig. 19). He holds the now-familiar brown Franciscan tunic in his outstretched arms, extending the garment to a kneeling man. To the saints' left, two more supplicants kneel in anticipation of ordination by Francis. Pages and retainers, all male, compose the remaining figures of the diorama. Immediately behind the saint and his followers, the surrounding fresco is more demographically diverse, including not only men but also women, and what appears to be a little girl. The spatial framework indicates an outdoor setting for the scene.

The upper walls are adorned with frescos depicting various notable members of the early order at the moment of their conversion. The arcade features personifications of the four essential Capuchin virtues: Poverty, Obedience, Meditation, and Mortification. Frescos on the vault depict the end times, when believers young and old, male and female, powerful and powerless, rich and poor, receive their crowns as they are ushered by the angels into the celestial heavens (see Fig. 20).

Fig. 20. Personification of the four essential Capuchin virtues: Poverty, Obedience, Meditation, and Mortification. Arcade frescos, Chapel V, Sacro Monte di Orta.

Fig. 21. The exterior of Chapel VI, St. Francis sends the First Disciples out to Preach & Miracles Confirm the Preaching. Sacro Monte di Orta.

Chapel VI. St. Francis Sends His First Disciples Out to Preach & Miracles Confirm the Preaching

The chapel was constructed in the classical style between 1614 and 1615, though the identity of the architect has been lost; he is described only as an "Honorable Father" from Milan.[29] An arched colonnade extends around three sides (front, left, and right) of the building. An apse defines the rear of the sanctuary (see Fig. 21). Blind windows, architectural molding, and (now faded) frescos decorate the exterior. Once again Prestinari and the Fiammenghini executed the artistic program of the chapel interior, which was completed by 1619. The residents of Orta financed the chapel. Later renovations introduced baroque additions, including the statues by Bussola (c. 1662) now seen in the nave. The result is two discrete dioramas, one (located in the apse) dedicated to the theme of Franciscan missions, the other (located in the nave) dedicated to the healing miracles that illustrate the order's divine sanction. This second theme comments on, and underscores the legitimacy of, the first.

According to the ocular plot, the pilgrim stands in the vestibule and gazes through the screen, and through the dynamic baroque scene of the nave into the apse (see Fig. 22). There, sober and static terracotta statues of the central diorama depict Francis and six followers. Despite the inherent risk of this new, global apostolic mission, the artists created a calm stillness that pervades the scene; to the pilgrim, the steadfast commitment of the friars is in no doubt. Frescos decorating the wall surface of the apse emphasize the noble purpose, and dangers, of Franciscan missions, dangers that according to the literary traditions were well understood by Francis:

Fig. 22. View from the vestibule into the Nave and Apse of Chapel VI. Sacro Monte di Orta.

"Go, my dear brothers," he said to them, "two by two through different parts of the world, announcing peace to the people and penance for the remission of sins. Be patient in trials, confident that the Lord will fulfill His plan and promise. Respond humbly to those who question you. Bless those who persecute you. Give thanks to those who harm you and bring false charges against you, for because of these things an eternal kingdom is prepared for us."[30]

In the fresco just above Francis, one sees Jesus sending his disciples to preach. The fresco directly behind Francis is more provocative: it is of Jesus' crucifixion. It implies, graphically, the possibility of painful persecution, but also eventual and anticipated sacred reward. Likewise, frescos in the vault depict various Old Testament scenes of persecution, such as Jonah thrown into the sea (Jon 1:15; see Fig. 23) and Jeremiah thrown into a cistern (Jer 38:6).

In the foreground, eleven terracotta figures compose the diorama of the nave, where the action is divided into two discrete scenes. To the viewer's left are six figures: two friars and four commoners (see Fig. 22). All the commoners are poorly clothed, physically impaired men. Two are in a state of mid-collapse, unable to stand, though their particular ailments are undisclosed. Both friars offer assistance; one gestures a benediction towards a pilgrim, the other makes the sign of the cross on the other pilgrim's forehead. Behind the friars stands a third pilgrim with multiple ailments: an amputated left leg, a bandaged head, a bandaged left arm, a withered right arm. Toward the front left a double amputee, a leper's horn tied around his waist, sits strapped to a sled (see Fig. 24). Meanwhile, one of the friars guides the viewer's gaze towards the right and to the second scene within the nave. In this episode a woman, held by one male companion and protected by another, collapses on the ground. Two friars, each with walking staff in one

Fig. 23. Painting of Jonah being thrown overboard. Chapel VI, Sacro Monte di Orta.

hand and gesticulating stage right with the other, draw the viewer's attention to the immediately adjacent wall fresco of Brother Sylvester and his famous vision of Francis' battle against a dragon: as the dragon attacks Assisi, Francis opens his mouth, emanates a golden cross, and expels multiple demons from the dragon's own opened mouth.[31] The miracle recounted in the painting is the encoded correlative of the diorama: a woman delivered of evil spirits. Such a subject would have been familiar to those versed in Franciscan legend, wherein Francis cures many individuals of demonic possession. Women were frequently portrayed as the victims of such possession, a condition, perhaps, that scholars now take to have been epilepsy or mental illness.[32]

The emphasis in this chapel on physical impairment reflects an important element of the Franciscan tradition. Francis suffered from a debilitating eye disease for over six years. By the time he died, he was blind. It is an important point towards understanding the Franciscan message at Orta as images of the physically impaired are present in both the central and peripheral spaces of numerous chapels (for example Chapels II, III, IV, IX, XIII, XVI, XIX, XX). But even when on the margin, the impaired are part of the community, the community of plastic and paint but also the community of the pilgrim. In Chapel VI, just as the foregrounded figures are spatially closer to the pilgrim, the figures of the impaired are emotionally immediate to the pilgrim. The figures of the physically impaired functioned as mediators and messengers of theological instruction: the suffering body was a step towards union with the suffering Francis, and therefore the suffering Christ.

Chapel VII. Pope Innocent III Gives His Approval of the Order

The *fabbriciere* of the Sacro Monte funded the construction of this chapel, and building took place largely between 1619 and 1625. The chapel is a rotunda, capped by a windowed, oval cupola, and fronted with a four columned portico (see Fig. 25). Engaged ionic columns surround the rotunda.

The interior frescos were painted by Antonio Maria Crespi and are dated by the artists' signature to 1629. Statues of the diorama were added in two phases: Giovanni and Melchiorre d'Enrico sculpted the cluster of cardinals, the pope, St. Francis, and a couple of the friars, c. 1634. In 1662, Bussola added additional friars, the Swiss Guard, and dignitaries, all executed in the baroque style. The ironwork screen (c. 1623–34) was designed by the Milanese craftsman Stefano Penaggio and its execution is attributed to various Milanese artists, including Penaggio, Ambrogio and Arbana.[33]

The diorama in the chapel is rather staid, with some baroque animation added by the later Bussola statues (see Fig. 26). From beyond the iron screen, the pilgrims' gaze is immediately drawn to the figure of the Pope flanked by cardinals and enthroned on a dais. A now-faded red frescoed canopy frames the figure of the Pope. Francis and the friars kneel before Pope Innocent III in humble submission, while the Pope's hand is raised in the sign of blessing. The few animated figures on the periphery of the diorama contrast with the stillness that is the focus of the pilgrims gaze. It is a stillness of dramatic intensity. Much was hanging in the balance for those first Franciscans, just as for the later Capuchin Reform.

The scene captures the moment that Pope Innocent grants the Friar's petition, officially sanctioning their order and allowing them to preach:

> He saw in a dream, as he recounted, the Lateran basilica almost ready to fall down. A little poor man, small and scorned, was propping it up with his own back bent so that it would not fall. "I'm sure," he said "he is the one who will hold up Christ's Church by what he does and what he teaches." Because of this, filled with exceptional devotion, he bowed to the request in everything and always loved Christ's servant with special love. Then he granted what was asked and promised even more. He approved the rule, gave them a mandate to preach pen-

Fig. 24. A friar ministering to an ill man, with a leper watching nearby. Chapel VI, Sacro Monte di Orta.

Fig. 25. Exterior of Chapel VII, Innocent III gives his Approval of the Order. Sacro Monte di Orta.

Fig. 26. The brothers receive approval from Pope Innocent III. Chapel VII, Sacro Monte di Orta.

Fig. 27. God looks down upon Moses in the Wilderness. Ceiling fresco, Chapel VII, Sacro Monte di Orta.

ance, and had small tonsures given to all the lay brothers, who were accompanying the servant of God, so that they could freely preach the word of God.[34]

It was a momentous occasion in the history of the order, and one not without controversy. In 1209, Francis wrote a *Rule* to guide the life of the brothers.[35] Francis' way of life was recognized by supporters as a move toward "Gospel perfection."[36] But critics had their suspicions. Francis founded his brotherhood during a period of schismatic heresies, such as those of the Cathars and Waldensians. What proof did Francis have that his movement was not just another heresy, especially given the similarity between his claim to apostolic poverty and that of the Waldensians? Jealousy also played a part in the criticism. The Franciscan way of life challenged the secular clergy's prerogative to preach, while their mendicancy rivaled that of the Dominicans. According to tradition, Francis allayed concerns about his intentions by taking along eleven brothers, which, when counting himself, made twelve brothers, thus modeling the twelve disciples of Christ. Bonaventure underscored the Order's divine approval by relating the story of Pope Innocent's dream of the Lateran. The Order was still defending their privilege centuries later, and the artistic program of the chapel reflects this position as the frescos in particular speak of the history, and orthodoxy, of the order. A fresco of the Last Supper, with the twelve disciples and covenant of communion, evokes the twelve friar's audience with Pope Innocent, a scene that is also painted on the walls. The Pope's Lateran vision, wherein Francis saves the Lateran by upholding the building pace his rebuilding of San Damiano (Chapel II) is also depicted. In both cases Francis supports the established church (both physically and metaphorically), he does not found a new one. Another covenantal relationship is found in the depiction of David and the Ark of the Covenant. Moses and the Mosaic Covenant feature prominently in the program as Moses stands with Jesus and Elijah (and in the company of Peter, John, and James), and then again when he is portrayed as leader of Israel (see Fig. 27). Moses points up, directing the pilgrim's eye to a portrait of God in the central ceiling medallion. God in turn points to the Pope. Another panel shows Francis' vision of the tree, representing the growth of the Order.[37]

The wall frescos are separated by *trompe l'oeil* marble columns that support standing portraits, though most of these are missing. The figures wear green tunics and carry banners inscribed with biblical passages. One of the figures is St. Rocco (d. 1327), identifiable by his lesions even though the torso and head are missing. Like Francis, Rocco was born to wealth but renounced his possessions to become a mendicant. He ministered to the ill, again, just like Francis. He carries a banner with the words "*Vacillantes Confirmaverunt Iob 4*," which refers the pilgrim to Job 4:4: "Your words have supported those who stumbled; you have strengthened faltering knees." A second figure, unidentifiable, carries a banner that quotes Psalm 77, which praises the God of Salvation, while a third missing figure holds banner referencing Deuteronomy 29, again affirming the covenantal relationship between God and His chosen people. The artists portray Francis and his *Rule* in distinguished company, as part of a long successive line of holy mediators between heaven and earth.

Chapel VIII. St. Francis on a Chariot of Fire

Chapel VIII captures the dramatic vision of Francis, embodied in a glowing orb, driving a chariot of fire. Thomas of Celano reports:

> One night the blessed father Francis was away from them in body. About midnight, some of the brothers were sleeping and others were praying in silence with deep feeling, when a brilliant fiery chariot entered through the little door of the house, and moved here and there

Fig. 28. Exterior of Chapel VIII, St. Francis on a Chariot of Fire. Sacro Monte di Orta.

Fig. 29. St. Francis drives his Chariot of Fire. Chapel VIII, Sacro Monte di Orta.

and was likewise funded by the *fabbriciere*. It was completed in 1629. The structure is polygonal, with an elevated porch accessible by steps from three different directions (see Fig. 28). An arcade surrounds the building. Above the roofline, a smaller domed polygonal cupola hints at the elevation of the interior vignette. Pilgrims are not allowed access to the interior, but can peer through one of the many windows in the exterior walls and doors. These portals allow the viewer multiple perspectives of the scene inside.

The d'Enrico brothers, who had done much of the diorama for Chapel VII, were commissioned for the nine terracotta figures of Chapel VIII as well. The suspended sculptures of St. Francis, the horses, and the chariot, all of which were carved of wood, were the special commission of Bartolomeo Tiberino (see Fig. 29). The wooden sculptures were painted by Christofo Martinoli (Il Rocca), who also painted the chapel's frescos. The artistic program was undertaken over the course of three years and was completed with the installation of the airborne chariot in 1641.

The nine terracotta figures are arranged along the back wall of the chapel, every other brother reclining (having been awakened by the brilliant light) or kneeling/standing (having been interrupted at prayer) (see Fig. 30). According to hagiographic accounts the vision took place in an abandoned hut, though no attempt has been made to replicate that setting. The floor of the chapel is barren, the walls paneled with frescoed scenes from Francis' life and, above, the chariot hangs suspended from an elaborately painted vault.

Although some of the frescos are in a poor state of repair, inscriptions along the lower register make it possible to identify the scenes at eye level. From the pilgrim's right to left: (1) Francis explains the vision of the chariot to the brothers (see Fig. 31); (2) Francis leads the souls of the saved; (3) Francis appears to Brother Leo and displays his stigmata; and (4) Francis appears before the brothers in Arles as they listen to St. Antho-

through the little house two or three times. On top of it sat a large ball that looked like the sun, and it made the night bright as day.[38]

Construction began on the chapel in 1624, just as that of Chapel VII was winding down,

CATALOGUE OF CHAPELS

Fig. 30. The friars are awakened by Francis in his Chariot of Fire. Chapel VIII, Sacro Monte di Orta.

ny preach about the crucified Christ. Each of these subjects stresses the relationship between Francis and Christ, indeed, Francis as a second Christ. Like Jesus appearing before his disciples (Matthew 28:16–20; Luke 24:13–52), so Francis appeared to his followers.[39] Furthermore, in making the connection even more explicit, Celano (and Bonaventure after him) notes that at Arles, Francis appeared "lifted up in the air with his hands extended as if on a cross."[40]

The frescos of the vault echo the connection between Francis and Jesus as well as Francis' privileged place among other mediators between God and humankind, at least according to the Franciscan tradition. There is a fresco of Jesus appearing before his disciples and another depicting the Last Supper. Elisha and Elijah are also prominent in the artistic program, for followers subsequently understood Francis as a new Elijah, who was borne to heaven in a horse-drawn chariot of fire (2 Kings 2:11–14). Bonaventure (c. 1221–74) elaborates on the connection between Francis and Elijah and their special commission:

> Like a second Elijah,
> God had made him
> a chariot and charioteer for spiritual
>   men.[41]

And that through this connection with Elijah, Francis was a legitimate (and orthodox) source of spiritual guidance:

> Shown to them by the Lord as one
> coming in the spirit and power of Elias,
> and as Israel's chariot and charioteer, he
> had been made leader for spiritual men.
> When the holy man rejoined his brothers,
> he began to comfort them concerning the
> vision they had been shown from heaven,
> probe the secrets of their consciences,
> predict the future, and radiate with
> miracles. In this manner, he revealed
> that the twofold spirit of Elias rested
> upon him in such plentitude that it was

Fig. 31. St. Francis explains the Vision of the Chariot of Fire. Wall fresco, Chapel VIII, Sacro Monte di Orta.

Fig. 32. Exterior of Chapel IX, St. Clare Takes the Veil. Sacro Monte di Orta.

absolutely safe for all to follow his life and teaching.[42]

For the followers of the saint, the vision underscores the authority granted Francis by God. And, as the episode follows shortly after his having received papal approval for the new order, it also affirms the decision of Pope Innocent (see Chapel VII).

Chapel IX. St. Clare Takes the Veil

The *fabbriciere* financed the construction of Chapel IX, which began in 1634 and ended in 1639, though the artistic program was not finished until almost 1650. Even then, a baroque remodeling sometime after 1661 saw the introduction of additional terracotta figures. The artists Melchiorre and Giovanni Righi (sculptors), Giacomo Ferro (sculptor), Cristoforo Martinoli (Il Rocca, painter), and later Dionigi Bussola (sculptor) decorated the interior, which replicates the nave of the church of St. Mary of the Angels, also known as the Porziuncola. The chapel is a rectilinear building with a squared, two-story porch affixed to a two-story nave (see Fig. 32). Pilgrims are allowed no further than the porch, but the ironwork doorway and its lunette, as well as the clerestory window of the nave, illuminate the interior for optimal viewing.

The chapel captures the conversion of Clare in 1212. As told in the anonymous *Legend of Saint Clare*:

> And so she ran to Saint Mary of the Portiuncula, leaving behind her home, city, and relatives. There the brothers, who were observing sacred vigils before the little altar of God, received the virgin Clare with torches. There, immediately after rejecting the filth of Babylon, she gave the world "a bill of divorce." There, her hair shorn by the hands of the brothers, she put aside every kind of fine dress.[43]

In the diorama, Clare, accompanied by her aunt, her sister, and a companion, kneels before Francis at the altar of the church (see Fig. 33). Her hair has been shorn and she has relinquished her fine coat. All of the figures in the immediate scene face Clare, with the exception of Francis, who looks out beyond the kneeling woman to the viewer. In the same way, the two figures on the periphery and closest to the viewer—an amputee to the viewers' left and a mother holding an infant with a toddler at her feet standing to the viewer's right—both look directly toward the pilgrim (see Fig. 34). The three figures, Francis, the amputee and the mother, form a triangular matrix that invites the viewer to participate in the scene, indeed in the conversion. While all other figures gesture toward Clare, these three figures gesture toward the viewer.

The frescos are dynamic with movement and action. Behind the altar is the statue of Our Lady of Assumption, surrounded by sculptural and frescoed putti and angels riding on the clouds of Heaven. The combination of these single- and three-dimensional images forms a distinctive multi-layered perspective. Just above Our Lady is a fresco of Christ and Mary sitting side by side on heavenly thrones (foreshadowing the imagery of the Porziuncola Indulgence of Chapels X and XI), each commending Francis and Clare respectively. In a post-Tridentine environment, the emphasis on Mary is clear affirmation of her very special place in Catholic theology. It also underscores the legitimacy of the Poor Clares.

Episodes from Clare's life line the walls of the chapel and include: (1) the cutting of her hair by Francis, (2) the moment her sister Agnes determines to join Clare, (3) the attempted kidnapping of Agnes by their uncle, (4) the arrival of Clare and her sisters at the Benedictine monastery at Monte Subasio and, finally (5) the sisters' arrival at San Damiano.

The artistic program of Chapel IX highlights not only Clare's story and her role as *alter Franciscus*, but also Clare's connection to other important women in biblical history and her role as successor of these strong figures and the virtues they represent. In the vaults and lunettes, there is Judith holding the head of Holefernes (symbolizing strength); the creation of Eve (identifying Clare as a helpmate for Francis) (see Fig. 35);

Fig. 33. St. Francis cuts off the hair of St. Clare as she becomes a religious. Chapel IX, Sacro Monte di Orta.

Fig. 34. An amputee engages the viewer outside the screen with a direct gaze. Interior of Chapel IX, St. Clare takes the Veil. Sacro Monte di Orta.

Fig. 36. Exterior of Chapel X, St. Francis Victorious over Temptation. Sacro Monte di Orta.

Chapel X. St. Francis Victorious over Temptation/Satan

Chapel X is a hexagonal building (c. 1648) with front steps leading to a doorway that is flanked by columns supporting an arched pediment (see Fig. 36). There is a square clerestory window above the pediment. At the pinnacle of the roof is an iron cross created by Pietro Ponti of Pettenasco in 1653. Upon entering the chapel, the pilgrim stands in a small, foreshortened vestibule separated from the diorama by an iron screen. The screen also dates to the mid-seventeenth century but the artist's name has been lost over time. The statues of the diorama have traditionally been thought the work of Dionigi Bussola, but are now considered by some scholars the work of Antonio Pini de Bellagio (c. 1654).[45] The frescos (c. 1665) are by Carlo Francesco and Giuseppe Nuvolone.

The central inspiration for Chapel X, "St. Francis Victorious over Temptation/Satan," is a story found in Arnald of Sarrant's *Chronicle of the Twenty-four Generals*. Driven by demonic temptations, Francis flees the Porziuncola to the nearby forest:

> When blessed Francis was in the middle of the woods, his flesh all stained and bloodied from the thorns, he said: "It is better for me to acknowledge the passion of my Lord Jesus Christ than to give in to the seduction of the deceiver."
>
> Then suddenly there was a great light in the midst of the forest and in that time of frost rose blossoms appeared right there where blessed Francis was. And a countless host of angels suddenly appeared both in the woods and in the said church next to the woods, and behold they cried with one voice: "Blessed Francis, hurry to the Savior and his Mother who await you in the church."[46]

Chapel X augments this story with three related subplots: (1) the striking drama of good versus evil in St. Francis' daily pursuit of

Miriam, along with Moses and Aaron, leading the Israelites in the desert (symbolizing leadership); and the wise woman of Tekoa advising King David (symbolizing wisdom).

Clare is extolled in the hagiographies of St. Francis, but the details of her life and her full conversion story are absent. The main source of her biography as it is depicted in the artistic program at Orta seems to be the thirteenth-century *Legend of Saint Clare*.[44] When, according to that *Legend*, on Palm Sunday of 1212 the wealthy Clare Offreduccio went before Francis at the altar of the Porziuncola to renounce her worldly possessions, what followed was her foundation of the first women's order to espouse poverty and the apostolic life. Clare and her followers represent the growth and influential reach of the Franciscan order. Clare, then, stands as an important symbol of inclusion, of both gender and social class, for pilgrims to the Sacro Monte di Orta.

Fig. 37. St. Francis lying on thorns between Devils and Angels. Chapel X, Sacro Monte di Orta.

the Gospel Life, (2) the earthly Grace given by God through the gift of indulgence and, at the end of time, (3) the ultimate redemption of humankind purchased through the sacrifice of Jesus Christ. The antagonists are the various temptations (often in the form of demons) that continuously challenge the saint's devotion. The legends documenting this struggle can be found in various thirteenth- and fourteenth- century Franciscan sources, with humankind's redemption in the final victory over Satan illustrated by the Book of Revelation (rather than the story of Christ's Passion, as is so often the case at Orta). Chapel X, more than any other chapel to this point, reflects the tremendous variety of influential medieval and Renaissance literary sources both for the Franciscan legend in general and for the message of Sacro Monte di Orta in particular.

The artistic program of Chapel X is an example in which the scenes, both painted and sculptural, do not form a unified vision but are nevertheless connected by theme and/or narrative trajectory. Though the pilgrim is first drawn to the dynamic (and fairly scary) diorama before them (see Fig. 37), the program as a whole flows nicely in a sequential spiraling narrative that crescendos, as the believer is guided through paintings of vari-

Fig. 38. Angels point the way to the Porziuncola. Chapel X, Sacro Monte di Orta.

ous demonic temptations, then again to the diorama of Francis' dramatic encounter with Satan outside the Garden of the Porziuncola, next on to Francis' theophany of Jesus and Mary inside the Porziuncola, where they bestow the gift of the Indulgence until, finally, the viewer, eyes raised aloft, meditates upon a vision of the Apocalypse and the salvific triumph of Christianity.

The diorama of Chapel X is breathtaking in its sublime portrayal of the battle between good and evil. Francis, naked, lies upon the barren and rocky ground in the wooded wilderness (pace Jesus in the wilderness; Matt 4) (see Fig. 37). To the viewer's left are three winged demons (see Chapter 5, Fig. 1). The most prominent demon is, at first glance, angelic in appearance, but horns, clawed hands and feet identify the figure as Satan, the fallen angel. To the viewer's right, a group of angels guide Francis toward the silk path and into the action of the wall painting of the Porziuncola Indulgence (see Fig. 38). Interspersed throughout the diorama are animals: rabbits, goats, a squirrel, a lion and a boar (the boar is symbol of greed and passion; it is replicated above the chapel door, where the animal is fighting an elephant, a Christian symbol of chastity).

Of the many temptations Francis encountered during his lifetime, the artists chose four illustrative episodes for the wall panels: (1) Francis driving away the devil (the temptation to lust) by rolling in the snow and performing a sign act by making snowball family;[47] (2) Francis kneeling at *prie dieu*, in front of which creeps a horned demon;[48] (3) the courtesan of Frederick II attempting to seduce Francis and failing (see Chapter 5, Fig. 5);[49] and, (4) Francis, having been pushed off a cliff at La Verna by the Devil, lands softly and unharmed.[50] The final wall panel of the reading line, the one to which the eye is drawn after the diorama, is not of temptation but rather of the outcome of Francis' dedicated fight against the temptations of Satan. It depicts Francis' vision of Jesus and Mary, and the subsequent gift of the Porziuncola Indulgence. [51] This panel is visually and narratively integrated into the action of the diorama.

Various allegorical and biblical figures in service of the narrative adorn the walls and ceiling. Not surprisingly we find Job, the perennial symbol of temptation and forbearance (see Chapter 5, Fig. 3). The cartouche inscription specifically references Job 7, a passage where Job laments the harshness of life, the futility of hope, and unavoidability of death. The accompanying fresco aptly portrays the Devil attacking Job. A second portrait illustrates Mathew 4:4, when Jesus, hungry in the wilderness, refuses the Devil's temptation to turn stones into bread. Also from Matthew 4 are depictions of Satan taking Jesus to the Jerusalem Temple (Matt 4:5–6) and Jesus driving Satan away with the admonishment to serve only the Lord (Matt 4:10). Nearby, Tobit refuses dinner and defies the Assyrian king in order to bury a fellow Israelite (Tobit 2; 12:13). The apocryphal story highlights piety, faithfulness and resilience in the face of tribulations. Personifications of Virtue and Temperance complete the portraits.

In a series of larger panels along the vault we see the woman of the Apocalypse with her crown of twelve stars (Rev 12:1, 2, 5), who is commonly identified as Mary or as the Church (see Chapter 5, Fig. 4). A portrait of St. John writing what is presumably the Book of Revelation appears in the corner of the painting. In an adjacent panel Mary protects the infant Jesus from a fiery dragon (the Devil) by giving him to God (Rev 12:5). Continuing the sequence of scenes from Revelation is a panel that features archangel Michael battling an apocalyptic dragon (Rev 12:7; see Fig. 39).

Fig. 39. Archangel Michael battles a dragon. Ceiling fresco, Chapel X, Sacro Monte di Orta.

Elsewhere on the walls are the portraits of female allegories. There is a young, barebreasted Temptation, a similarly barebreasted Penance holding an instrument of self-mortification as well as the palm of martyrdom, and Virtue holding a crown of laurel leaves, all patterned on the iconography detailed in Cesare Ripa's *Iconologia,* a reference work used by the designers of the Sacro Monte.[52] The depiction of Virtue calls to mind Francis' "A Salutation of the Virtues," in praise of Wisdom, Simplicity, Poverty, Charity, Humility, and Obedience.[53]

The context of the central narrative concerns one of the ongoing controversies in the medieval-Renaissance church: the historicity of the Porziuncola Indulgence. According to tradition, in the year 1216 Francis received a vision of Jesus, Mary and the Angels, wherein Jesus granted pilgrims to the church of Mary of the Angels (the Porziuncola) freedom from retribution for all sins. Days later, an astounded Pope Honorious III confirmed the indulgence. The indulgence is still in effect to this day on the first Sunday of August at any Franciscan church or shrine. Nevertheless,

Fig. 40. Exterior of Chapel XI, The Indulgence of the Porziuncola. Sacro Monte di Orta.

the earliest documentation of this indulgence dates some sixty years after the reported events and obviously extended a popularity and authority to Franciscanism that other religious orders of the time found enviable. Stories circulated to enhance the authenticity of the event, including the one found in Sarrant's *Chronicle of the Twenty-four Generals*.[54] The artistic program of Chapel X, then, simultaneously asserts Francis' conformity to Christ, his special status with respect to the Holy Family, and the historical and spiritual veracity of the Porziuncola Indulgence, which itself is the focus of the following Chapel XI. For pilgrims, this chapel encapsulates the struggle against earthly temptations in the lives of all humans, the temporal salvation selflessly requested by Francis on behalf of all believers, and the eternal salvation awaiting all the faithful at the end of days.

Chapel XI. The Indulgence of the Porziuncola

Chapel XI is one of the earlier chapels of the sacred mountain, designed by Father Cleto of Castelletto Tricino and constructed in 1606–1607. The financier of the chapel was the vice-mayor of Orta, a lawyer named Giovanni Antonio Martelli whose name and family crest appear on the façade. The exterior stone statues were executed by Christoforo Prestinari, and Giovani and Melchiorre d'Enrico (completed by 1630). Only traces remain of the exterior frescos by Giacomo Filippo Monti (1623). The interior terracotta statues were the work of Christoforo Prestinari (c. 1615–17), while the frescos were painted by Pier Francesco Mazzucchelli (il Morazzone) (1616–17) and Giacomo Filippo Monti (1623). The elaborate and very beautiful iron screen is attributed to Giovanni Battista Contini (1688).

The exterior of Chapel XI reproduces the huge Basilica Santa Maria degli Angeli in Assisi, which was built around the Porziuncola and, as such, this sanctuary is one of the more elaborate buildings of the Sacro Monte (see Fig. 40). The large portico rests upon four freestanding columns, two on each side of the doorway, while a broken pediment, with a statue niche and a demilune window above, caps the door. A narrow architrave supports the arched vault of the frieze above the entrance and flanking statue niches. A central carved medallion decorates the triangular pediment. Along the left and right side of the building runs a portico decorated with ornamental frescos and terminating in a statuary niche. The statues of the façade are Saint Francis, Saint Giulio, the Virgin Mary, God, and two allegorical figures; angels perch on the rooftop. Inside is a replica of the little Porziuncola, with only a nave and an apse; the nave, separated from the apse by an elaborate iron screen, functions as a vestibule for pilgrims.

Chapel XI culminates the story of Chapel X, where Francis triumphs over satanic temptation and finds himself invited into the Porziuncola, into the presence of Jesus Christ and Mary, where Jesus gives Francis the opportunity to make one request:

> There then appeared to him a straight path as if of decorated silk going up to the church, and blessed Francis took from the rose patch twelve red roses

Fig. 41. God and Christ in ceiling center, surrounded variously by Putti, angels. The female figures standing upon plinths are personifications of the Beatitudes. Ceiling frescos, Chapel XI. Sacro Monte di Orta.

and twelve white roses and entered the church. He proceeded to the altar and placed on it the roses he had brought with him in joined hands. There he saw Jesus Christ standing with his Mother at his right with a great multitude of angels. Then Francis found himself dressed in a very beautiful garment before the Savior and his Mother, and the Savior said to him: "Francis, ask whatever you will for the enlightenment of the nations and the consolation of souls, to the honor and reverence of God, for you have been designated a light to the nations and the repair of the earthly church, that is the Church Militant."[55]

In response, Francis asks for an indulgence, that is, the remission of the temporal punishment of sins that have been subject to the Sacrament of Confession.[56] That indulgence is known to this day as the Porziuncola Indulgence and occurs on the first Sunday of August at any Franciscan church or shrine.

The walls of the vestibule in Chapel XI are covered with a narrative sequence of frescos depicting the events that led to papal approval of the indulgence (see Chapter 7, Fig. 1): (L to R) Francis prays before the crucifix just prior to demonic temptation (cf. Chapel X); an angel invites him to the church of Porziuncola where Jesus and Mary await him; Pope Innocent III dreams of several friars physically supporting the Lateran church;[57] Francis petitions Honorious III for the indulgence; Francis, in the presence of an angel, kneels before the altar of the Porziuncola and prays for the souls of all sinners; Francis announces the Porziuncola Indulgence before the pope, bishops, and a crowd of onlookers.

At the center of the vaulted ceiling above the vestibule is an octagonally-framed fresco of God and Christ in heaven, surrounded by pillowy clouds and frolicking putti (see Fig. 41). There are four triangular panels on the

Fig. 42. Jesus and Mary enthroned. Chapel XI, Sacro Monte di Orta.

dome, each with a white-robed angel holding a censer. Directly beneath these four triangular panels are lunettes; three of these contain frescos, one encases a leaded window. One lunette depicts a woman breastfeeding a child while tending two other children, another features a woman holding yet another incense burner, and a final lunette fresco is too damaged to make out. Each of the four triangular panels, and their respective lunettes, are flanked by two painted female figures each standing on an inscribed plinth. These figures are allegorical representations of the beatitudes as articulated in Matthew 5:3–10. The figures are not in the biblical sequence and some of the cartouches are illegible, but as best as we can discern based upon the remaining inscriptions and iconography they are: a woman in a tattered garment representing the poor in spirit (Matthew 5:3); a woman holding an ermine, whose white coat symbolizes purity and moderation, representing the meek (Matthew 5:5); a pious woman with her hands clasp in prayer representing the persecuted (5:10); Lady Justice with sword and scale representing the righteous (Matthew 5:6); a very sad looking woman representing those who mourn (5:4); a woman with three young children may represent the peacemaker (5:9) (this artist clearly had a sense of humour!); a serene and untroubled looking woman who seems to represent the pure of heart (5:8); and, finally, a woman standing over a dead child who may represent the merciful, who were often called to tend the sick and deceased (5:7).

Jesus and Mary are the central figures of the diorama in the apse and are flanked by four terracotta angels to either side (see Fig. 42 and Chapter 7, Fig. 2). Jesus and Mary are equally enthroned on a dais and sit beneath a gilt canopy trimmed with red, green and gold fringe. Mother and son engage each other through gaze and posture, while Jesus' extended hand invites Francis into conversation. In front of the dais is an altar, covered with a real linen cloth used during mass.[58] Frescos on the apse walls portray bucolic landscapes, *trompe l'oeil* architectural elements such as columns, and, directly behind the holy family, a radiating sun. The vault of the apse is decorated simply and sparsely with geometric designs and portraits of winged putti.

Centuries of criticism, from Wycliff and Hus to Luther, called not only the sale of indulgences but the theological underpinnings of the indulgence system into question. In Session 25, the Council of Trent, while proscribing the sale of indulgences, reaffirmed the doctrine. The artistic program of Chapel XI argues for the divine origin and legitimacy of indulgences in general, and of the Porziuncola Indulgence in particular. For the faithful, the chapel stands as testimony to the efficaciousness of Francis' mediation and the special favour shown the Franciscan Order by both the papacy and the Divine.

Chapel XII. God Reveals the Rule to St. Francis

Fig. 43. Exterior of Chapel XII, God Reveals the Rule to St. Francis. Sacro Monte di Orta.

Built between 1591 and 1597, Chapel XII, also known as the Roman Chapel because it was paid for by native Ortans living in Rome, was one of the first chapels constructed on the mount. The original chapel is an elegant two-story circular structure built upon a squared foundation (see Fig. 43). The upper story is decorated with engaged columns and is pierced by a tall rectangular lead-glass window and several small round windows. Its gently sloping roof is topped with a circular cupola. A heavy, rectilinear neo-classical portico was added in the late eighteenth century. Inside, a small vestibule allows just enough room for a few pilgrims at a time to peer upward through the wooden screen and toward the elevated diorama perched upon a faux mountaintop. Christoforo Prestinari sculpted the terracotta figures. The current frescos were painted in 1772 by Giovanni Battista Cantalupi and are characterized by the artist's sensitive and delicate rendering of the regional landscape on the walls and heavenly landscape on the vault above.

As followers joined Francis in community, he realized that, like other holy orders, his group needed a *Rule*. He first drafted a statement that was presented to and verbally affirmed by Pope Innocent III in 1209/10. This *Earlier Rule* was revised and expanded until 1221, when a second *Rule* (the *Later Rule*) was written to better serve the needs of what was, by then, a large and robust order. The *Later Rule* was authorized by the Bull of Pope Honorius III in 1223. There are multiple sources that document the development of the rules, but they are singular in asserting that the rules were the work of God, received by Francis in divine revelation, thereby underscoring the authority of the rules. Commenting on the inception of the *Rule*, Francis wrote:

> And after the Lord gave me some brothers, no one showed me what I had to do, but the Most High Himself revealed to me that I should live according to the pattern of the Holy Gospel. And I had this written down simply and in a few

Fig. 44. Francis receives the Rule, delivered through the Holy Spirit. Sacro Monte di Orta.

Fig. 45. Joshua, Caleb, and Moses (Num 13–14). Ceiling of Chapel XII, Sacro Monte di Orta.

words and the Lord Pope confirmed it for me.⁵⁹

Bonaventure elaborates on the audience before Pope Innocent III, also emphasizing the divine origin of the Franciscan way of life. He relates that Francis worried about the papal audience but while on the road to Rome, God sent him a reassuring vision. Francis saw a tall tree and, as he flew to the top of the tree, the tree bent over before him. The vision thus signified Pope Innocent yielding to his request and, indeed, the Pope gave verbal approval for the Order.⁶⁰

Continued growth of the Order as well as challenges from critics necessitated written confirmation of the *Rule*. As Francis considered approaching Pope Honorius with this request, he received yet another vision. In this vision, among other things, the *Rule* was equated to the communion host— in other words the *Rule* was indispensable divine nourishment for the soul. The vision further claimed divine origin of the *Rule* as Francis was advised to record the Rule as dictated by the Holy Spirit:

> He went up to a certain mountain led by the Holy Spirit, with two of his companions, to condense it [the Rule] in a shorter form as the vision had dictated. There he fasted, content with only bread and water, and dictated the rule as the Holy Spirit suggested to him while he was praying. When he came down from the mountain, he gave the rule to his vicar to keep. After a few days had elapsed, the vicar claimed that it had been lost through carelessness. The holy man went off again to the place of solitude and rewrote it just as before, as if he were taking the words from the mouth of God. And he obtained confirmation for it, as he had desired, from the lord Pope Honorius, in the eighth year of his pontificate.

> Fervently exhorting the brothers to observe this rule,
> Francis used to say
> that nothing of what he had placed there came from his own efforts
> but that he dictated everything
> just as it had been revealed by God.
> To confirm this with greater certainty by God's own testimony,
> when only a few days had passed,
> the Stigmata of our Lord Jesus were imprinted upon him
> by the finger of the living God,
> as the seal of the Supreme Pontiff, Christ,
> for the complete confirmation of the rule and the commendation of its author…⁶¹

Within the diorama are eight terracotta friars in various pious attitudes (see Fig. 44). Though the overall timber of the diorama is static, no two statues are identical. Each figure has a distinctive expression, unique physical features, and an individualized pose. Through the variety of gestures, stances, and expressions, Prestinari manages to convey a sense of earnestness among the friars that lends dynamism to the otherwise staid scene.

The artists created a unified field of vision by having the mountaintop vignette of the diorama blend into the scenic landscape of the frescos. Frescoed friars, rocks, and trees elaborate the narrative of the diorama in the near view while in the distance grasslands and a cityscape expand the illusion. The landscape of the lower walls flows upwards into a pink-orange sky and, above that, in the center of the vault, heaven. Christ, seated among the clouds and accompanied by the angelic host and putti, looks upon the diorama below and gives his approval to the formative work of the Order.

On the vault just below Christ is a cartouche bordered by a gold-trimmed green curtain held aside by four putti (see Fig. 45).⁶² The curtain reveals a gray monochromatic scene of a story from the Old Testament book of Numbers. In the story, a scouting party returns to the wilderness encampment

Fig. 46. Exterior of Chapel XIII, The Humility of St. Francis. Sacro Monte di Orta.

with bounty from the Promised Land but sadly report that the enemy is too strong to overcome; only Joshua and Caleb stand firm on God's plan for conquest. The people rend their clothes, lament their circumstance, and threaten to stone the two men of faith. While Moses' intervention saves the people from God's wrath, Joshua and Caleb alone are destined to enter the Promised Land as reward for their faithfulness (Num 13–14). The fresco encapsulates the story in a single scene, depicting the moment of the scouts' return, the people's mourning, and the people arming themselves with stones. Moses, arms outstretched, entreats God, who appears on a cloud over the Tent of Meeting. The theme of the biblical story is obedience to God's command, a lesson echoed in the story of the Franciscan Rule. As Bonaventure repeatedly asserts in his version of events, Francis was only a passive recipient of God's command, and that command was the Rule. According to this belief, and reflected in the program of the chapel, the Rule, and thus the Franciscan Order, was divinely conceived and ordained, and should not be contravened.

Chapel XIII. The Humility of St. Francis

Chapel XIII was constructed between 1670 and 1690. The heart of the chapel is a two-story rectilinear nave, with a single-story rectilinear porch on the front and a one-and-a-half story rectilinear apse at the rear (see Fig. 46). To each side of the chapel are one-and-a-half story circular apses. The chapel is topped with a tall octagonal cupola. The lateral and vertical movement between angles and curves gives the exterior added interest and an eye-pleasing symmetry. A lunette window over the front double doors, another over the porch, and a window in the cupola provide light to the interior.

Inside, pilgrims view the magnificently elaborate interior from a small vestibule separated from the diorama by an ironwork screen. Over sixty terracotta figures of men and women, children, horses and other animals, compose the diorama (see Fig. 47). A marble column, stairs, and a wooden post (the work of sculptors Bernardo Falconi and Giuseppe Rusnati) add architectural dimension to the scene. The Grandi brothers (Giovanni Battista and Gerolamo), along with Federico Bianchi, are responsible for the frescos. The chapel was funded by a Milanese knight cum Franciscan Capuchin named Constanzo Besozzo, whose family crest is worked into the iron screen.

Francis maintained a strict discipline focused on denial of the flesh. This took many forms, from bodily mortification (such as wearing a hair shirt) to eating a minimal, vegetarian diet. On one rare occasion, he ate a small bit of chicken in order to regain his health. For this he held himself in disdain, in spite of what was quite understandable in light of illness:

> Once, because he was ill, he ate a
> little bit of chicken. When his physical
> strength returned, he entered the city of

Fig. 47. Carnival celebrants surround (and largely ignore) St. Francis. Chapel XIII, Sacro Monte di Orta.

Assisi. When he reached the city gate, he commanded the brother who was with him to tie a cord around his neck and drag him through the whole city as if he were a thief, loudly crying out: "Look! See this glutton who grew fat on the flesh of chickens that he ate without your knowledge." Many people ran to see this grand spectacle and, groaning and weeping, they said: "Woe to us! We are wretches and our whole life is steeped in blood! With excess and drunkenness we feed our hearts and bodies to overflowing!" They were touched in their hearts and were moved to a better way of life by such an example.[63]

Francis seems to have taken a verse from First Corinthians to heart: " But I punish my body and enslave it, so that after proclaiming to others I myself should not be disqualified" (I Cor 9:27). For him eating meat was a great hypocrisy; it was an act of gross indulgence that crossed the line from venial to mortal sin. Francis, who reportedly described himself as "the greatest sinner in the world," was renowned for his humility.[64] For this sin of eating meat, Francis humbled himself in contrition before God. But ever the teacher, Francis turned his personal repentance into a teachable moment with a very public message. In the vein of the Old Testament prophets his humiliation became a sign act; he dramatized his confession through symbolic action as he had himself loudly condemned and dragged through the streets of Assisi.

The diorama of Chapel XIII illustrates this moment, as four friars lead Francis, whose hands are bound with rope, through the city plaza. There are reflections of Christ's passion, as Francis' humble entry into Assisi recalls Jesus' entrance into Jerusalem upon a humble donkey. Reminiscent of Zaccheaus who climbed a tree to better see Jesus as he rode in (Luke 19:4), in Chapel XIII a man clings to a tall post to better see Francis (see Chapter 6, Fig. 2). Scattered throughout the chapel are small intimate groupings, figures clustered in

Fig. 48. St. Francis sharing a meal with social outcasts. Wall fresco, Chapel XIII, Sacro Monte di Orta.

Fig. 49. Brother Bernard, in obedience, steps on St. Francis. Wall fresco, Chapel XIII, Sacro Monte di Orta.

conversation, either nonchalantly looking on or disconcertingly unaware of the pious spectacle. Figures who gesture toward Francis control the pilgrim's gaze and provide the reading lines for the artistic program. At the center front, a beggar points to Francis and by looking directly at the viewer, arrests the viewers' attention. To the viewer's right, three separate family groups look or gesture toward Francis, while to the viewer's left, the figure clinging to the post rises above the fray below and directs attention back to the friars. These reading lines are necessary, for the dynamic, colorful and frenetic activity of carnival celebrants surrounds the friars and can distract the viewer's eye. To the viewer's right are a rearing horse, a dwarf, a monkey, and two drunken revelers tussling on the ground (see Chapter 6, Fig. 1). To the left are running children, dogs, and the rearing horse of King Carnival (see Chapter 6, Fig. 2). To both the right and left are cross-dressing men, a practice popular during carnival and representing the inverse social mores of the hedonistic festivities. There are representations of otherness; there are blacks, the old and the unattractive, the physically impaired, a Jewish prisoner, and a dwarf. Along the chapel walls, the paintings extend the illusion of the city plaza with additional figures and building façades. There are elements of whimsy with women and men peering out of windows and from balconies, leaning over pillars and around columns, and looking down from a rooftop parapet. One man waves a greeting to the pilgrim. And in the far distance soldiers go about their normal duties standing guard on battlements. We see clearly the influence of the Brueghel family (Pieter the Elder, Jan the Elder and Jan the Younger) and Peter Paul Rubens who made these crowded, exotic, animal-filled landscapes popular in the sixteenth and seventeeth centuries.[65] More importantly, the extravagance of the scene serves an important function as it contrasts the humility of Francis with the indulgent excess surrounding him.

Four ceiling medallions emphasize the humility of Francis in imitation of Christ. One depicts Francis sharing a meal of broth with society's marginalized, in this case poor and physically impaired men (see Fig. 48). Below is a banner referencing Jesus' comforting words to the oppressed: "Take my yoke upon you, and learn from me; for I am gentle and humble in heart, and you will find rest for your souls" (Matt 11:29). A second medallion depicts Francis lying on the ground while Brother Bernard steps upon him (see Fig. 49). The source of this episode is *The Little Flowers of Saint Francis*. After he had an unkind thought against Brother Bernard, Francis lay on the ground and ordered Bernard to place one foot on the saint's neck and the other over his mouth. Bernard was to do this three times while admonishing Francis to be humble.[66] The banner for this medallion contains an excerpt from Psalm 36:11 (Ps 35:12 Vulgate): "Let not the foot of the arrogant tread on me, or the hand of the wicked drive me away." A third medallion is simply inscribed with the theme of the chapel "Humility," which is, not coincidentally, also the motto of the Borromeo family. A final medallion graces the center wall just above the terracotta portrait of Francis and directly in the sightline of a pilgrim entering the chapel. It is bordered with a fringed green curtain and replicates the frame of an earlier fresco in Chapel XII. The scene is Jesus led before Pilate, in the same exact pose as Francis below in the diorama; Jesus is half-naked, bound at the hands, and taken for judgment (see Fig. 50). The accompanying banner is inscribed: "He humbled himself," excerpted from Philippians 2:8 which reads in full "He humbled himself and became obedient to the point of death—even death on a cross." The decoration of the center vault shows a multitude of angels rejoicing in Francis' embrace of the core Gospel message.

The artistic program of Chapel XIII is a visual buffet of color and texture, costume and decorative detail, gesture and expression. And, as with so many of these chapels,

Fig. 50. Jesus is taken before Pontius Pilate. Wall fresco, Chapel XIII, Sacro Monte di Orta.

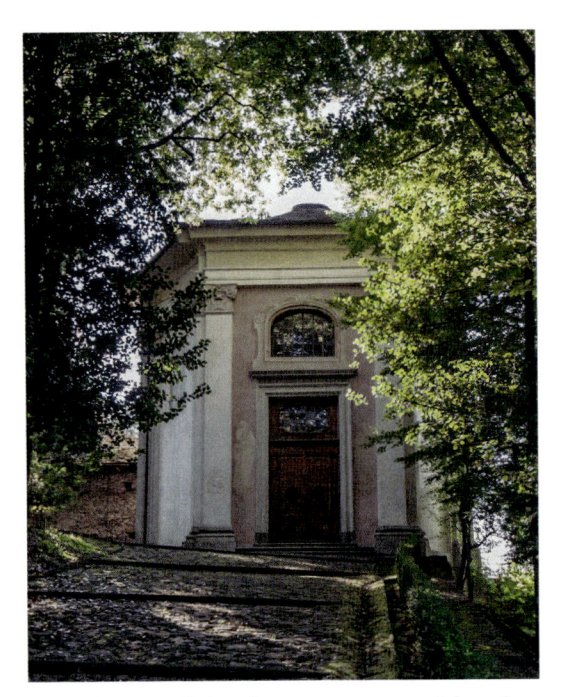

Fig. 51. Exterior of Chapel XIV, St. Francis and the Sultan. Sacro Monte di Orta.

the mise-en-scène is sophisticatedly multivalent. Archbishop Carlo Borromeo was a chief critic of Carnival with its secular focus and libertine excess.[67] In keeping with the Tridentine didacticism of the Sacri Monti and Borromean influence in design, the Carnival setting of Francis' humble contrition is apt. We have already noted the nod to the Borromean family motto "Humility," as it connects Francis to Christ, to the great Tridentine reformer, to the Capuchin ascetic life, and, finally to the theme of the chapel. Furthermore, we see Francis' sin, eating a meager portion of meat, innovatively juxtaposed to the celebration of *carnevale*, the Latin etymology of which means literally "putting away flesh" (from *carne* and *levare*). This season "without meat" is inversely celebrated by gluttonous feasting. In the textual tradition, Francis' sign act is efficacious. The crowd recognizes their own transgressions; they are reflective, remorseful and contrite. This is not so with the crowd portrayed in the chapel. With the exception of four brethren, few of the celebrants are struck by the call to repent. The responsibility now falls upon the pilgrim, who stands in the vestibule of Chapel XIII, to heed the message.

Chapel XIV. St. Francis and the Sultan

Constructed in the mid-eighteenth century (1757–59), Chapel XIV is the last completed chapel of the Sacro Monte. It is a hexagonal, neo-classical building with expected classical elements: Greco-Roman styled statuary, columns, and capitals (see Fig. 51). Despite its classicism, the exterior has unexpectedly extravagant elements. Two multi-paned windows, vertically related, rest above the entrance. Frescos, executed in pastels, exude rococo grace and elegance. Inside, one encounters indisputably rococo (and late baroque) design. Sculptor Carlo Beretta is responsible for the over fifty terracotta statues. Artist Federico Ferrari painted the frescos.

The artistic program of Chapel XIV recounts Francis' participation in the Fifth Crusade (1213–21). Fervent in his wish to imitate Christ, Francis yearned for martyrdom and to that end traveled to the Egyptian port city of Damietta during the siege of 1218. He and his companions[68] were taken captive, tortured, and presented to the Sultan. Francis attempts to convert the Sultan and offers a series of challenges, each of which the Sultan rebuffs:

> "If you wish to promise me that if I come out of the fire unharmed," the saint said to the Sultan, "you and your people will come over to the worship of Christ, then I will enter the fire alone. And if I shall be burned, you must attribute it to my sins. But if God's power protects me, you will acknowledge Christ the power and wisdom of God as the true God and the Savior of all." The Sultan replied that he did not dare to accept this choice because he feared a revolt among his people. Nevertheless he offered him many precious gifts, which the man of God, greedy not for worldly possessions but the salvation of souls, spurned as if they were dirt. Seeing that the holy man so completely despised worldly possessions, the Sultan was overflowing with admiration, and developed an even greater respect for him.[69]

Francis, realizing the futility of his errand, one in which he would accomplish neither martyrdom nor conversion of the Sultan, returns to Italy.[70]

When entering the chapel, the statue of Sultan al-Malik al-Kâmil, who sits on a richly canopied throne, voluptuously robed, and crowned with a royal turban, immediately attracts the pilgrim's eye (see Fig. 52). Given the eighteenth-century European penchant for turquerie, it is not surprising to find the scene imitative of a Turkish court. Surrounding him are heavily armed soldiers, boys, a dog, and four friars in a highly animated scene. In the confusion that the presence of Francis and the three friars with him have no doubt provoked, there are several identifiable scenes from the hagiography.

Francis, standing before the Sultan, is seen rejecting the Sultan's gift of gold coins. To the right of Francis, and walking away from him, one sees the back of an imam trying to quickly absent himself from Francis' challenge by fire. He carries a large text, presumably a Quran. Also to the right of Francis and just beyond are two Muslims stoking and feeding the fire that Francis proposed for the ordeals. To the viewer's left are three friars and various Muslim guards, both frescoed and sculpted. The friar closest to the viewer holds communion hosts in his right hand and extends them towards the Sultan (see Fig. 52).

Unlike other artistic representations of this event that put dramatic focus on Francis' bold challenge and willingness to step into the fire,[71] at Orta Francis is not paying attention to the fire at all. Indeed, the fire ordeal seems an ancillary element. Francis' attention is focused on the Sultan and his brethren, as he looks and gestures with his left hand toward the communion hosts extended by the brother and with his right hand toward the Sultan. These gestures are the reading lines of the viewer, guiding their gaze and focusing

Fig. 52. St. Francis before the Sultan. Chapel XIV, Sacro Monte di Orta.

Fig. 53. St. Francis preaches to Muslims (below) and Jesus preaches in the synagogue (above). Wall fresco, Chapel XIV, Sacro Monte di Orta.

Fig. 54. Francis rejects offering of gold (foreground), a Native American watches as the friars are taken captive on the shores of Damietta (background fresco). Chapel XIV, Sacro Monte di Orta.

their attention on an invitation to repentance and conversion.

The surrounding wall fresco offers a panoramic view of the port of Damietta where distinct episodes of Francis' Egyptian mission are collapsed within the scene: we observe the friars landing at the port and their immediate capture; we witness the beating of the friars; we watch as the friars are escorted to the Sultan; and, in the largest of the depictions, we see Francis preaching to Muslims.[72] Above this particular vignette is a cartouche with a parallel scene of Jesus preaching to a hostile congregation of Jews (see Fig. 53). The quotation inscribed on the banner above is from Mark 1:39, "And he went throughout Galilee, proclaiming the message in their synagogues and casting out demons." The artist underscores the rejection of Francis through a forced comparison with Jesus, for this Gospel account nowhere indicates that Jesus was amongst a hostile audience in that moment, nevertheless the artist here portrays Jewish men gathering stones to hurl at Jesus, with one man even drawing a sword. The bodily danger to those who believed they were God's messengers, whether Jesus, Francis, or Franciscan friars, was very real. The challenge reverberates in another interesting element in the panorama: the insertion of a Native American reclining on the shores of the port city and silently observing the arrival and capture of the Franciscans (see Fig. 54). This anachronistic element, an editorial comment of the artists' own day, testifies to the global reach of Franciscan missions and the dangers of such work. Meanwhile, the ceiling of the chapel is covered with angels and putti frolicking among billowy clouds. The movement

Fig. 55. Exterior of Chapel XV, St. Francis receives the Stigmata. Sacro Monte di Orta.

Fig. 56. The Seraph appears to St. Francis. Ceiling fresco, Chapel XV, Sacro Monte di Orta.

and energy of the heavenly audience echoes the dynamic action of the scene below.

Though Francis failed in his goals for the mission to Egypt, the episode is instructive and was put to use by the architects of the Sacro Monte. By placing Francis' audience with the Sultan immediately following the Carnival scene of Chapel XIII, they make a damning indictment of their fellow Christians: while the imam recognized the power of the holy man, while Muslim crowds heard him preach, while the Sultan was impressed (to such a degree that by some accounts he desired conversion), the Italians of Assisi largely spurned the saint and his message. Francis suffered the same rejection that Jesus had experienced within the Jewish community of Roman Palestine. The foreign mission was then a type of success: the Muslims at least recognized Francis' saintliness. This recognition foreshadows the final acceptance of Francis by his fellow townsmen (Chapel XVI) and the eventual successes of international Franciscan missions.

Chapel XV. St. Francis Receives the Stigmata

Chapel XV is dedicated to the tradition of Francis' miraculous reception of stigmata, the climactic spiritual event in his faith-filled life. One of the earliest chapels on the mount, it was designed by Father Cleto and constructed between 1591 and 1597.[73] The first story of this round chapel is surrounded by an arched portico supported by smooth Doric columns (see Fig. 55). Trace evidence of paint upon the vaulted ceiling of the portico testifies to frescos long eroded. A blind, engaged arcade decorates the second story with a single leaded window at the front to light the interior. The chapel is topped with a cylindrical cupola that reinforces the verticality of the building. Six steps lead up to the front entrance, above which is a niche containing the bust of the donor, Giulio Maffioli, a financier from Orta. A filigreed iron screen bisects the circular interior, separat-

Fig. 57. Peter, Paul, Noah, and David. Ceiling fresco, Chapel XV, Sacro Monte di Orta.

ing the vestibule from the tableau. The terracotta statues are by Christoforo Prestinari, while the original wall decoration was lost in the late eighteenth century when painter Riccardo Donnino was commissioned to update the frescos in the baroque style.

Within the tableau the floor rises sharply to mimic the mountainous terrain of La Verna. The figure of Saint Francis kneels while that of Brother Leo cowers, both looking upward toward the frescoed seraphic Christ and heavenly host (see Fig. 56 and Chapter 4, Fig. 3). Other figures on the rocky ground include small terracotta animals and sparse metal flora. The ceiling fresco surrounding the seraph and above the diorama depicts numerous saintly, angelic, and biblical dignitaries, including Peter, Paul, Noah and David (see Fig. 57). The frescoed decoration behind the viewer (and opposite the diorama) is composed of equally sparse foliage and angels. There is significant damage and decay to this portion of the wall and ceiling frescos.

In Chapel XV, Francis' spiritual journey culminates in his transposition to a new Christ. According to Franciscan tradition, Francis was in the midst of a personal struggle immediately prior to the transformative experience at La Verna. By 1223, Francis had become withdrawn and reclusive.[74] His Order of the Friars Minor was growing, but not in the direction he wanted; Francis was disappointed as he watched the movement become embroiled in Papal bureaucracy. Eventually he, along with a few companions, moved to the mountainside retreat at La Verna, where according to tradition Francis received the stigmata:

According to Bonaventure, at that moment Francis was "totally transformed into the likeness of Christ crucified."[76]

The landscape of the diorama in Chapel XV conveys the emotional desolation Francis experienced during this period of his life. The landscape also alludes to locations relevant to Christ's Passion: the Mount of Olives in general and the Garden of Gethsemane in particular.[77] Animals dotting the mountainside convey the danger and violence of the wilderness: a mountain cat attacks a wild boar; a large lizard with open jaws lurks menacingly nearby. This wildlife imbues a measure of fear in the viewer.[78] Francis kneels on the bleak mountainside, arms outstretched, gazing intently at the seraphic Christ figure. Francis bears the five wounds of the Crucifixion. According to Celano and Bonaventure, Francis' response to the vision was a mixture of fear and joyful incredulity, followed in turn by a great epiphany once the stigmata were realized. Prestinari captures this latter moment of clarity in the figure's pose and expression; it is a moment of decisive response, with Francis at once joyful in his union with Christ and accepting of the suffering it requires.

Brother Leo is absent from the literary accounts of the miracle, but commonly included in artistic renderings.[79] Given that the veracity of Francis' stigmatization was challenged throughout the centuries and in many quarters, the presence of Brother Leo is essential in providing witness to the miraculous event. Given the experiential nature of the chapels at Orta, Leo's presence as witness invites each pilgrim to be a witness as well.

The stigmatization was a particularly important theme in art of the Renaissance-era Franciscans. Its promulgation asserted the fact of the event, whose historicity even five hundred years later was controversial. The miracle illustrated the unique relationship between Francis and Christ, and by implication the special status of his order. It also distinguished the Franciscans from the rival mendicant order of the Dominicans, whose

Fig. 58. Exterior of Chapel XVI, St. Francis, nearing Death, returns to Assisi. Sacro Monte di Orta.

For immediately the marks of nails began to appear in his hands and feet just as he had seen a little before in the figure of the man crucified. His hand and feet seemed to be pierced through the center by nails, with the heads of the nails appearing on the inner side of the hands and the upper side of the feet and their points on the opposite sides. The heads of the nails in his hands and his feet were round and black; their points were oblong and bent as if driven with a hammer, and they emerged from the flesh and stuck out beyond it. Also his right side, as if pierced with a lance, was marked with a red wound from which his sacred blood often flowed moistening his tunic and underwear.[75]

founder, St. Dominic, received no similar divine favour. Like images of the stigmatization in earlier twelfth- and thirteenth-century Franciscan art, we can say that the stigmatization of Chapel XV functioned as "visual proof" of the event.[80]

Chapel XVI. St. Francis, Nearing Death, Returns to Assisi

Construction of this chapel, designed by Federico Bizzozzero, began in 1640 and was completed with the addition of a portico in the early 1690s. Undulating curves of the baroque façade echo in column niches and the quatrefoil window, the entrance archway, the frescoed door-surround, and cartouche of the pediment (see Fig. 58). The curves play against the many angles of the roofline and open pediment. A single engaged column with elaborated vegetative capital stands to either side of the archway surrounding the rectangular double door. The façade retains much of its original painted decoration including cherubs and the anthropomorphized figures of Prayer and Love, as well as *trompe l'oeil* architectural elements. The inscription within the cartouche above the doorway is Luke 6:19, "And all the people tried to touch him," referring to Jesus' reputation as a healer. This biblical passage on the exterior forecasts the message of the interior program: the recognition of Francis' saintliness, manifest in his healing powers, by his contemporaries: "The city rejoiced at the arrival of the blessed father and all the people with one voice praised God, since the whole multitude of the people hoped that the holy of one of God would die close to them, and this was the reason for such great rejoicing."[81]

For the interior of the chapel, Dionigi Bussola sculpted roughly two-dozen terracotta figures. Stefano Maria Legnani's frescos, with their soft colors and florid embellishments, reflect a late-baroque/rococo influence. As the pilgrim peers through the ornate grille separating the vestibule from the tableau, the eye is immediately drawn to Francis and his messianic entrance into Assisi astride a donkey *pace* Christ's entry into Jerusalem (cf. Matt 21:2; Mark 11:2; Luke 19:30; John 12:14) (see Fig. 59). Gazing upward towards heaven, Francis' countenance is of pain-filled exhaustion. Three men hover next to Francis, close but not touching, and through pointing gestures draw the viewer's attention to his stigmata. Two figures in the crowd have obvious physical impairments (one a goiter, the other a muscular atrophy) and reach out toward Francis, hoping, one can assume, for a cure. Each figure emotively captures the viewer's gaze and redirects it to the figure of Francis. Surrounding these main figures are men, women, children, horses, and dogs who simultaneously normalize the street scene while underscoring (through movement and gaze) the extraordinary saint in their midst. The throng of people replicates the literary descriptions of crowds in Luke 6 and in Celano's account of Francis' return home. It is a scene that culminates a narrative ark begun in Chapel XIII and told over the course of the next three chapels. In Chapel XIII, the Carnival-goers overwhelmingly ignore the holy man. The story line moves to Chapel XIV with Francis' audience before the Sultan, one point being that, in contrast to the residents of Assisi, even a Muslim such as the Sultan recognized the special nature of the holy man. In Chapel XV, Francis receives the stigmata, again underscoring in the most powerful way the holy nature of the mendicant friar, and sets the stage for his celebrated return home, as depicted in Chapel XVI. His special relationship to Christ can no longer be denied, since the miracle of the stigmata convinces even the most intemperate individuals of Francis' sanctity; the citizens of Assisi rush to embrace him. The stark contrast between the reception of Francis by his fellow citizens in Chapel XIII with that of Chapel XVI models the experience (according to tradition) of Jesus, whose true identity, though repeatedly revealed through healing miracles, was only gradually understood by those around him (cf. the Gospels of Mark and John).

Fig. 59. St. Francis, blind and terminally ill, enters into Assisi surrounded by supporters. Chapel XVI, Sacro Monte di Orta.

The *trompe l'oeil* paintings at eye-level extend the scene of the diorama with additions to the crowd and of the built environment of Assisi. Interrupting the contemporaneous scene is a vignette within the wall painting, just above and behind the statue of Francis, that depicts Christ healing the hemorrhaging woman (Matt 9:20–22; Mark 5:25–29; Luke 8:43–48) (see Fig. 60). She is modest in depiction; her disability is not graphic. Nor for that matter is biblical passage. Her identity is only indicated by the painting's caption. Her inclusion in the artistic program at Orta is curious, where women are often helpmeets

Fig. 60. Jesus and the Hemorrhaging Woman (Matt 9:20–22, Mark 5:25–34, Luke 8:43–48). Wall fresco, Chapel XVI, Sacro Monte di Orta.

and bystanders rather than the center of narrative action (Claire and Mary notwithstanding). Among the depictions of the physically impaired, women are a significant minority. But the woman with an issue of blood was a common subject in early Christianity, from catacombs and sarcophagi to reliquary caskets (such as the Brescia Box).[82] While the subject may have declined in popularity with Renaissance artists, there are examples from the period.[83] We can speculate that the image was included at Orta because it played a role in advancing the Tridentine agenda. According to Eusebius and early Christian tradition, there was a bronze statue of Christ with this woman, erected by the woman herself, at the gates of Ceasarea Phillipi.[84] Alexander Nigel points out that the statue is important evidence in the Catholic Reformation defense of images, as it provided proof for the use of images in early Christian practice.[85] There may have been additional reasons for the artist's inclusion of the image. By the medieval period, the bleeding woman was associated with St. Veronica, who was said to have loaned her veil to Christ to wipe his brow as he carried his cross. Her story is greatly expanded in the Golden Legend, wherein Veronica presents the veil, a mandylion preserving the image of Christ, to emperor Tiberius, who looked upon it with devotion and was miraculously healed.[86] In Latin, Veronica (from *vera icon*) means "true image." At Orta, then, this depiction of the bleeding woman could function with triple meaning: she represents the power of Christ (even his image) to miraculously heal, she represents the Tridentine argument for images, and as a literal vera icon, signifies Francis as the true image of Jesus. Meanwhile, in the vault above, an-

Fig. 61. The ornate grill separating the vestibule and the nave of Chapel XVII. Sacro Monte di Orta.

Fig. 62. Exterior of Chapel XVII, The Death of St. Francis. Sacro Monte di Orta.

poor—recognized Francis' miraculous powers before his death. Such tacit recognition furthered the Order's claim to the veracity and legitimacy of Francis' sainthood.

Chapel XVII. The Death of St. Francis

The hexagonal chapel, designed by architect Federico Bizzozzero, was constructed in the mid–seventeeth century. The small vestibule was separated from the diorama by an ornate floral grille in 1695 (see Fig. 61) and the chapel was fully completed, including the statues (Dionigi Bussola) and frescos (Carlo Francesco and Giuseppe Nuvolene, and Giovanni Battista Grandi), by 1698. In 1850, the northern Italian architect Paolo Rivolta added the building's neo-classical façade and parapet (see Fig. 62).

This chapel chronicles the death of St. Francis on October 3, 1226, about which Bonaventure relates:

> In all things
> he wished without hesitation
> to be conformed to Christ crucified,
> who hung on the cross poor, suffering,
>   and naked.
>
> Naked he lingered before the bishop
> at the beginning of his conversion;
> and, for this reason, at the end of this
>   life, he wanted to leave this world
>   naked.
>
> And so he charged the brothers assisting
>   him,
> under the obedience of love,
> that when they saw he was dead,
> they should allow him to lie naked on the
>   ground
> for as long as it takes to walk a leisurely
>   mile.
>
> O truly the most Christian of men,
> who strove by perfect imitation to be
>   conformed
> while living to Christ living,

gels lead the stigmatic towards heaven, foreshadowing Francis' death—and the theme of the next chapel, Chapel XVII.

Francis' return to Assisi is illustrated through stories of pain and healing. By focusing on the ways in which Francis' life imitated that of Jesus, both the suffering and the miraculous, the chapel furthers the Franciscan narrative by demonstrating that the people of the day—young and old, rich and

CATALOGUE OF CHAPELS

Fig. 63. St. Francis receiving the Last Rites. Chapel XVII, Sacro Monte di Orta.

Fig. 64. Lady Jacoba tending the feet of St. Francis. Chapel XVII, Sacro Monte di Orta.

dying to Christ dying,
and dead to Christ dead
and deserved to be adorned
with an expressed likeness.[87]

The central focus of the diorama is Francis recumbent on the ground, per his dying wish, and surrounded by friars, priests, secular notables and their attendants (see Fig. 63); a wooden bedframe stands discarded against the chapel wall, just as Francis distained bedding in the story. Of the figures in closest proximity to the saint, a priest stands with arms posed in benediction as he administers sacraments to the dying man; another priest stands over Francis sprinkling holy water with an aspergillum (brush);[88] a friar cradles Francis' head upon Lady Jacoba's cushion; and Lady Jacoba reaches to caress and bathe his wounded feet in the manner of Mary Magdalene (see Fig. 64).[89] Around these main figures cluster a friar offering Francis his patchwork robe—an iconic symbol of the saints' true poverty;[90] a friar kneeling in prayer and gazing toward the wall fresco depicting Francis' ascent into Heaven;[91] a well-dressed Black man, presumably part of Lady Jacoba's Roman contingent, inclining his head towards the two friars and gesturing animatedly; a friar—presumably having just read the Passion narrative in John 13 to the assembled group—holding a Bible; and Lady Jacoba's personal retinue.

The *leitmotif* of Franciscan hagiography is Francis' conformity to Christ. The diorama of Chapel XVII replicates this theme in plastic: Francis, as *alter Christus*, lay naked on the ground; prominent rendering of the stigmata and the friar's Bible evoke the Passion narrative of John 13; and Lady Jacoba models the Magdalene.

Despite the seeming simplicity of the chapel (it lacks the illusionistic and impressive "built environment" of Chapels XI, XIII,

Fig. 65. David enters Jerusalem with the head of Goliah (above); St. Francis welcomed into Heaven (below). Wall frescos, Chapel XVII, Sacro Monte di Orta.

and XVI for example, or the dramatic terrain of Chapels X, XII, and XV), Chapel XVII has a far more complex artistic program than meets the eye. Beyond the diorama, upon the walls, a variety of Old and New Testament images underscore Francis' selection as one specially chosen by God. Some parallels are presented in pairs of frescos that are to be read as one-on-one correlates: the depiction of Jacob's blessing of Ephraim (Gen 48) along the upper wall is echoed in Francis' blessing of Brother Bernard on the wall below;[92] Jacob, on his deathbed, predicting the destiny of his children (above) parallels a friar's deathbed vision of Francis' ascension (below); the fresco of the upper wall depicting Thomas's examination of Christ's wounds (John 20:24–29) pairs with the fresco along the lower wall depicting Jerome's certification of Francis' stigmata;[93] finally, just as Christ leads souls from purgatory (above), so does Francis (below). Other frescos evoke such parallelism not through illustrated pairs but through symbolism: David's entry into Jerusalem with the head of Goliath symbolizes Francis' defeat of death and his entry into Paradise (see Fig. 65); Habbakuk's delivery of food to Daniel in the lion's den embodies, in the works of Bonaventure, the ardent desire of both Daniel and Francis for humility and God's mercy;[94] the portrayal of Elijah riding his chariot of fire illustrates Bonaventure's description of Francis as "a second Elijah" and "a chariot and charioteer for spiritual men."[95] The remaining scenes detail the final days of Francis: Lady Jacoba, her sons, and

Fig. 66. Exterior of Chapel XVIII, The Vision of St. Francis in the Crypt. Sacro Monte di Orta.

Fig. 67. Exterior of Chapel XIX, Miracles at the Saint's Tomb. Sacro Monte di Orta.

Fig. 68. Exterior of Chapel XX, The Canonization of St. Francis. Sacro Monte di Orta.

the while maintaining the saint's connection to the people and peninsula of Italy.

Previously we have noted that figural placement, pose, and perspective are designed to direct the pilgrims' visual (and ergo affective) experience. Here in Chapel XVII the artists incorporate numerous reading lines to such purpose. The pilgrim's gaze is arrested by the figures of two priests and a servant that look directly at the viewer, inviting the pilgrim into the drama; Francis, too, faces the viewer, so that they become a witness to his death. As the drama unfolds, three women, two noblemen, and two friars direct the pilgrim's gaze to Lady Jacoba and her emotive caress of Francis' stigmatized feet. The prone body of the saint is presented to the viewer three times, once, of course, in the diorama itself and twice in the surrounding wall frescos. The repetition reinforces the message of "[Francis] dying to Christ dying." The artists shift the viewer's focus from death to resurrection through the Black nobleman, whose red tunic and upward pointing gesture replicates the red tunic and gesture of Francis in fresco just behind. These upward hand gestures, coupled with the upward gesture of the priest's benediction, actualize the concept of ascendancy. The message of salvation echoes in the pose of the kneeling friar who guides the pilgrim's eye to the fresco of Francis' heavenly reception, as well as in the fresco immediately behind the kneeling friar, one of a variant tradition, where another friar witnesses the saintly soul's ascent to heaven.

Chapels XVIII, XIX, and XX: The Basilica of Assisi

Although Francis was originally buried in Assisi at the Church of St. George, his body was later moved to the crypt of the basilica built in his honor, the Basilica of St. Francis, also in Assisi. Pope Gregory IX laid the cornerstone of the Basilica in Assisi one day after the canonization of Francis (July 16, 1228), just two years after the saints' death.

retinue attending Francis; Francis' blessing of the friars; Francis dictating his testament; and Francis ascending to Heaven. The fresco cycle weaves a narrative that binds Francis to patriarch and prophet, king and Christ, all

Bonaventure describes the translation of the body:

> While that sacred treasure was being carried,
> marked with the seal of the Most High Kinds,
> he whose image Francis bore
> deigned to perform many miracles
> so that through his saving fragrance
> the faithful in their love
> might be drawn to run after Christ.
> It was truly appropriate
> that he who was pleasing to God and beloved by him
> in his life;
> who, like Enoch,
> had been borne into paradise
> by the grace of contemplation
> and carried off to heaven
> like Elijah in a fiery chariot;
> now that his soul is blossoming
> in eternal springtime
> among the heavenly flowers
> it was, indeed, truly appropriate
> that his blessed bones too
> should sprout with the fragrant miracles
> in their own place of rest.[96]

The design of Chapels XVIII, XIX, and XX at the Sacro Monte di Orta is intended to replicate the three levels of the Basilica: the crypt (Chapel XVIII), the lower church (Chapel XIX), and the upper church (Chapel XX), with Chapel XVIII literally beneath Chapel XIX. All three chapels were designed by Father Cleto and their construction began in 1591. Chapel XVIII was completed by 1624, while Chapels XIX and XX were not completed until 1670. A bust (now missing) of Abbot Amico Canobio of Novara (c. 1532–92), who originally developed the idea of the Sacro Monte di Orta and funded Chapel XX from his own estate, once stood in the interior lunette above the door of Chapel XIX. He laid the cornerstone of Chapel XX in 1591.[97]

The pilgrim approaches Chapels XVIII and XIX though partially enclosed, vaulted

Fig. 69. Pope Nicholas V has a vision of St. Francis while visiting his crypt. Chapel XVIII, Sacro Monte di Orta.

Fig. 70. The sarcophagus of St. Francis. Chapel XVIII, Sacro Monte di Orta.

corridors. Doorways lead into very small vestibules; iron grilles and kneelers separate the pilgrim from the dioramas. The façade of the Chapel XX (the only one of the three chapels with an exterior architectural style *per se*) is an example of Renaissance classicism (see Figs. 66, 67, and 68). The interior of Chapel

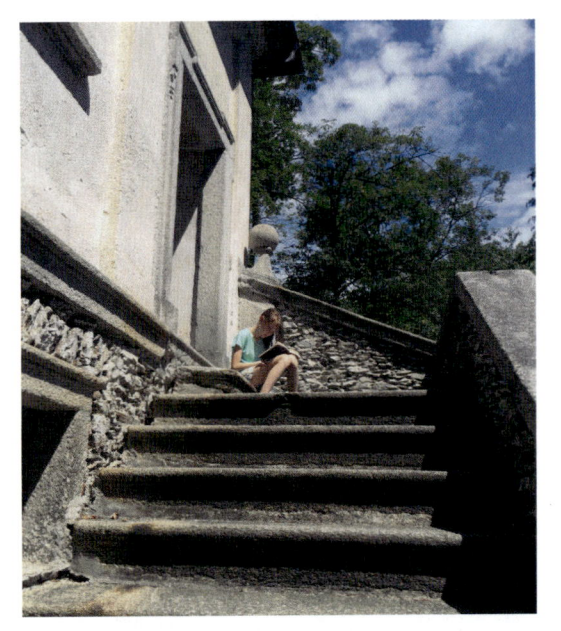

Fig. 71. Stairway from Chapel XVIII to Chapel XIX. Sacro Monte di Orta.

Fig. 72. Miracles cure the crowds who gather at the crypt of St. Francis. Chapel XIX, Sacro Monte di Orta.

XVIII ("the crypt") is, predictably, quite dark. A local Ortan artist named Giacomo Filippo Monti painted the frescos though few of the largely ornamental designs survive. The frescos of Chapels XIX (again, largely ornamental motifs) and XX (narrative and figural) were done by Antonio Busca. Dionigi Bussola created the statues in Chapels XVIII and XX, while Giuseppe Rusnati crafted the figures in Chapel XIX. The frescos of Chapels XIX (again, largely ornamental motifs) and XX (narrative and figural) were done by Antonio Busca. The ironwork of both Chapels XIX and XX was crafted by Giuseppe Malcotto da Borgomanero.

Chapel XVIII. The Vision of Francis in the Crypt

Chapel XVIII (constructed ca. 1591–1624) commemorates the visit of Pope Nicholas V to the tomb of St. Francis in 1449. According to the mid-sixteenth-century account by Mark of Lisbon, as the Pope and his retinue (which included the Cardinal Archbishop of Milan, Enrico Rampini) knelt before the tomb, Francis appeared before them in a vision—standing, looking heavenward, crying tears of devotion, with bleeding stigmata. "With great fear and reverence," the Pope kissed the stigmata of the Holy Saint.[98] This vision is reminiscent of Christ's miraculous post-resurrection appearances (Matt 28: 16–17; Mark 16:14; Luke 24:33–37; John 20: 19–20) and serves to underscore for the pilgrim the parallel lives of Christ and St. Francis, the *alter Christus*. The connection between Francis and Pope Nicholas is important as well, for both men revived and rebuilt the Church spiritually and physically.[99]

In this chapel, the figure of Nicholas kneels before Francis, his left hand holds his *zucchetto*, his right arm reaches toward the saint as his hand seeks to touch the cord of Francis' belt, intimating a connection with both Francis and the Franciscan Order that is, once again, both figural and literal (see Fig. 69). As Bradley Franco notes, the inclusion of church authorities in Franciscan artworks, as in this case a pope, bespeaks a close relationship between the saint, his order, and the institutional church.[100]

There are five cartouche inscriptions among the ornamental and architectural frescos of the chapel walls: (1) an Old Testament quotation from Isaiah 11:10, "And his rest shall be glorious"; (2) a quotation from St. Anthony of Padua, "His conveyance is acceptable to God"; (3) an identifying marker above a life-sized faux sarcophagus, "The burial of some companions of Seraphic Father S. Francesco with their bodies intact" (see Fig. 70); (4) a quote from Deuteronomy 34:5 referencing Moses' death: "And he died by the mouth [kiss] of the Lord"; and, (5), an identifying marker just behind the statue of St. Francis, "The Sepulcher of Father Francis."

Chapel XIX. The Miracles at the Saint's Tomb

As pilgrims ascend the stairway from Chapel XVIII to Chapel XIX (ca. 1591–1670) (see Fig. 71), through verisimilitude they move from the crypt to the Lower Basilica of Assisi with its ornamental frescos and white marble statues of Peter, David and Solomon. Chapel XIX celebrates the healing power of St. Francis, extolled by Bonaventure, among others. In a series of small vignettes set around a railing (where an opening to the crypt below would normally be), the almost two-dozen statues depict pilgrims at various moments during their petitions (see Fig. 72). The demographics represented by the statues reflect many different strands of society: male and female, adult and child, rich and poor, white and Black, soldier and civilian, and even a large dog (see Fig. 73). Throughout the chapel's vignettes, body positions create intimate conversations all the while gestures point toward the opening to Francis' crypt. Thus the pilgrim's gaze is guided through each vignette, but is ultimately directed back to the tomb of the saint. The central focus remains on St. Francis as the chapel promulgates his reputa-

Fig. 73. A woman brings a dog to the crypt of St. Francis. Chapel XIX, Sacro Monte di Orta.

tion as a miracle-worker and serves to promote the continued observation of his cult.

Chapel XX. The Canonization of St. Francis

Chapel XIX (the "Lower Basilica of Assisi") shares interior space in the apsidal choir area with Chapel XX (the "Upper Basilica of Assisi"), which is immediately adjacent. This final chapel (ca. 1591–1670) is the triumphal celebration of the day Pope Gregory IX "came personally to Assisi in the year of the Lord's Incarnation 1228 on Sunday, July 16, and inscribed our blessed father in the catalog of the saints, in a great and solemn ceremony that would be too long to describe."[101] Where words failed Bonaventure, the artists at the Sacro Monte Di Orta succeeded in capturing

Fig. 74. Pope Gregory IX canonizes St. Francis before prelates and a body of onlookers. Chapel XX, Sacro Monte di Orta.

Fig. 75. Crowds attend the canonization of St. Francis. Wall fresco, Chapel XX, Sacro Monte di Orta.

the drama in a dynamic recreation of the moment the Pope handed the official document of canonization to the Minister General of the Friars Minor, Giovanni Parenti. More than fifty statues of friars, pageboys, papal guards, cardinals and other prelates flank either side of the enthroned pope, who is seated before an altar (see Fig. 74). Vivid *trompe l'oeil* portraits of citizens of Assisi along the sidewalls further the illusion of a crowded scene and add heightened intensity (see Fig. 75). Pilgrims are encouraged to stand or kneel in order to peer through peepholes in the elaborate iron grille encrusted with florets and vines. Several of the terra cotta figures actively engage the viewer through gestures and eye contact, inviting pilgrims into the crowd and into the moment (see Fig. 76).

Antonio Busca's wall and ceiling frescos are as spectacular as Bussola's diorama. Engaged columns and arches frame three large frescoed panels on each sidewall. The scenes echo or replicate images already presented elsewhere in the Sacro Monte but are intended to reiterate and underscore important points. The first fresco to the viewer's immediate right depicts Mary holding the infant Jesus toward St. Francis' outstretched arms. The three are surrounding by a host of cherubs. It illustrates the special closeness Francis enjoyed with the holy family. In the second fresco, Francis appears in a heavenly vision to revivify a dead child cradled in the lap of his grief-stricken mother (see Fig. 77). It is representative of the miraculous healing power afforded Francis. The third fresco to the viewer's right, and the one in closest proximity to the altar (and the Pope) portrays the seraphic presence at the moment of Francis' stigmatization. Brother Leo, in the capuchin robe, hides his eyes. This scene reiterates the saint's devotion to the crucified Christ and his conformity to Christ.

On the viewer's immediate left, Francis is attacked by demons who try to throw him down a precipice.[102] Pilgrims here are asked to recall his struggles against temptation. The scene of the middle left fresco depicts Francis

Fig. 76. A peephole in the ironwork screen separating the vestibule from the nave in Chapel XX. The terracotta figure directly engages the viewer through eye contact. Chapel XX, Sacro Monte di Orta.

Fig. 77. St. Francis raising a child from the dead is evidence of a posthumous miracle. Wall fresco, Chapel XX, Sacro Monte di Orta.

Fig. 78. Mary, Francis, and Dominic intercede with an angry Christ on behalf of the world. Wall fresco, Chapel XX, Sacro Monte di Orta.

The ceiling fresco is operatic. Herald angels and cherubs surround Francis as he is welcomed to Paradise by the Holy Trinity. Christ crowns Francis with garland; God offers a golden crown (see Fig. 79 and Foreword, Fig. 1). Around the perimeter of the scene, several of the heavenly host play musical instruments. Inscribed upon an unfurled banner in lower left corner are lines from the fourteenth-century Gregorian chant "O sanctissima anima" ("O Most Holy Soul") used for centuries in the Franciscan rite of *Transitus*, the "crossing" of Francis from earthly death to eternal life, celebrated on Oct 3: "O sanctissima anima, in cujus transitu coeli cives occurrunt, Angelorum chorus exultat, et gloriosa Trinitas invitat, dicens: Mane nobiscum in aeternum" ("O most holy soul, at your departure the heavenly host comes to meet you, the angelic choir rejoices and the glorious Trinity welcomes you, saying: remain with us forever").

The New Chapel

In early plans, Chapel XVI was devoted to Francis' *Canticle of the Creatures*, but as work on the Sacro Monte took place over the centuries, and not necessarily in narrative sequence, construction on the *Canticle* chapel was initiated only toward the end of the eighteenth century and, as history unfolded, it was the last of the chapels to be built. Only the neo-classical exterior, designed by Santini of Lagna, was completed when in 1795 construction was halted amidst the political turmoil of the Napoleonic Era (see Fig. 80). The suppression of religious orders eventually brought about the expulsion of the site's guardians—the Capuchin monks of the Sacro Monte—and the end of any new construction on the Mount; the so-called New Chapel was never completed. Today the three-storey circular building, located between Chapels XV and XVI, serves as an exhibition space with an observation deck (see Fig. 81). Meanwhile, the *Canticle of the Creatures* is nevertheless represented in the names of the various paths

performing a variety of miracles. The crowd of penitents includes parents with a dead infant, a pregnant woman, a man with a head wound, and a man suffering with a goiter, an arm injury and an impaired ability to walk. The final fresco of the series, once again the painting in closest proximity to the altar, portrays Christ, angry at humanity and ready to strike the earth, along with Mary, who stays his anger by introducing Saints Francis and Dominic who, in turn, kneel beside a globe and entreat Christ to spare humankind (see Fig. 78).[103] The fresco illustrates the intercessory power of the saints, an important point within the Catholic Reformation program.

CATALOGUE OF CHAPELS

Fig. 79. The magnificent, operatic ceiling of Chapel XX, depicting St. Francis' ascension into Heaven. Sacro Monte di Orta.

and piazzas along the pilgrimage route, such as Viale di Frate Vento (Avenue of Brother Wind) near Chapel V (see Fig. 82) and Piazale di Frate Sol (Brother Sun Square) near Chapel XIII (see Fig. 83).

Fig. 80. Exterior of the New Chapel, whose completion was disrupted in 1795 by Napoleon's elimination of religious orders. Sacro Monte di Orta.

115

Fig. 81. Observation deck of the New Chapel. Sacro Monte di Orta.

CATALOGUE OF CHAPELS

Fig. 82. The Canticle of the Creatures is evidenced in the name of paths and piazzas of the Sacro Monte. Here we see the sign for the Avenue of Brother Wind. Sacro Monte di Orta.

Fig. 83. As with the previous figure (Fig. 82) we see The Canticle of the Creatures represented in the name of this piazza: Brother Sun Square. Sacro Monte di Orta.

117

Endnotes

1. Bradley R. Franco, "The Functions of Early Franciscan Art," in *The World of St. Francis of Assisi: Essays in Honor of William R. Cook*, eds. Bradley R. Franco and Beth Mulvaney (Leiden: Brill, 2015), 31–32.

2. Fedele Merelli, O.F.M. Cap., "Father Cleto from Castelletto Ticino Cappuccino (d. 1619): Notes for a Biography," *Communicare Network: Radio Missione Francescana*, http://www.comunicare.it/ofmcap/archivio/p.cleto/pcleto.html.

3. Ibid.

4. See, for example, Angelo Maria Manzini, O.F.M. Cap., *Sacro Monte of Orta* (Orta: Community of the Franciscan Friars, Custodian of the Sacro Monte of Orta, 2006), 26. Bascapè was also intimately involved in the (re)design of the Sacro Monte di Varallo. There he had to mediate the ongoing disputes between the guardians of the sacred mountain, the Franciscan Observants, and the *fabbriciere*. Eventually, the bishop ordered the removal of the Observants and the installation of the Capuchins. See Geoffrey Symcox, *Jerusalem in the Alps: The Sacro Monte of Varallo and the Sanctuaries of North-West Italy* (Turnhout: Brepols, 2019).

5. The Reformation-era contestation over the role of images and pilgrimage resulted in Tridentine efforts to "control both the visual and embodied experience," and Carlo Borromeo was central to these efforts. Carla Benzan, "Alone at the Summit: Solitude and the Ascetic Imagination at the Sacro Monte of Varallo," in *Solitudo: Spaces, Places, and Times of Solitude in Late Medieval and Early Modern Cultures*, eds. Karl A.E. Enenkel and Christine Göttler (Leiden: Brill, 2018), 343–45.

6. See Margaret Bell, "Image as Relic: Bodily Vision and the Reconstitution of Viewer/Image Relationships at the Sacro Monte di Varallo," *California Italian Studies* 5, no. 1 (2014): 303–31.

7. For a discussion of somaesthetic style, see Allie Terry-Fritsch, "Performing the Renaissance Body and Mind: Somaesthetic Style and Devotional Practice a the Sacro Monte di Varallo." *Open Arts Journal* 4 (Winter 2014–2015): 111–32.

8. Paul Davies, "The Lighting of Pilgrimage Shrines in Renaissance Italy," in *The Miraculous Image in the Late Middle Ages and Renaissance*, eds. Erik Thunø and Gerhard Wolf (Rome: L'Erma di Bretschneider, 2004), 64, 79.

9. See Charlotte Hubbard and Peta Motture, "The Making of Terracotta Sculpture: Techniques and Observations," in *Earth and Fire: Italian Terracotta Sculpture from Donatello to Canova*, ed. Bruce Boucher (New Haven: Yale University Press, 2001), 83–95, and Bruce Boucher, "Italian Renaissance Terracotta," in ibid., 27–28.

10. Hubbard and Motture, "The Making of Terracotta Sculpture, Techniques and Observations," 94.

11. See, for example, the story told by Mark of Lisbon: "Before his birth, his mother endured very much being many days in labor of delivery, meanwhile there came a poor pilgrim to the door of the house, who having received alms, said to him that brought it: 'Cause that woman who endures such pain of travail to be carried to a stable, and she shall be incontinently delivered.' Once done, she was instantly delivered and for that respect there built a chapel, where in memory of the birth of this Saint the history of the this miracle was depicted; he whom our Lord Jesus Christ would in regard of his birth in a poor and contemptible place, make like unto himself." Mark of Lisbon, *The Chronicle and Institution of the Order of the Seraphicall Father S. Francis Conteyning his Life, his Death, and his Miracles, and of all his Holie Disciples and Companions*, 2 vols., trans. William Cape (England: John Heigham, 1618), 1:3. [Note that this is not the same volume as the two Italian editions referenced in this work as *Croniche*, 1605 or 1680. Spelling and some phrasing adapted for a contemporary audience by the authors of this book.]

12. E. de Filippis and F.M. Carcano, *Guide to the Sacro Monte of Orta* (Novara: Riserva Naturale Speciale del Sacro Monte di Orta, 1991), 15, and Manzini, *Sacro Monte of Orta*, 22.

13. See Arnald of Sarrant, *Kinship of St. Francis*, in *Francis of Assisi: Early Documents*, 3 vols., eds. Regis Armstrong. O.F.M. Cap., et al. (New

York: New City Press, 1999–2001), 3:695–96; and Bartholomew of Pisa, *De Conformitate*, eds. the Fathers of the College of Saint Bonaventure, Analecta Franciscana 4 (Quaracchi: Collegium S. Bonaventurae, 1906), 56. See also, *A Book of Exemplary Stories (c. 1280–1310)*, in *Francis of Assisi: Early Documents*, 3:800.

14 According the to the *Legend of the Three Companions*, the Holy Spirit told Francis to enter a dilapidated church. Once inside, Francis saw a crucifix and "began to pray intensely before an image of the Crucified, which spoke to him in a tender and kind voice: 'Francis, don't you see that my house is being destroyed? Go, then, and rebuild it for me.' Stunned and trembling, he said: 'I will do so gladly, Lord.' For he understood that it was speaking about that church, which was near collapse because of its age. He was filled with such joy and became so radiant with light over that message, that he knew in his soul that it was truly Christ crucified who spoke to him." See the *Legend of the Three Companions*, in *Francis of Assisi: Early Documents*, 2:76.

15 Francis of Assisi, *The Testament*, in *Francis of Assisi: Early Documents*, 1:124.

16 Bonaventure of Bagnoregio, *Major Legend of Saint Francis*, in *Francis of Assisi: Early Documents*, 2:532. The stories and sequence vary in the other sources; in Thomas of Celano's *Life of Saint Francis*, Francis suffers illness, dreams of knightly armament and success, later refuses to go on military mission to Apulia, then kisses a leper; in *Legend of the Three Companions*, Francis dreams of knightly armament and success, donates clothes to the bedraggled knight, departs for Apulia, has a second dream of Christ telling him to return home, goes to Rome and begs for alms, returns home and kisses the leper; in *The Remembrance of the Desire of a Soul*, Francis gives clothes to a bedraggled knight, dreams of knightly armor and success, departs for Apulia, has second dream telling him to return home, goes to Rome and begs alms, returns to Assisi and dines with friends, has a vision of an ugly woman, and kisses the leper.

17 Krijn Pansters, "Dreams in Medieval Saints' Lives: Saint Francis of Assisi," *Dreaming* 19, no. 1 (2009): 56.

18 *Instruzzione al Divoto Lettore che Desidera Visitare il Sacro Monte di S. Francesco D'Orta*, in *Antiche Guide del Sacro Monte di Orta*, ed. Loredana Racchelli (Orta: Ente di Gestione delle Reserve Naturali Speciali del Sacro Monte di Orta, del Monte Mesma e del Colle della Torre di Buccione, 2008), 155.

19 On Giovanni Righetti, see Alfredo Papale, *Cultura Materiale del XVIII secolo. Le Botteghe di Tessuit di Giovanni Righetti ad Orta e Miasino. Estr. orig. da Boll. Stor. per la Prov. di Novara*, 1, 1979. (Novara: Tip. La Cupola Novara, 1979).

20 Thomas of Celano, *The Remembrance of the Desire of a Soul*, in *Francis of Assisi: Early Documents*, 2:251.

21 The biographers state that Francis stripped nude. That Francis appears here in a hairshirt is consistent with the penitential practices of the Capuchins, for whom wearing a hairshirt was an important method of daily mortification. See Paul Hanbridge, O.F.M. Cap., trans., *The Capuchin Reform, A Franciscan Renaissance: A Portrait of Sixteenth-century Capuchin Life, An English Translation of La bella e santa riforma by Melchiorre da Pobladura, O.F.M. Cap.* (Delhi: Media House, 2003), 198–99.

22 See Kimberly Rivers, *Preaching the Memory of Virtue and Vice: Memory, Images, and Preaching in the Late Middle Ages* (Turnhout: Brepols, 2010), 218–19. Though the Franciscan artistic tradition owes much to the work of Giotto, with many of his innovative compositions becoming normative over the succeeding centuries, it is interesting that the virtues enumerated by Giotto at the Arena Chapel in Padua bear little, if any, resemblance to the virtues depicted in the Capuchin program of Chapel III here at Orta. See Douglas Lackey, "Giotto in Padua: A New Geography of the Human Soul," *The Journal of Ethics* 9, nos. 3–4 (2005): 551–72.

23 The *Fasciculus Morum* was a Franciscan guide for sermons which cataloged virtues and vices, a list that became a standard index within the Order. See Siegfried Wenzel, *Fasciculus Morum: A Fourteenth Century Preacher's Handbook* (University Park: Pennsylvania State University Press, 1989).

24 As Capuchin brother Antonio Corse (d. 1585) declared, "The mortifications of our

Father Saint Francis enriched heaven and earth. Through them came so much light that it was as if another sun were shining, giving light to the whole world. The Lord would never have brought Francis' exemplary life and that of his Order to such heights of perfection had he not striven so mightily to mortify himself. Therefore, if we are unwilling to mortify ourselves a little, we inflict great damage on ourselves and on those who seek enlightenment." Hanbridge, *The Capuchin Reform*, 48. Twentieth-century Franciscan scholar Melchiorre da Pobladura further explains, "The body is a powerful enemy that needs to be brought into servitude, otherwise it will prepare some dangerous ambushes for us. Therefore the Capuchins, as true athletes of penance and austerity, nourished themselves with the most frugal meals, wore the most humble habits, slept little (and on bare boards), and punished their bodies with harsh sackcloth and bloody disciplines...Their external penance was nothing else but a departure point to attack a stronger, battle-hardened enemy: self-love, which is conquered with internal mortification—the annihilation of self-will to conform it to the will of God." Ibid., 175.

25   Bonaventure of Bagnoregio, *Major Legend of Saint Francis*, 2:542.

26   De Filippis and Carcano suggest that the local artist Giacomo Gilippo Monti of Orta was responsible for painting the frescos. *Guide to the Sacro Monte of Orta*, 23.

27   See the discussion regarding the squirrel in Giovanni Bellini's *St. Jerome Reading*, in D.A. Brown and S. Ferino-Pagden, *Bellini, Giorgione, Titian, and the Renaissance of Venetian Painting* (New Haven: Yale University Press, 2007), 132.

28   Bonaventure of Bagnoregio, *Major Legend of Saint Francis*, in *Francis of Assisi: Early Documents*, 2:543.

29   De Filippis and Carcano, *Guide to the Sacro Monte of Orta*, 28.

30   Thomas of Celano, *Life of Saint Francis*, in *Francis of Assisi: Early Documents*, 1:207.

31   The recurring dream eventually prompted Sylvester to join the Franciscan order. The dream echoes the tradition of the fourth-century Pope Sylvester, who defeats a dragon threatening the city of Rome. See Jacobus de Voragine, *The Golden Legend, or, Lives of the Saints*, 7 vols., ed. F.S. Ellis, trans. William Caxton (London: J.M. Dent, 1922), 2:101–2.

32   See Nicole Kelley, "'The Punishment of the Devil Was Apparent in the Torment of the Human Body': Epilepsy in Early Christianity," in *Disability Studies and Biblical Literature*, esd. Candida Moss and Jeremy Schipper (London: Palgrave Macmillan, 2016), 205–21.

33   See Manzini, *Sacro Monte of Orta*, 34.

34   Bonaventure of Bagnoregio, *Major Legend of Saint Francis*, in *Francis of Assisi: Early Documents*, 2:548.

35   This is called the *Earlier Rule*, or *First Rule*, subsequently supplanted by Francis with the *Later Rule* (written c. 1221, approved by Pope Honorius III, c. 1223) to reflect evolving circumstances within the Order and the Church.

36   Bonaventure of Bagnoregio, *Major Legend of Saint Francis*, in *Francis of Assisi: Early Documents*, 2:526.

37   Thomas of Celano, *Life of Saint Francis*, in *Francis of Assisi: Early Documents*, 1:212–13.

38   Thomas of Celano, *Life of Saint Francis*, in *Francis of Assisi: Early Documents*, 1:224.

39   Bonaventure also compares Francis to Ambrose, who was said to have appeared at the funeral of St. Martin while simultaneously at Mass elsewhere. See Bonaventure of Bagnoregio, *Major Legend of Saint Francis*, in *Francis of Assisi: Early Documents*, 2:557.

40   Thomas of Celano, *Life of Saint Francis*, in *Francis of Assisi: Early Documents*, 1:225, Bonaventure of Bagnoregio, *Major Legend of Saint Francis*, in *Francis of Assisi: Early Documents*, 2:557.

41   Ibid., 2:552.

42   Bonaventure of Bagnoregio, *Major Legend of Saint Francis*, in *Francis of Assisi: Early Documents*, 2:692.

43   *The Legend of Saint Clare*, in *Clare of Assisi, The Lady: Early Documents*, ed. Regis Armstrong (New York: New City Press, 2006), 286. The authorship of the *Legend of St. Clare*, though uncertain, is generally attributed to Thomas of Celano.

44   Ibid., 285–86.

45 Marina Dell'Omo, "Antonio Pino da Bellagio al Sacro Monte di Orta," *Sacri Monti* 2 (2010): 97–103.

46 Arnald of Sarrant, *Chronicle of the Twenty-four Generals*, in *Francis of Assisi: Early Documents*, 3:810–11.

47 Thomas of Celano, *Remembrance of the Desire of a Soul*, in *Francis of Assisi: Early Documents*, 2:324–25.

48 Perhaps based on a story from "The Considerations on the Holy Stigmata," in Brown, ed. and trans., *The Little Flowers of Saint Francis* (New York: Image Books/Doubleday, 1958), 175.

49 From Bartholomew of Piza's *De Conformitatae* as told in Léopold de Chérancé, O.F.M. Cap., *Saint Francis of Assisi*, trans. R.F. O'Connor (London: Burns and Oates, 1880). This story and scene are reminiscent of the story in *The Little Flowers of Saint Francis* of the Sultan sending a woman to tempt Francis. See the story in various translations: Ugolino Boniscambi, *The Little Flowers of Saint Francis*, in *Francis of Assisi: Early Documents*, 3:606.

50 *Considerations of the Holy Stigmata*, in *The Little Flowers of Saint Francis*, 184.

51 See Arnald of Sarrant, *Chronicle of the Twenty-four Generals*, in *Francis of Assisi: Early Documents*, 3:810–11.

52 Pier Giorgo Longo, "Immagini e immaginario di San Francesco al Sacro Monte di Orta," in *Antiche Guide del Sacro Monte di Orta*, ed. Loredana Racchelli (Orta: Ente di Gestione delle Reserve Naturali Speciali del Sacro Monte di Orta, del Monte Mesma e del Colle della Torre di Buccione, 2008), 54; Cesare Ripa, *Baroque and Rococo Pictorial Imagery: The 1758–60 Hertel Edition of Ripa's "Iconologia," Dover Pictorial Archives*, ed. Edward A. Maser (New York: Doubleday, 1971); Merelli, *Father Cleto from Castelletto*.

53 See Francis of Assisi, *Salutation of the Virtues*, in *Francis of Assisi: Early Documents*, 1:164–65.

54 Arnald of Sarrant, *Chronicle of the Twenty-four Generals*, in *Francis of Assisi: Early Documents*, 3:810–12.

55 Ibid., 3:811.

56 Ibid., 3:810–11.

57 For an early version of the prophetic dream, see *Legend of the Three Companions*, in *Francis of Assisi: Early Documents*, 2:97–98.

58 Chapel XI is the only chapel of the Sacro Monte di Orta that is consecrated for services.

59 Francis of Assisi, *The Testament*, in *Francis of Assisi: Early Documents*, 1:125.

60 Bonaventure of Bagnoregio, *Major Legend of Saint Francis*, in *Francis of Assisi: Early Documents*, 2:547–49.

61 Ibid., 2:557–59.

62 The style of this cartouche is imitative of the seventeenth-century curtained cartouche of Chapel XIII painted by the Grandi brothers.

63 Thomas of Celano, *Life of Saint Francis*, in *Francis of Assisi: Early Documents*, 1:228.

64 Bonaventure of Bagnoregio, *The Evening Sermon on Saint Francis*, in *Francis of Assisi: Early Documents*, 2:725. Francis' humility is yet another echo in *imitatio Christi*, for as Bonaventure describes, "Christ's cross is the sign of the most perfect humility and self-abasement because on the cross he humbled and abased himself to such an extreme for us" (726). In his perfect imitation of Christ, Francis too was marked with the greatest humiliation—the stigmata.

65 See especially Pieter Brueghel's *The Fight between Carnival and Lent* (1559) and Jan Miense Molenaer's *Battle between Carnival and Lent* (1633), which must have influenced the designers of Chapel XIII (especially Molenaer's two men tussling in the foreground), though admittedly there is no explicit record of a link.

66 Boniscambi, *The Little Flowers of Saint Francis*, in *Francis of Assisi: Early Documents*, 3:46–48.

67 Jennifer Mara DeSilva, *The Sacralization of Space and Behavior in the Early Modern World* (London: Routledge, 2015), 138.

68 The thirteenth-century sources vary as to the number of companions traveling with Francis. Celano and Bonaventure record only one companion while the expansive account in *The Little Flowers of Saint Francis* records twelve.

69 Bonaventure of Bagnoregio, *Major Legend of Saint Francis*, in *Francis of Assisi: Early Documents*, 2:603.

70 Thomas of Celano and Bonaventure of Bagnoreggio understand this turn of events as God's plan to reserve for Francis the greatest of all honors—stigmatization. Ugolino Baniscambi, author of *The Little Flowers of Saint Francis*, once again expands the tradition asserting that the Sultan wanted to convert and in fact did convert years after Francis' death and with his own death in sight. Bartholomew of Pisa follows suit. See Baniscambi, *The Little Flowers of Saint Francis*, 93–96.

71 See the depictions of this event by Giotto (1291–1299; Upper Basilica of Assisi and Bardi Chapel of Santa Croce in Florence); Gaddi (1330–1335; Santa Croce in Florence); Sassetta (1444; San Sepolcro Altarpiece); and Gozzoli (1450–1452; Montefalco).

72 According to some traditions, the Sultan was so impressed with the holy man that Francis was given permission to preach to the Muslims throughout his empire. See Baniscambi, *The Little Flowers of Saint Francis*, 94. The story is repeated by Bartholomew of Pisa and Mark of Lisbon. See Mark of Lisbon, *The Chronicle and Institution of the Order of the Seraphicall Father S. Francis Conteyning his Life, his Death, and his Miracles, and of all his Holie Disciples and Companions*, 1:123–26.

73 The seventeenth- to eighteenth-century pilgrim guide *Instruzzione al Divoto Lettore che Desidera Visitare il Sacro Monte di S. Francesco D'Orta* mistakenly attributes the design to "the famous architect and painter Buonarroti," presumably Michelangelo, though the dates are off by half a century. In *Antiche Guide del Sacro Monte di Orta*, ed. Racchelli, 219.

74 Michael Robson, *The Franciscans in the Middle Ages* (Woodbridge: Boydell Press, 2006), 18, 44; André Vauchez, *Francis of Assisi: The Life and Afterlife of a Medieval Saint*, trans. Michael Cusato (New Haven: Yale University Press, 2012), 131.

75 Bonaventure of Bagnoregio, *Major Legend of Saint Francis*, in *Francis of Assisi: Early Documents*, 2:632–33.

76 Ibid., 2:632.

77 For discussion of these visual references to Christ's Passion, see Arnold Davidson, "Miracles of Bodily Transformation, or How St. Francis Received the Stigmata," *Critical Inquiry* 35, no. 3 (Spring 2009): 464–65.

78 On the inducement of such emotions in the viewer, see Jill Bennett, "Stigmata and Sense Memory: St. Francis and the Affective," *Art History* 24, no. 1 (2001): 1–16.

79 See Robert Kiely, "Further Considerations of the Holy Stigmata of St. Francis: Where Was Brother Leo?" *Religion and the Arts* 3, no. 1 (1999): 20–40.

80 Franco, "The Functions of Early Franciscan Art," 24.

81 Thomas of Celano, *Life of Saint Francis*, in *Francis of Assisi: Early Documents*, 1:274.

82 Peter and Linda Murray, *A Dictionary of Christian Art, Oxford Quick Reference* (Oxford: Oxford University Press, 2004), 620.

83 Gertrud Schiller, *Iconography of Christian Art*, 2 vols. (London: Lund Humphries, 1972), 1:178–79.

84 Eusebius, *History of the Church: From Christ to Constantine*, ed. Andrew Louth, trans. G.A. Williamson, rev. edn. (London: Penguin Classics, 1990), 233–34.

85 Alexander Nagel, *The Controversy of Renaissance Art* (Chicago: University of Chicago Press, 2011), 135. The statue was also used as evidence to support the use of images during the iconoclastic controversy of the Byzantine era. See Leslie Ross, *Medieval Art: A Topical Dictionary* (Santa Barbara: Greenwood Publishing Group, 1996), 257.

86 See Jacobus de Voragine, *The Golden Legend*, 212.

87 Bonaventure of Bagnoregio, *Major Legend of Saint Francis*, in *Francis of Assisi: Early Documents*, 2:642–43.

88 Mark of Lisbon, *The Chronicle and Institution of the Order of the Seraphicall Father S. Francis Conteyning his Life, his Death, and his Miracles, and of all his Holie Disciples and Companions*, 1:342.

89 St. Francis referred to Lady Jacoba de Settesoli (c. 1190–1273), a wealthy noblewoman of Rome, as Brother Jacoba. This close friend had privileged access to the saint. He summoned her to his deathbed and she was allowed to mourn by his side along with the friars. The earliest biographical account to include her story is Thomas of Celano's *Treatise on the Miracles of*

Saint Francis (c. 1250). Bonaventure does not include her at Francis' deathbed, but her story is found later in *The Deeds of Blessed Francis and His Companions* (c. 1330) and then *Considerations of the Holy Stigmata* (c. 1390). According to tradition, Lady Jacoba was a member of the Third Order (a group of lay Franciscans). At Orta, she is indeed dressed in the humble robes and veil of a tertiary both in the diorama and in a wall fresco behind the diorama. Lady Jacoba is buried in the crypt of the Basilica of St. Francis in Assisi, near the tomb of the saint. See Thomas of Celano, *Treatise on the Miracles of Saint Francis*, in *Francis of Assisi: Early Documents*, 2:417–19; Boniscambi, *The Deeds of Blessed Francis and His Companions*, in *Francis of Assisi: Early Documents*, 3:471–74; *Considerations of the Holy Stigmata*, in *The Little Flowers of Saint Francis*, 203–6.

90   See *The Assisi Compilation*, in *Francis of Assisi: Early Documents*, 2:123.

91   Thomas of Celano, *Life of Saint Francis*, in *Francis of Assisi: Early Documents*, 1:278; Julian of Speyer, *The Life of Saint Francis*, in *Francis of Assisi: Early Documents*, 1:414; *Legend of the Three Companions*, in *Francis of Assisi: Early Documents*, 2:106, and *An Umbrian Choir Legend*, in *Francis of Assisi: Early Documents*, 2:475 all report that an anonymous brother attendant at the moment of Francis' death saw the saint's soul carried heavenward on a cloud. Variant accounts, similar but not identical, record that Brother Augustine witnessed the ascension (Bonaventure of Bagnoregio, *Major Legend of Saint Francis*, in *Francis of Assisi: Early Documents*, 2:644) as did Brother Angelus (Mark of Lisbon, *The Chronicle and Institution of the Order of the Seraphicall Father S. Francis Conteyning his Life, his Death, and his Miracles, and of all his Holie Disciples and Companions*, 343–44).

92   See Boniscambi, *The Little Flowers of Saint Francis*, in *Francis of Assisi: Early Documents*, 2:576–79.

93   *Considerations of the Holy Stigmata*, in *The Little Flowers of Saint Francis*, 206.

94   Bonaventure of Bagnoregio, *The Evening Sermon on Saint Francis*, in *Francis of Assisi: Early Documents*, 2:725; and *The Morning Sermon on Saint Francis*, in *Francis of Assisi: Early Documents*, 2:754.

95   Bonaventure of Bagnoreggio, *Major Legend of Saint Francis*, in *Francis of Assisi: Early Documents*, 2:552.

96   Bonaventure of Bagnoreggio, *Bonaventure: The Soul's Journey into God, The Tree of Life, The Life of St. Francis*, trans. Ewert Cousins, The Classics of Western Spirituality, ed. Richard Payne (New York: Paulist Press, 1978), 326.

97   Manzini, *Sacro Monte of Orta*, 78.

98   Mark of Lisbon, *Croniche de gli Ordini istituiti dal P.S. Francesco: Nella quale si contiene la sua vita, la morte, & I suoi miracoli, e de'suoi discepoli*, 3 vols., trans. Horation Diola of Bologna (1605), 3:302.

99   Pope Nicholas V embraced the revitalizing current of Renaissance humanism and intellectualism, and also undertook successful remodeling and building programs at the Vatican. For more on Pope Nicholas in this regard, see, for example, F. Donald Logan, *A History of the Church in the Middle Ages* (London: Routledge, 2012), 339–40.

100   Franco, "The Functions of Early Franciscan Art," 31.

101   Bonaventure of Bagnoreggio, *Bonaventure*, 326.

102   This episode is from a lesser-known tradition but one that is highlighted previously in Chapel X.

103   Dominic also figured in the frescos of Chapel I. The pairing of Francis with Dominic bookends the pilgrimage, from Chapel I to Chapel XX.

3

The Birth of St. Francis

Chapel 1

A close study of the first chapel along the devotional path of the Sacro Monte di Orta, "The Birth of Francis" allows us to see the Franciscan and Tridentine epistemological agenda in action: carefully controlled art which facilitates the pilgrim's encounter with Christ through Francis.

The exterior of Chapel I, constructed between 1592 and 1604, was once decorated with portraits of Francis and Giulio, the patron saints of the lake, as well as a topographical landscape of the region painted by Stefano Maria Legnani.[1] Only traces of the paintings are left, but there are still landscapes on the inner walls of the chapel surrounding the doorway. These landscapes create the "image and place" required by Ignatius' *Spiritual Exercises*, while also reflecting Federico Borromeo's desire to glorify nature (see Chapter 1). The square chapel has only one entrance, which leads into an interior space equally divided into two parts: a vestibule with frescoed walls and the nativity scene behind a wooden screen. A local artist named Giacomo Filippo Monti, with assistance from his brother Bernardo, was responsible for the frescos. The workshop of sculptor Christoforo Prestinari executed the diorama. The artists created naturalistic representations so as to enhance the pilgrim's affective experience of the event. In the tableau area, for example, the ceiling painting imitates wood, the walls simulate stone, and a hayloft hangs on the back wall. While there is no hay there now, it seems probable that there once was. The initial impression of exterior combined with interior is that this place is Orta, it is Assisi, it is Bethlehem, it is everywhere.

The audience's view of the diorama is controlled by a seven-foot carved wooden screen with four oval openings (see Catalogue of Chapels, Fig. 4). The addition of grilles was a profound physical alteration in the fabric of the Sacro Monte and represents a significant change in both its intended purpose and its function. The original chapels incorporated the viewer as participant, creating an enhanced liminality, but the Tridentine focus on didacticism and authority necessitated a change in the way the sites operated. The grilles supported the authority of the church by delimiting the place of the pilgrim, dissolving any potential ambiguity.[2] That being said, the actual experience of gazing through the portholes is not very limiting and the goal of such focused looking—a contemplative union with the divine—is not inhibited.

While thirteenth-century biographies provide few details of the saint's birth, beyond noting that his father was away on a business trip, and that the baby originally had two names (first John and then Francis), fourteenth-century biographies amplify the story surrounding his birth. Francis' nativity becomes a product of biographers who aggressively began to portray Francis as a saint who lived in perfect conformity with Christ in all the moments of his life. Typically, these

SACRED VIEWS OF SAINT FRANCIS

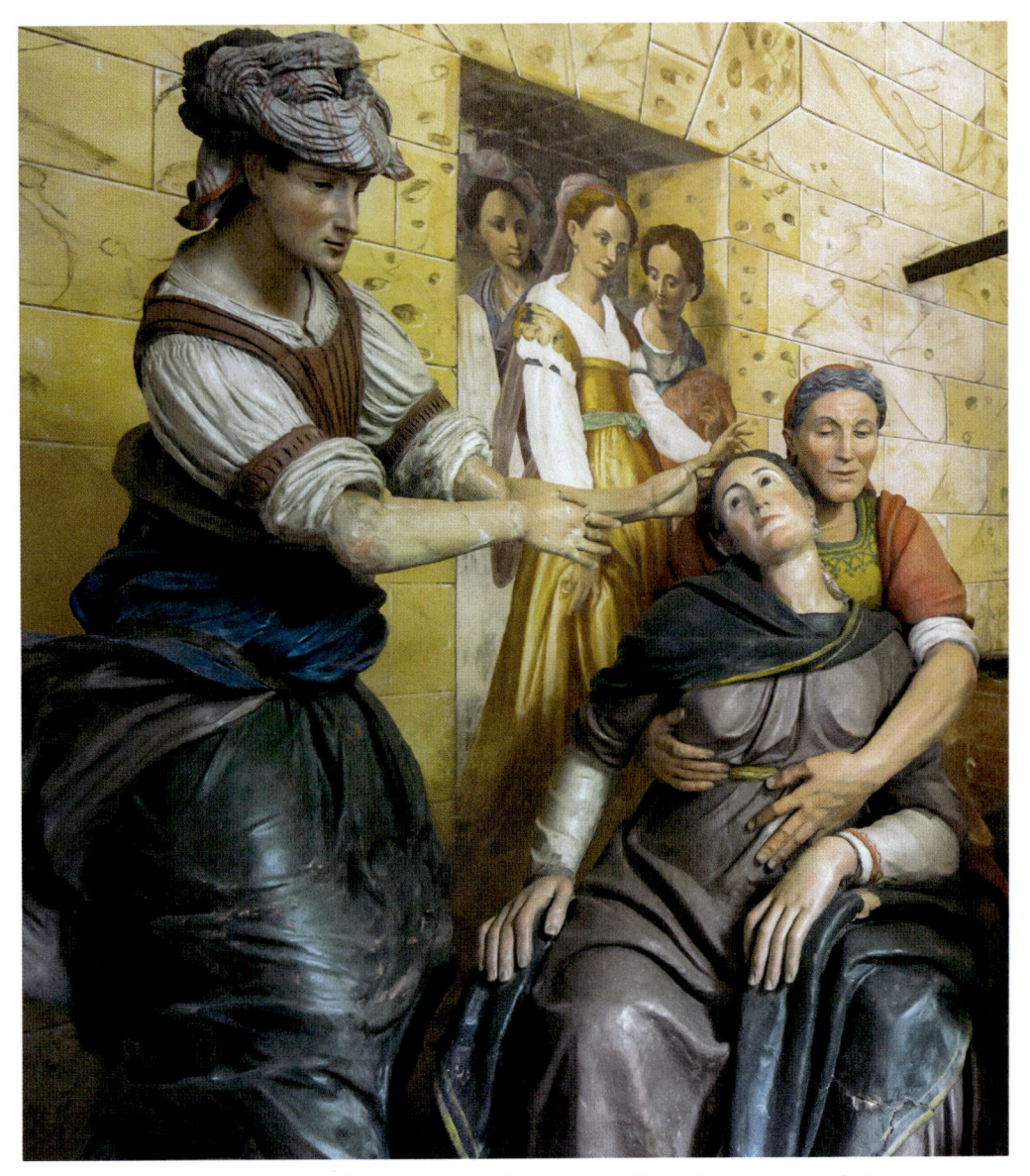

Fig. 1. The Nativity of St. Francis: Lady Pica giving birth in a stable. Chapel I, Sacro Monte di Orta.

later versions of Francis' birth have three narrative parts. First, a wide variety of people foretell the importance of Francis and his birth; second, Francis' mother, because of problems with her labor, gives birth in the stable; and third, a pilgrim comes to the house. With an unusual assertiveness, this beggar/pilgrim demands to see the newborn baby. When Lady Pica (the nickname for Francis' mother, because she was supposedly from Picardy) allows this, he proclaims Francis' greatness in contrast to another Assisi-born boy (never named) who won't turn out so well.

Arnald of Sarrant's *The Kinship of Saint Francis* (written in 1365) is probably the source for the first motif, prophecy. Arnald's entire work illustrates that Francis' life is in direct conformity in nine points of the life of Jesus. While Bonaventure's *Major Legend* articulated the nine primary virtues of Francis' life, Arnald nuances this idea further and shows that Christ's life became a form to which Francis was called to conform. In his story of the birth, he includes predictions by Abbot Joachim, Saint Dominic, Innocent III, Brother Elias, Brother Pacifico, an unnamed abbot in "regions over the seas," and an unnamed devout man of Assisi. In his *De Conformitate*, Bartolomew of Pisa then takes Arnald's nine autobiographical parallels and spins them into eighty: forty events from Jesus and forty from Francis, the foretelling of Francis' birth included.[3]

The second event, the birth of Francis in a stable, is one of the latest medieval Franciscan legends. The first surviving evidence for this story is an inscription on the archway above the entrance to the oratory San Francesco Piccolino which reads "*Hoc oratorium fuit bovis: et asini stabulum in quo natus est sanctus Franciscus mundi speculum*" ("This oratory was the stable of the ox and ass in which was born Saint Francis, the mirror of the world"). According to the Franciscan scholar Giuseppe Abate, this inscription dates from the mid-fourteenth-century.[4] Meanwhile, H.W. van Os identifies the earliest literary account of this story as the late-fourteenth-century *Vita Bruxellensis*.[5] The story was well enough established to be part of Benozzo Gozzoli's painting "Scenes from the Life of Saint Francis" (1452). Accompanying the fresco, which cleverly shows the three narrative units in one artistic frame, is the inscription: *Qualiter b. F. Fuit denu(n)tiatus a xro i(n) forma peregrini quod debebat nasci sicut ips(e) in stab(u)lo qualit(er) quida(m) fatuu(s) p(ro)ste(r)nebat b. F. Vestime(n)tu(m) in via* ("How St. Francis was announced by Christ in the form of a pilgrim, and that he, like Christ himself, had to be born in a stable. And how a certain simple man spread his clothes out where St. Francis was walking.")[6]

The third event, a prophet-pilgrim who appears after the birth of Francis, seems to appear first in *A Book of Exemplary Stories* (1280–1310) attributed to a report by Brother Nicholas of Assisi, whose family home was next door to the Bernardones.[7] Arnald, in *The Kinship of Saint Francis*, explains the typological meaning: "As we read that Christ was carried by Simeon in his arms and that he also prophesied many things about Christ, thus, on the same day Francis was born, a pilgrim made his way to the door of his family's house."[8]

In Chapel I, the story of Francis's birth is told by seven human and three animal statuary figures of this early, fairly simple chapel. In a group of three on the left (see Fig. 1), the immediately post-partum mother of Francis, dressed in a simple rose dress and greenish-blue cloak, reclines against the older and seemingly wise midwife. Another female helper reaches out to her, as do the painted female attendants who appear on the left wall. Pica gazes heavenward with a supernatural calmness that expresses her foreknowledge of the meaning of the event. Francis' mother is clearly *imitatio Mariae* in both her serene gaze and symbolic clothing. The medieval Virgin Mary often wears a dark blue mantle, blue having replaced purple as the color of royalty in the Western European art.[9] Beginning in the tenth-century Mary also wears red, symbolic of nobility, suffering and passion. From these two evolved the classic representation of the Blessed Virgin Mary with a red robe and a blue mantle. The simplicity of Lady Pica's clothing and hair is particularly noteworthy when compared to the strikingly elaborate costumes and coiffures of the other women.

In the middle group, a kneeling woman holds the baby Francis (see Fig. 2). The baby gazes directly at the viewer. Naked, except for swaddling across the genitals, Francis holds his hands in a benediction: left hand across the heart, and right hand raised in blessing. This evocative hand gesture, called a *moti* in Gian Paolo Lomazzo's *Trattato dell'arte* (1584), indicates Francis' saintly character and creates the central gesture of the group.[10] To the right, one elaborately dressed woman moves toward the baby, folding down her bodice to

Fig. 2. The infant Francis with hand held in benediction, surrounded by attendants. Chapel I, Sacro Monte di Orta.

expose her breast. Her hair is in an elaborate coiffure intertwined with ribbons and a medallion. Her costume, which includes a broad red girdle and an intricate apron of seemingly expensive material over a full dark skirt is clearly a fine garment. The careful detail with which it is painted certainly suggests that a popular style is being referenced: it resembles those in near-contemporary bourgeois portraits recorded by Racinet as well as surviving local antique costumes of the Ossolano valley.[11] As such, these material objects bring home the meaning to the female viewer—that she, too, can affectively imagine motherly attentions to the baby. Here, the explicit exhortation to venerate Francis, and through him Jesus, is made in the relationship among the particulars of the story, the general truth it illustrates, and the devotional response of the audience. This chapel makes the birth real in an almost photographic evocation of the past reality.[12]

At the right, a servant woman simply holds a bowl of water. Next to her, another woman gazes at the scene and thus directs the viewer's sight. She holds linens and is not really a necessary member of the ensemble except that she provides meta-narrative guidance. Her gaze confirms the didactic stability of Truth of the historical event and its artistic representation. Acting as an embedded interpreter, she reads on behalf of the viewers, who are also engaged in the effort to understand the correlations of the tableau.

Three animals make important appearances as well. Directly behind Francis is an ass with a rope tied around his neck (see Catalogue of Chapels, Fig. 5). He seems hidden, until the viewer looks through one of the ovals in the screen, and then the ass gazes di-

Fig. 3. Fresco of Lady Pica giving bread to the prophesying pilgrim (right), and Lady Pica is escorted to the stable for the birth of Francis (left). Chapel I, Sacro Monte di Orta.

rectly at the viewer with what must have been intended to be a look of compassion. Francis' frequent reference to the body as "Brother Ass" makes this an obvious iconic connection, and the rope foretells Chapel XIII when Francis is lead through the streets with a noose around his own "Brother Ass." Tucked in next to the ass is a horned ram, also gazing at the viewer and also iconographically linked with the saint. Francis especially loved sheep throughout his life for the simplicity of their way of life. By grazing and eating from the hands of their owners, the sheep reflect the Franciscans' alms-based economy. And of course Christ is the Lamb of God, and in loving sheep Francis expresses his love of Him. In a circle of reciprocal references, Christ is like a lamb, the lamb is like Francis, and thus Francis is like Christ.[13] Looking over the servant's shoulder is a large horse. He, too, gazes at the baby Francis with an anthropomorphic grin and adoring eye. In the traditions (but not biblical texts) of Christ's nativity, the ass, ox, and the sheep keep watch.[14] Rather than an ox, here the more courtly horse is present, perhaps reflecting Francis' later acclaim as "soldier of Christ."[15]

In the vestibule area of the chapel, where the viewer stands, the walls are decorated with frescos outside the invented space of the faux-crèche. On the viewer's right Lady Pica gives bread to the visiting pilgrim (identified by his staff and pilgrim badges), and two servants carry the pregnant Lady Pica into the stable (see Fig. 3). The implication here is that the angel/pilgrim is the one who tells Francis' mother to forsake her wealthy bedchamber and deliver her baby in the stable. On the viewer's left the pilgrim, now with the wings of an angel, holds the naked baby Francis. At one time an oil painting of the "Birth of Christ" executed by Camillo Procaccini (c. 1618) hung overhead; it is now in the Church of San Nicolao (also on the Sacred Mount), on the right side of the presbytery. Procaccini is famous for his adoration of the shepherds' motif, which he employs here as well. This early master of the Baroque evokes a reality of the experience in a way expressly encouraged by Federico Borromeo.[16] In Chapel I, the painting originally served to underscore one of the parallels between the lives of Christ and Francis.

Viewers knowledgeable in the life of Francis might be surprised that there is no chapel at Orta dedicated to one of the most memorable events in Francis' life, his creation of the Christmas nativity scene at Greccio. Both Thomas of Celano and Bonaventure relate that Francis created a living nativity scene to celebrate Christmas Eve in 1223. In the woods of Greccio he arranged hay, an ox, an ass, a manger, and a baby (perhaps a doll, perhaps a real sleeping child). Francis' "tableau vivant" re-created the real atmosphere of the stable in Bethlehem and movingly touched the emotions of the audience. Thomas of Celano, in one of his interesting tense shifts, exclaims: "out of this is made a new Bethlehem."[17] Celano probably means that Francis popularized an already existing tradition which is now re-enacted each year; he certainly also means that Francis has created a scene to demonstrate a new distinctly "Franciscan," affective viewing practice. But, Chapel One at Orta *is* the Greccio scene, as the baby Francis in a stable again recreates the birth of Christ and remakes Assisi a new Bethlehem as well. In another loop of self-referentiality, Francis' own birth recalls the nativity scene at Greccio, the nativity scene remembers the first Christmas, and Christ's nativity provides the foundation for Francis' *imitatio Christi*.

Endnotes

1. E. de Filippis and F. M Carcano, *Guide to the Sacro Monte of Orta* (Novara: Riserva Naturale Speciale del Sacro Monte di Orta, 1991), 16.

2. Ryan Gregg, "The Sacro Monte of Varallo as a Physical Manifestation of the Spiritual Exercises," *Athenor* 22 (2004): 49–55.

3. Carolly Erickson, "Bartholomew of Pisa, Francis Exalted: De conformitate," 273.

4. P. Guiseppe Abate, *La Casa Natale di S. Francesco e la Topografia di Assisi nella prima metà del secolo XIII* (Rome: Miscellanea Francescana, 1966), 9.

5. H.W. Van Os, "St. Francis of Assisi as a Second Christ in Early Italian Painting," *Simiolus* 7, no. 3 (1974): 132.

6. See Diane Cole Ahl, *Benozzo Gozzoli: Tradition and Innovation in Renaissance Painting* (New Haven: Yale University Press, 1996), 230.

7. *A Book of Exemplary Stories* (c. 1280–1310), in *Francis of Assisi: Early Documents*, 3 vols., eds. Regis Armstrong. O.F.M. Cap., et al. (New York: New City Press, 1999–2001), 3:800.

8. Arnald of Sarrant, *The Kinship of Saint Francis*, in *Francis of Assisi: Early Documents*, 695–96. See Bartholomew of Pisa, *De Conformitate*, eds. Fathers of the College of Saint Bonaventure, Analecta Franciscana 4 (Quaracchi: Collegium S. Bonaventurae, 1906), 56.

9. John Gage, *Color and Meaning: Art, Science, and Symbolism* (Berkeley: University of California Press, 2000), 15. On the symbolism of the color blue, see Lisa Jardine, *Wordly Goods: A New History of the Renaissance* (New York: W.W. Norton and Co., 1998), 15. See also P. Dronke, "Tradition and Innovation in Medieval Western Colour-Imagery," in *The Realms of Colour: Lectures Given at the Eranos Conference in Ascona from August 23rd to 31st, 1972*, eds. Adolf Portmann and Rudolf Ritsema (Leiden: Brill, 1974), 51–107.

10. Fredrika Jacobs, *The Living Image in Renaissance Art* (Cambridge: Cambridge University Press, 2005), 18.

11. Auguste Racinet, *The Costume History* (Cologne: Taschen, 2003), 109. Also see Penny Howell Jolly, "Learned Reading, Vernacular Seeing: Jacques Daret's Presentation in the Temple," *The Art Bulletin* 82 (2000): 428–52.

12. Critics who discuss this phenomenon in two different ways are Karl-Heinz Stierle, "Story as Exemplum—Exemplum as Story: On the Pragmatics and Poetics of Narrative Texts," in *New Perspectives in German Literary Criticism*, eds. Richard Amacher and Victor Lange (Princeton: Princeton University Press, 1979), 75–93; and Roland Barthes, *Camera Lucida: Reflections on Photography*, trans. Richard Howard (New York: Hill & Wang, 1981), 88.

13. Lisa Kiser, "Animal Economies: The Lives of St. Francis in Their Medieval Contexts," *Isle: Interdisciplinary Studies in Literature and Environment* 11 (2004): 126.

14. David Salter, *Holy and Noble Beasts. Encounters with Animals in Medieval Literature*, (Woodbridge: D.S. Brewer, 2001), 33.

15. See for example, Thomas of Celano, *Life of Saint Francis*, in *Francis of Assisi: Early Documents*, 1:189 and 1:214.

16. Nancy Ward Neilson, "Etched Transfiguration," *Burlington Magazine* 118 (1977): 699.

17. Thomas of Celano, *Life of Saint Francis*, in *Francis of Assisi: Early Documents*, 1:85.

4

The Framework of St. Francis' Spiritual Journey

Chapels II and XV

Chapel II and Chapel XV both depict mystical, theophanic, and, indeed, miraculous experiences attributed to St. Francis, one at the beginning of his mission and one toward the end. The chapels feature moments along St. Francis' spiritual journey as he perfected an imitation of Christ (*imitatio Christi*). The idea that Francis imitated Christ with such devotion that he became a second Christ (*alter Christus*) dominates the didactic theme of the Sacro Monte di Orta (see Chapter 1). The devotional path upon the sacred mountain dedicated to St. Francis begins at Chapel I with the saint's nativity—in a stable— explicitly establishing the mimesis of Francis and Christ, and establishing the Franciscan agenda, from the outset. It is Chapel II (St. Francis before the San Damiano Cross) and Chapel XV (St. Francis receives the Stigmata at La Verna) that provide the spiritual framework of the saint's ministry, his life of living the Gospel. They highlight two periods of struggle for discernment in his life, and the transformative role that total submission and thankful praise may play in the life of the Christian. Chapels II and XV are thematically united in celebrating what Catholic tradition holds as the initial wound of God's love in St. Francis' heart and the culminating wounds of that love in Francis' flesh.

Chapel II

As the second stop of the Sacro Monte's "pilgrimage within a pilgrimage," the iconographic program of Chapel II focuses on a visionary encounter between Francis and Christ crucified in the San Damiano Church, an encounter long considered by his early hagiographers a decisive moment in Francis' conversion. In the thirteenth-century *Legend of the Three Companions*, we read:

> A few days had passed when, while he was walking by the church of San Damiano, he was told in the Spirit to go inside for a prayer. Once he entered, he began to pray intensely before an image of the Crucified, which spoke to him in a tender and kind voice: "Francis, don't you see that my house is being destroyed? Go, then, and rebuild it for me." Stunned and trembling, he said: "I will do so gladly, Lord." For he understood that it was speaking about that church, which was near collapse because of its age. He was filled with such joy and became so radiant with light over that message, that he knew in his soul that it was truly Christ crucified who spoke to him.[1]

The conversion of Francis did not happen at one precise moment but in a series of events.[2]

Nevertheless, early followers and biographers considered the tradition of the theophany of the Cross of San Damiano an important turning point. Again, from the *Legend of the Three Companions*, we read:

> From that hour, therefore, his heart was wounded and it melted when remembering the Lord's passion. While he lived, he always carried the wounds of the Lord Jesus in his heart. This was brilliantly shown afterwards in the renewal of those wounds that were miraculously impressed on and most clearly revealed on his body.[3]

Similarly, Celano writes:

> Francis was more than a little stunned, trembling, and stuttering like a man out of his senses. He prepared himself to obey and pulled himself together to carry out the command. He felt this mysterious change in himself, but he could not describe it. So it is better for us to remain silent about it too. From that time on, compassion for the Crucified was impressed into this holy soul. And we honestly believe the wounds of the sacred Passion were impressed deep in his heart, though not yet on his flesh.[4]

The belief that a person could bear the signs of Christ's Passion (internally or externally) was not an innovation of the medieval Franciscans. In Galatians 6:17, Paul writes: "I bear the stigmata of the Lord Jesus in my body." Usually the Church Fathers understood these marks to be metaphorical, indicating the hardships Paul endured for his faith. Alternatively, Paul's comment could be considered indicative of the physical penance that Paul performed as a Christian.[5] The comment was rarely, however, understood to mean a literal replica of Christ's stigmata. Similarly, early medieval Latin writers use the term "stigma" in a general sense to denote any bodily mark derived from self-inflicted wounds in the course of penitential Christian devotion, as in the cases of Bishop Silvinus of Therouanne and William of Gellone.[6] Other marks were considered signs of miraculous intercession or signs of great faith, as with the wounds of Pope Leo IX, the martyr Theodard, and the bodies of some Crusaders.[7] Medieval commentators sometimes understood the marks of Paul as the tattoo of a soldier—a soldier of Christ—a term by which Francis is also repeatedly identified.[8] Even in such contexts, the wounds suffered by the especially devout could be internal, like that described in Francis' encounter with Christ at San Damiano, echoing 2 Corinthians 4:10: "We always carry around in our body the death of Jesus, so that the life of Jesus may also be revealed in our body." Just so, in the eleventh century, Peter Damian prayed that his soul be marked with the cross.[9] In the fourteenth century, Bartholomew of Pisa outlined two types of "transformational similitude" to the wounds of Christ; his typology encompassed the range of interpretative tradition: one transformation (common to mystics) occurred in the soul, while a second type occurred in both soul and body, as with Francis.[10] However, as traditions about Christ's Passion began to emphasize His human suffering, and artistic representations changed to more naturalistic depictions of the dying Christ, "stigmata" came to denote more narrowly the wounds of the Passion.[11] It is in this context that Bartholomew of Pisa understands the external, bodily stigmata of Francis, and the way in which his biographers wish us to understand the events on La Verna (Chapel XV).[12]

Whether internal or external, stigmata are wounds that Catholics believe indicate intense physical and spiritual connection with the divine. By all accounts Francis was overwhelmed by the great mystery of the Passion; he was known for weeping openly as he wandered the streets, overcome by Christ's sacrifice.[13] The intensity of Christ's suffering moved Francis deeply, as the crucified Christ became for him the model of his own spirituality and of his devotion to the Church.

Francis' emphasis on the crucified Christ was not unusual for the period and reflected the popularity of Passion devotion in the Middle Ages. Medieval Passion devotion aroused "powerful feelings of compassion, and the interiorization of these emotions. In the process, a much greater emphasis came to be laid on the sense of the suffering humanity of Christ, and the wonder and awe with which Christians in earlier centuries had regarded the Son of God was complemented by powerful sensations of compassionate love."[14] Like others who were said to have been made "new" through devotion to the Passion experience, Francis' status within his social world—his family and the community—was altered, but his biographers also said he experienced a significant internal change in his very nature, as his priorities, beliefs and worldview became focused on a mission to imitate Christ.[15] The post-Tridentine Church embraced St. Francis' renewal as emblematic of the Church's program of rejuvenation, which made St. Francis one of the most popular saints of the Catholic Reformation.

Medieval hagiographers and contemporary scholars situate St. Francis firmly in the mystical tradition.[16] However, his place in the history of Christian mysticism is complex. A mystical experience is in its essence one in which the devotee has an alteration of consciousness during what they believe to be an immediate encounter with the divine.[17] (A mystical text can likewise transform the consciousness of the believer by encouraging what they regard as a similarly intimate connection.) Through prayer, bodily mortification, and theophany (e.g., the events of San Damiano, the vision of the stigmatic Seraphim, and the vision of Christ at Porziuncola), St. Francis is said to have experienced many such mystical encounters. What is unusual about Francis' place in the history of Christian mysticism is that he was orthodox in his support for the established Church. Mysticism is typically described as "the paradigm of religious individualism and radicalism,"[18] with mystics as peripheral to the mainstream establishment:

> The mystic, it is said, is the great religious rebel who undermines the orthodox establishment, placing his own experience above the doctrines of the accepted authorities, and who not infrequently engenders serious opposition even to the point of being put to death for heresy.[19]

It is true that Francis was radical in his break with contemporary monastic tradition and in his embrace of abject poverty, but in these moves he still sought and submitted to Roman authority.[20] According to the medieval testimony he embraced the veneration of angels, the primacy of the Virgin Mary, the transubstantiation of the Eucharist, the cult of relics, and the granting of indulgences.[21] Saint Francis urged "fidelity to the Roman Church because it perpetuates the reality of the Incarnation through the religious buildings, sacred vessels and especially the Eucharist, and thus renders visible the presence of God among men and women."[22]

As for the crucified Christ's directive that Francis rebuild the Church, this too would have lasting import for the saint's mission and his legacy in the Reformation Church. According to André Vauchez, for Francis churches, the buildings themselves, mediated communion with God. Within such sacred space, in prayer and contemplation, Saint Francis knew the immediacy of God through the sacrifice of His Son.[23] Thus churches, and especially the crucifix, became important reference points of holiness for Francis. Yet his medieval hagiographers (and perhaps even Francis himself) understood Christ's message to mean he should work beyond the walls (and limits) of material structure, as Bonaventure reports: "the principal intention of the words referred to that which Christ purchased with his own blood, as the Holy Spirit taught him and as he himself later disclosed to the brothers."[24] In other words, Francis was charged with rebuilding the universal

Fig. 1. Francis kneels beneath the San Damiano Cross. Chapel II, Sacro Monte di Orta.

Fig. 2. Christ on the San Damiano Cross. Chapel II, Sacro Monte di Orta.

church, a theme that we encounter in several of the chapels at the Sacro Monte di Orta, especially Chapels II and XV.

The diorama of Chapel II captures the essence of the mystical event laid out by medieval hagiographers. In a dimly lighted nave, Francis kneels below the crucified Christ, pleading for direction and guidance (see Fig. 1). Though in anguish, Francis does not appear in a state of ecstasy, nor does he appear unnerved. In this way, the depiction seems to follow the account of the *Legend of the Three Companions* rather than Celano's *The Remembrance of the Desire of a Soul* or Bonaventure's *The Major Legend of Saint Francis*. Meanwhile, the figure of Christ is imposing in both its authority and its sorrow (see Fig. 2). As blood drips from His wounds, Christ locks eyes with Francis. The quiet intensity of their mutual gaze is accentuated by the flurry of activity around them, as the stableman attends the frisky horse and three dogs give chase to a hare.[25] To their goal, the artists have effectively executed a moment of profound divine communion amidst the mundanity of life.

The representation of St. Francis' encounter with the crucified Christ at Sacro Monte di Orta differs in important ways from the medieval accounts as found in *Legend of the Three Companions*, *The Remembrance of the Desire of the Soul*, and the *Major Legend of Saint Francis*. One significant difference is that the crucifix of the chapel is not the San Damiano Cross. The San Damiano Cross is an icon in the Italo-Byzantine style.[26] Icons can tell the story of an event, and the San Damiano Cross tells the entire story of the Passion: death, resurrection and ascension. The icon portrays the crucified Christ, witnesses to the death of Jesus, the empty tomb (represented by the black background), Christ's ascension to heaven, and the hand of God with fingers held in benediction. But the scene of Chapel II features a sculpted crucifix of terra cotta with only angels (of terra cotta and fresco) attendant (see Chapter 2, Catalogue of Chapels, Fig. 7). The substitution for the San Damiano icon, the emblem of the Franciscan order to this very day, of the simpler version of the crucifix is perhaps best understood when we consider the general function of the icon. Through the icon, the viewer becomes psychologically engaged in the Passion story, becoming one of the eyewitnesses among the disciples, women, children, centurions, and saints. Chapel II of the Sacro Monte, constructed within a hundred years of when the popularity of Passion devotion had reached an all-time high (c. 14th–16th centuries), would then affect the intensely emotional experience of the Passion.[27] Such an experience would seem fitting for a pilgrimage site that was expressly devotional and influenced as it was by Ignatius of Loyola's *Spiritual Exercises* (1548). The story the artists of Orta want to effect, however, is not that of the Passion, but rather the story of Francis' encounter with the crucified Christ. The emphasis of the chapel is on Francis and an important moment in his spiritual conversion—the formal beginning of his ministry and life as a new man. It is the tradition of his mystical and visionary experience that the post-Tridentine Church embraces as an exemplar of adoration and devotion, with an emphasis on justification though good works in imitation of Christ. It was precisely this psychological engagement that the architect and artists of Chapel II wanted to effect, rather than that of the Passion, and the use of the traditional crucifix as found in the chapel facilitates this focus. It is a specific example of an occasion at the Sacro Monte when the historical-literary tradition is subsumed by the interests of the didactic tableau.

The second unusual feature of Chapel II is that the setting of the encounter between the crucified Christ and Francis takes place not in the church of San Damiano but outdoors. This divergence from the tradition may reflect an interpretation that developed over time: that the commission Francis received was to have universal applicability. Christ told Francis not just to rebuild the crumbling San Damiano, but to rebuild the Catholic Church, to bring it back to a Gospel centered mission. It is the universality of this message that is reflected in the artistic program of Chapel II. The crucified Christ and the saint, and most importantly the message, are not constrained to one location. The notion of particularity is displaced as the physical walls where the encounter happened are torn down and replaced with a panoramic landscape that is everywhere and anywhere. The message is literally reframed in Chapel II to create an affective corollary echoing Jesus' own universal message that was spoken from a mountain top—the Sermon on the Mount—just as the message of Francis is spoken from the Sacro Monte. The landscape provides a powerful mimesis for the pilgrim, who is able to project themselves into this imaginary, universal landscape just as the deliberate use of seventeenth-century dress encouraged pilgrims to see themselves as participants in a contemporary scene.

The landscape perspective of Chapel II directs the pilgrim's gaze from rugged *terra firma* to the angelic heavens of the frescoed walls. This visual movement from foreground to background, low to high, is accentuated by the bleakness of the rocky terrain against the bright colors of the elevated features. The figure of the stableman with the animals epitomizes the banal and mundane; the heavenly host and crucified Christ are God manifest. Meanwhile the figure of St. Francis kneeling on the barren ground, in the posture of contrition, visually mediates the earthly and heavenly realms.

Chapel XV

In Chapel XV, Francis' spiritual journey, begun in the church of San Damiano where he became a "new man," ends in his transformation into a new Christ. And as in the narrative tradition surrounding his conversion at San Damiano, Francis was in the midst of a personal struggle just prior to the transformative experience at La Verna. At this point, the biographers, as Paul Sabatier notes,

show us Francis distressed for the future of the Order, and with an infinite desire for new spiritual progress. He was consumed with the fever of saints, that need of immolation which wrung from St. Theresa the passionate cry, 'Either to suffer or to die!' He was bitterly reproaching himself with not having been found worthy of martyrdom, not having been able to give himself for Him who gave himself for us.[28]

By 1223, Francis was withdrawn and reclusive;[29] his order grew, but not in the direction he had envisioned. Eventually he, along with a few companions, moved to La Verna—an uninhabited, isolated wilderness in Tuscany. Celano recounts that,

While he was staying in that hermitage called La Verna, after the place where it is located, two years prior to the time that he returned his soul to heaven, he saw in the vision of God a man, having six wings like a Seraph, standing over him, arms extended and feet joined, affixed to a cross. Two of his wings were raised up, two were stretched out over his head as if for flight, and two covered his whole body. When the blessed servant of the most High saw these things, he was filled with the greatest awe, but could not decide what the vision meant for him. Moreover, he greatly rejoiced and was much delighted by the kind and gracious look that he saw the Seraph gave him. The Seraph's beauty was beyond comprehension, but the fact that the Seraph was fixed to the cross and the bitter suffering of that passion thoroughly frightened him. Consequently, he got up both sad and happy as joy and sorrow took their turns in his heart. Concerned over the matter, he kept thinking about what this vision could mean and his spirit was anxious to discern a sensible meaning from the vision. While he was unable to perceive anything clearly understandable from the vision, its newness very much pressed upon his heart. Signs of the nails began to appear on his hands and feet, just as he had seen them a little while earlier on the crucified man hovering over him.[30]

Bonaventure adds additional details in his version of the event:

> On a certain morning about the feast of the Exaltation of the Cross, while Francis was praying on the mountainside, he saw a Seraph having six wings, fiery as well as brilliant, descend from the grandeur of heaven. And when in swift flight, it had arrived at a spot in the air near the man of God, there appeared between the wings the likeness of a man crucified, with his hands and feet extended in the form of a cross and fastened to a cross. Two of the wings were raised above his head, two were extended for flight, and two covered his whole body. Seeing this, he was overwhelmed and his heart was flooded with a mixture of joy and sorrow. He rejoiced at the gracious way Christ looked upon him under the appearance of the Seraph, but the fact that He was fastened to a cross pierced his soul with a sword of compassionate sorrow...
>
> ...As the vision was disappearing, it left in his heart a marvelous fire and imprinted in his flesh a likeness of signs no less marvelous. For immediately the marks of nails began to appear in his hands and feet just as he had seen a little before in the figure of the man crucified. His hands and feet seemed to be pierced through the center by nails, with the heads of the nails appearing on the inner side of the hands and the upper side of the feet and their points on the opposite sides. The heads of the nails in his hands and his feet were round and black; their points were oblong and bent as if driven with a hammer, and they emerged from the flesh and stuck out beyond it. Also his right side, as if pierced with a lance, was marked with a red wound from which his sacred blood often flowed moistening his tunic and underwear.[31]

For his biographers, the reception of the stigmata marked a fitting end to Francis' spiritual transformation, as the trials of the recent years had become his own "personal passion." According to Bonaventure, Francis was "totally transformed into the likeness of Christ crucified."[32]

The stigmatization of Francis, a stunning claim of mimesis,[33] was controversial throughout both the medieval and Renaissance periods. André Vauchez documents the early critics, noting that opposition to the claim was derived from various motivations.[34] Some hostility originated in the clash between the secular clergy and the perceived arrogance of the Franciscans. The Dominicans on the other hand were jealous of the exclusive prerogative claimed by the Franciscans. For others, the dramatic break with tradition, wherein only the Son of God had stigmata, and the innovative claims about Francis' holiness created deep suspicions.[35] In the end, according to Vauchez, lasting resistance to the stigmatization of Francis was caused by "...the fact that his followers were 'divinizing' him."[36] From Peter John Olivi to Bartholomew of Pisa, many Franciscans claimed that the saint was truly, and literally, another Christ.[37] While for other devout Christians, the popular Franciscan belief that Francis was an *alter Christus*, or second Christ, was simply too strong a claim.

But the Franciscans and the papacy pushed back against the critics. Between 1237 and 1291, the Vatican issued nine papal bulls authenticating the stigmatization and condemning the critics.[38] Meanwhile, Franciscan writers elaborated on the tradition by adding greater detail and underscoring its miraculous nature. This elaboration can be found in the artistic program of ensuing centuries as well.

Arnold Davidson traces the representational evolution of Francis' stigmata.[39] He begins with earliest known depiction of the account, a scene from Bonaventura Berlinghieri's *Francis of Assisi* (c. 1235) from the church of San Francesco in Pescia. In this panel painting, the artist has moved Francis outside the hermitage of La Verna and onto the mountainside. He no longer stands, but kneels in a prayerful attitude before the Seraph. Through these changes, the artist is making an "unmistakable iconographical reference to Christ's Agony in the Garden,"[40] on the Mount of Olives, thus furthering Franciscan identification of Francis as *alter Christus*. Also noteworthy is that Francis is stigmatized while in the presence of the Seraph. Though Celano's account leaves the reader to put together cause and effect, Berlinghieri straightforwardly connects the appearance of the Seraph with the appearance of the stigmata. Davidson goes on to assert that the writings of Bonaventure and the frescos of Giotto further accentuate the miraculous nature of the stigmata and the special standing of St. Francis.[41] In his *Major Legend of Saint Francis*, Bonaventure recounts that Francis was praying on the mountainside when a Seraph, *who was Christ*, appeared before him. As the vision disappeared, it left imprinted upon him the stigmata. Though as in Celano's *Life of Francis* the marks appear after the departure of the Seraph, nonetheless Bonaventure avers an explicit causal connection between the two.[42] Bonaventure's description of the event established a new paradigm for artistic representations going forward, as exemplified by the work of Giotto.[43] As with Bonaventure's account, the painter's fresco of the stigmatization at the Basilica of Assisi (c. 1300) shows Francis on bended knee in prayerful attitude on the mountainside. The Seraph appears above him, the wings revealing a human form from the ribcage upwards. The figure is unmistakably Christ. Giotto was innovative as well, in ways that came to dominate future representations.[44] In order to visually illustrate the causal connection between the Seraph and the stigmata of Francis, Francis' stigmatization occurs in the presence of the Christ-Seraph, not after the vision had disappeared; the artist has collapsed the chronological sequence of events. Furthermore, Giotto painted rays of light emanating from the stigmata of the Christ-Seraph and terminating in the marks of Francis. There is no question but that the viewer is to understand the miraculous and divine origin of Francis' stigmata. A second innovation was the inclusion of a witness to the stigmata, Brother Leo. We have seen that in the earliest depictions of the event (such as that of Berlinghiri, discussed above) there was no second figure, in keeping with the account of Celano's *Life of Francis*. Indeed, Celano stresses Francis' desire to keep the stigmata a secret; only two brothers are named as having seen the wounds during Francis' lifetime.[45] It was Bonaventure who introduced the explicit testimony of witnesses in *The Major Legend of Saint Francis*, when he wrote that Francis was compelled to reveal his experience in order to share "the Lord's sacrament."[46] These witnesses were said to have seen the stigmata for themselves and heard about the vision directly from the saint. Bonaventure writes:

> Now
> Through these most certain signs,
> Corroborated
> Not by the sufficient testimony of two or three witnesses,
> But by the superabundant testimony of a whole multitude,
> God's testimony about you and through you
> Has been made overwhelmingly credible,
> Removing completely from unbelievers
> The veil of excuse,
> While they confirm believers in faith
> Raise them aloft with confident hope
> And set them ablaze with the fire of charity.[47]

The addition of witnesses functioned to lend confirmation to the event and provide authenticity in the face of both Catholic and Protestant critics.[48] Following Bonaventure's account, Giotto underscores the authenticity of the miracle by including just such a witness in his artistic program. And what began with Giotto in 1300, adding a witness to the scene, was commonplace by the fifteenth and sixteenth century.[49] The choice of Leo as witness in Giotto's work (and those paintings subsequently influenced by his innovation) is also important. Though other friars accompanied Francis to La Verna, it was Leo who became, in the textual tradition, his most trusted companion. In *Little Flowers* of the late fourteenth century, Leo is portrayed as a complex character; he is tempted, frightened, sceptical, devoted, and good.[50] He strives and sometimes fails. And in his fragility of spirit, he provides for believers a reflection of themselves.

At the Sacro Monte di Orta, the setting of Chapel XV conveys the emotional and geographical desolation of Francis' La Verna experience. Figures of small animals dot the landscape, underlining the danger and violence of the wilderness: a mountain cat attacks a wild boar, while a large lizard with open jaws lurks menacingly nearby, producing a measure of discomfort and fear in the viewer.[51] The artistic program of Chapel XV reflects the textual vision of Bonaventure and the artistic vision of Giotto. Francis, echoing the penitential posture of the terra-cotta Francis in Chapel II, kneels on a bleak and rocky mountain with his arms outstretched at waist level, looking in awe at the Christ figure, a Seraph (see Fig. 3). Francis bears the stigmata; blackened flesh like "nail heads" mark the palms of the hands, and the skin surrounding the blackened flesh is red with irritation. In the *Life of Francis*, followed by *The Major Legend of Saint Francis*, Francis' response to the vision was characterized by a mixture of joyousness, fearfulness, and incomprehension, followed at last by understanding. Prestinari captures this latter moment of clarity; it is a moment of decisive response, with Francis at once joyful in his share of Christ's Passion, but also accepting of the suffering it entails.

Fig. 3. Francis and Brother Leo on La Verna at the moment of the Seraph's appearance and Francis' stigmatization. Chapel XV, Sacro Monte di Orta.

In the diorama, Brother Leo accompanies Francis. In contrast to St. Francis' posture of attention, the witness leans away from the Seraph in fear while shading his eyes from the blinding vision (see Fig. 3). Leo's posture thus amplifies the emotional pitch of the occasion by creating a tension between his attitude and that of Francis. Davidson examines the dynamics of the witness as depicted in painting. In Giotto's Assisi fresco (c. 1300), Brother Leo sits to the side reading a book. The friar seems to take no notice of the encounter occurring before him.[52] In Giovanni Bellini's Pesaro altarpiece (c. 1470), Leo, book in hand, rests his head with his eyelids closed, mimicking the disciples of Christ who slept in the Garden. (473)[53] Davidson concludes:

Fig. 3. The Seraph from the Stigmatization of Francis. Ceiling Fresco, Chapel XV, Sacro Monte di Orta. The Seraph from the Stigmatization of Francis. Ceiling Fresco, Chapel XV, Sacro Monte di Orta.

The contrast between Francis praying and Leo reading invokes the contrast between prayer and the study of sacred theology made by Francis in his letter to Anthony of Padua...Furthermore, Bonaventure has Francis contrast reading and studying with prayer...As in Christ's life, prayer takes precedence over reading, so Francis prays on the mountainside while Leo reads, and Francis's praying culminates in his stigmatization, while Leo's reading distracts him from a vision of the supernatural.[54]

In other works, such as the *Stigmatization of St. Francis* by Domenico Ghirlandaio (c. 1430), the *Stigmatization of St Francis* by Benozzo Gozzoli (c. 1450), and the *Stigmatization of St. Francis* by Federico Barocci (c. 1560–1580), Leo looks up from his book to watch the event.[55] In our chapel, too, Leo clearly had been reading his book but was distracted by the vision. If Davidson is correct about the contrast between reading and prayer, it seems that in our chapel, as in the paintings by Ghirlandaio, Gozzoli, and Barocci, the need for authentication and eyewitness testimony was more imperative for these artists than the theological debate between reading and prayer. In terms of viewership and experiential participation at this critical moment in the life of St. Francis, the presence of Leo (or of *a* Leo) in the scene of Chapel XV invites each pilgrim to be a witness as well.

We do not know what the original frescos in Chapel XV looked like; they were replaced approximately one hundred and seventy-five years after the chapel was completed, probably because of decay. The current frescos were painted in 1783 by Riccardo Donnino (alt. Donini), and feature the gentle pastels, curving lines, cherubs, and pastoral landscapes typical of the rococo style. Despite this later renovation, the artistic program remains unified and compelling. The wall frescos sweep the viewer's eye up toward the heavens, where the heavenly host, who ride swirling clouds, make their way (see Chapter 2, Catalogue of Chapels, Fig. 55). Golden rays of light emanate from the Christ-Seraph, who is surrounded by a mandorla (see Fig. 4). The body and wings are highlighted in a soft red and gold while the stigmata are a deep black that is striking against the softer background.

Unusually, Donnino depicts an infant Christ-Seraph on the wall of Chapel XV. The six wings are present but diminutive and do not cover the infant's body. Such a depiction may have had its roots in the Renaissance-era popularity of Roman putti, or cherubs, in iconography. Most commonly associated with love, the putti were also known as *spiritello*, little sprites.[56] By the fifteenth century in Italy and France, putti could be found festooning church entrances, hanging garlands on altars, and sitting vigilantly upon tombs. The Florentine sculptor Donatello (c. 1386–1466) is credited with the earliest sculptural examples of Renaissance putti. His putti are chubby, male and winged, typically having only two wings. As Charles Dempsey notes, there were medieval precedents to Donatello's putti but, static in their execution, they served a minor decorative role. Dempsey emphasizes the celebratory role of the Renaissance putti and the development of "appealingly childish" personalities of their own.[57] Sally Struthers credits Donatello with restoring their respectability, using them in a positive light, and infusing them with Christian meaning.[58] Donatello's putti romp, play instruments, dance, laugh and even show fear. They attended Christ at his Incarnation and at his death. But most striking in Donatello's reinvention of the putto is its ability to be "a participant in [a scene's] larger meaning, and even an independent bearer of meaning itself."[59]

Though putti and seraphim belong to different orders of the angelic hierarchy (seraphim being the highest order), in Renaissance iconography there was fluidity between angels, cherubim (which biblically speaking were composite creatures, part human, part animal, with multiple wings; cf. Ezek 1:5–10), putti and seraphim. The illuminated seraphim of the fourteenth century *Petites Heures de Jean de Berry* are infants rather than adults. In Benozzo Gozzoli's *Virgin and Child* (c. 1460), infant seraphim surround Mary and Jesus. Infant seraphim are also associated with St. Francis in fifteenth-century painting. In Taddeo di Bartolo's *St. Francis of Assisi* (c. 1403), St. Francis is surrounded by a mandorla of putti-seraphim. Domenico Ghirlandaio replicates this image of the seraphic infant mandorla in his *St. Francis in Glory* (c.1440). Similarly, Ghirlandaio uses a mandorla of infant seraphim around the crucified Christ-Seraph of his *Stigmata of St. Francis* in the Sassetta Chapel in Florence (c. 1483–85). By the end of the fifteenth century, putti *cum* seraphim have become a common motif.

Donnino's innovation, influenced by the precedent of putti-seraphim with perhaps a dash of rococo playfulness, need not be a purely flamboyant or superficial one. The Christ child calls to mind Bartolomeo of Pisa's parallel between the infancy narratives of Christ and Francis, vividly illustrated at the Sacro Monte di Orta in Chapel I. It also brings Francis' transformation as a "new man" full circle by juxtaposing spiritual growth from birth to death. At the very least, the infant represents purity and innocence of both the divine and the saint. In this presentation, the stigmatization of Francis was a miracle in its purest form.

In addition to the infant Christ-Seraph, the ceiling fresco of Chapel XV is crowded with biblical and Church figures, interspersed with assorted angels, both children and adults. To the viewers' left as one approaches the diorama is the Prophet Jeremiah and his assistant Baruch, both holding Scripture. Continuing to the right a helpful putto catches the toppled mitre of a male church figure. Next to them a second church figure has a five-star halo, which identifies him as Saint John Nepomuk (d. 1393; see Fig. 5).[60] Though the inclusion of an eighteenth-century Bohemian saint in the artistic program of Chapel XV seems incongruous at first, the canonization of John in 1729 by Pope Benedict XIII played a very important role in the post-Tridentine Church. According to tradition, when King Wenceslaus ordered John to betray the seal of the confessional and reveal the sins of his queen, John refused. King Wenceslaus subsequently had John killed. Thus John became a symbol for the inviolability of the confessional, an upholder of the sacrament of Penance, and a defender of the autonomy of the Church. His popularity increased with his canonization, and his image spread throughout Catholic Europe. At Orta, St. John Nepomuk's inclusion in the

Fig. 5. Saint John Nepomuk and Moses among the Heavenly Host. Ceiling Fresco, Chapel XV, Sacro Monte di Orta.

late eighteenth-century fresco of Chapel XV serves as an example of the post-Tridentine program at work on the Sacri Monti.

Adjacent to St. John Nepomuk, one immediately recognizes Moses with shining horns and holding the tablet of the Ten Commandments. Behind Moses is another church figure looking down upon Francis and swinging a smoking incense burner. An adult angel hovers over a knife-wielding Abraham who leans towards a pale youth (Isaac) who holds a *fasces* across his body, perhaps symbolizing the salvific power and protection of God. The artist's design leads the eye further upward and to the right, where the viewer encounters Eve and Adam modestly draped in greenery. Above them are the figures of Joseph and Mary, both gesturing toward the Holy Trinity who occupy the highest register. The figure of Christ is depicted as having just been removed from the adjacent cross; his seminude body is crumpled but sitting upright, with one hand, clearly displaying a stigma, raised aloft. God the Father sits enthroned, a pyramidal nimbus surrounding his head, and rests his hand upon the *globus cruciger* symbolic of authority and dominion. Both God and Christ look down on the scene below. The white dove flies above Christ and God, with rays of light emanating in all directions from its body. The painting of the Trinity is directly above the terra-cotta statue of St. Francis. Adjacent to the Trinity, putti bear a large cross, reminding the pilgrim of the glory of the Resurrection.

Continuing again to the right around the circumference of the ceiling and at a register just below Joseph and Mary, Donnino included additional New Testament figures who appear to be John the Baptist, Simon, James, and Bartholomew. Bartholomew, just below James, is engaged with yet another church figure. The design on the ornate vestment of the church representative is that of three men in a boat, thus recalling the biblical stories of Luke 5:1–11 and John 21:1–14. For Catholics, Church leadership, like the disciples, functions as fishers of men (Mark 1:17), with special emphasis on the pope, who from the thirteenth century until the mid–nineteenth

144

century, wore the Fisherman's Ring to seal official documents. This particular papal figure is anonymous, his back to us; he personifies the papacy. His inclusion among the disciples speaks to the importance and authenticity of the papacy, and church authority in general. The unnamed pope is in conversation with a fair, golden-haired young man holding the martyr's palm. Given the presence of a putto holding a book nearby, the iconography indicates that the youth is St. John the Evangelist. Moving again upward and to the right, King David plays a harp, and next to him Noah sits in an ark and holds an olive branch. Below Noah are Peter, dressed in white and holding a key to heaven, and Paul, also dressed in white, holding a sword (see Chapter 2, Catalogue of Chapels, Fig. 56). A putto sits with them, holding Paul's book of letters in one hand and a second key to heaven in the other. Donnino's willingness for innovation is also found in these representations: Paul is beardless, John the Baptist is not in animal skins, and Adam and Eve are depicted in a positive light, content in Eden.

While the ceiling fresco with its swirling clouds and heavenly host commands attention, a rather washed-out landscape fills the eye-level register surrounding Francis and Leo. There is no hermitage in the vicinity of the friars; the ground level is a continuation of the rocky terrain of the diorama. Most unusually, however, the setting seems to be seaside foothills rather than an isolated mountaintop. While a tall mountain range appears in the far distance, the pilgrim finds Francis and Leo near the shore with a panoramic view of buildings, a bridge, and four tall sailing ships (see Chapter 2, Catalogue of Chapels, Fig. 55). Though the water is evocative of the beautiful Lake Orta immediately below the Sacro Monte, the presence of large seagoing vessels takes the viewer away from the central Piedmont region to coastal Mediterranean Italy. This move echoes Chapel II, where the historical location of the encounter, the Church of San Damiano, is replaced with an outdoor landscape that could be anywhere. Given the rococo predilection for bucolic landscapes, perhaps this substitution of the coast for La Verna is simply a whimsical innovation that conjures any number of locations throughout Italy. On the other hand, it is possible that Donnino is making a connection between the universal message of St. Francis and the universal—literally global—mission of the Franciscans during the late eighteenth century. These ships of Chapel XV are sailing away from land; they are going out into the world. And by this time, Franciscan missionaries were active in all parts of the known world, including Mexico, Peru, Brazil, Venezuela, Florida and the American Southwest; Japan, Mongolia, China; Goa, Sumatra, Java and Borneo; the Guinea Coast and the Congo. Such missionary zeal reverberates especially with the theme and message of Chapel XI, St. Francis and the Sultan.

Despite the juxtaposition between the simple figures of Francis and his companion and the far more flamboyant frescos of the ceiling and the imaginary landscape of the sea, the focus of the chapel remains firmly on Francis and his spiritual connection to the Seraph, emphasizing the miracle of his transformation. And, in the midst of action (the threatening beasts, the cowering friar, the swirling heavens and radiating Seraph), Francis, in his stillness, provides a profoundly dramatic moment.

Conclusion

These two chapels of Orta, Chapel II and Chapel XV, capture pivotal moments in the tradition of Francis' spiritual journey. The hagiographic accounts of his experiences at San Damiano and La Verna provided the architects and artists of the Sacro Monte di Orta the framework of his missionary activity. The differences between the literary accounts of these two transformational events in Francis' life and their representation in the chapels of Orta reflect a duality of meanings embedded in the pilgrimage site at large. Each event held meaning for the life of Saint Francis and additional meaning for the Counter Reformation Church, but both messages were part of a Franciscan love story. The *Legend of the Three Companions* asserts that the wounds of Christ were initially inscribed upon Francis' heart as the young man prayed in adoration before the Cross of San Damiano. Toward the end of his life, through the seraphic spirit (love), Francis received the wounds externally in his flesh. Francis' *conformitas Christi* signifies his role as mediator between God and humankind in Franciscan tradition from Celano, for whom Christ represents sacrifice and the Seraph represents the contemplative life—both pillars of the Franciscan Order—to Francis de Sales, an affiliate of the Capuchins, who wrote of Francis:

> Love then drove the interior torment of this great lover S. Francis to the exterior, and wounded the body with the same dart of pain with which it had wounded the heart; but love being within could not well make the holes in the flesh without, and therefore the burning seraph coming to its help, darted rays of so penetrating a light, that it really made in the flesh the exterior wounds of the crucified which love had imprinted interiorly in the soul.[61]

Endnotes

1   *Legend of the Three Companions*, in *Francis of Assisi: Early Documents*, 3 vols., eds. Regis Armstrong, O.F.M. Cap., et al. (New York: New City Press, 1999–2001), 2:76. The *Legend of the Three Companions* (c. 1245–46) is a compilation of episodes from the saint's life intended to fill in gaps left by Thomas of Celano's *Life of Saint Francis*. It is presumably based on the collected memories of those who knew Saint Francis in his lifetime. Later, Celano includes the story in his revised and expanded version of his Francis biography, entitled *Desire of Remembrance of a Soul* (c. 1250) in which he relied upon the *Legend of Three Companions*. Celano notes the story again in his *Miracles of St. Francis* (c. 1254), as does Bonaventure in his official biography of St. Francis, *Major Life of St. Francis* (c. 1260).

2   See Jacques Le Goff, *St. Francis of Assisi*, trans. Christine Rhone (London: Routledge, 2004), 26; see also Pierre Brunette, *Francis of Assisi and His Conversions*, trans. P. Lachance and K. Krug (Chicago: Franciscan Press, 1997).

3   *Legend of the Three Companions*, in *Francis of Assisi: Early Documents*, 2:76.

4   Thomas of Celano, *Remembrance of the Desire of a Soul*, in *Francis of Assisi: Early Documents*, 2:249. Celano's *Life of Saint Francis* makes no mention of the encounter between Francis and Christ at San Damiano.

5   Carolyn Muessig, "Signs of Salvation: The Evolution of Stigmatic Spirituality before Francis of Assisi," *Church History* 82, no. 1 (2013): 42–43.

6   Giles Constable, *Three Studies in Medieval and Religious and Social Thought* (Cambridge: Cambridge University Press, 1995), 198–99.

7   Ibid., 200.

8   Muessig, "Signs of Salvation," 45.

9   Constable, *Three Studies in Medieval and Religious and Social Thought*, 202.

10 Carolly Erickson, "Bartholomew of Pisa, Francis Exalted: De conformitate," *Mediaeval Studies* 34 (1972): 268.

11 Ibid., 199, 201.

12 By tradition, Francis is the first case of external stigmata (in the narrow sense) in Christianity. Catherine of Siena (1327–80) is also said to have experienced stigmata, but that when she prayed God would make them invisible, her prayer was granted.

13 *Legend of the Three Companions*, in *Francis of Assisi: Early Documents*, 2:76. See also *The Assisi Compilation*, in *Francis of Assisi: Early Documents*, 2:180–1.

14 "Introduction" to *The Broken Body: Passion Devotion in Late-Medieval Culture*, eds. A.A. MacDonald, H.N.B. Ridderbos, and R.M. Schlusemann (Groningen: Egbert Forsten, 1998), ix.

15 The identification of Francis as a "new man" appears frequently in Thomas of Celano's *Treatise on the Miracles of St. Francis*, in *Francis of Assisi: Early Documents*, 2:399–400.

16 See, for example, Ewert Cousins, "Francis of Assisi: Nature, Poverty, and the Humanity of Christ," in *Mystics of the Book: Themes, Topics, and Typologies*, ed. R.A. Herrara (New York: Peter Lang, 1993), 203–17, and Jay M. Hammond, "Saint Francis's Doxological Mysticism in Light of His Prayers," in *Francis of Assisi: History, Hagiography and Hermeneutics in the Early Documents*, ed. J.M. Hammond (Hyde Park: New City Press, 2004), 105–52.

17 For discussion, see Hammond, "Saint Francis's Doxological Mysticism in Light of His Prayers," 106–11.

18 Steven T. Katz, "The 'Conservative' Character of Mystical Experience," in *Mysticism and Religious Traditions*, ed. Steven T. Katz (Oxford: Oxford University Press, 1983), 3.

19 Ibid., 3. Katz challenges this traditional image of the mystic and of mysticism, arguing that the relationships between mysticism and established religion "are far more varied and dialectical than is usually appreciated." Nevertheless, the traditional understanding of the relationships seems to still apply within the history and scholarship of medieval European Christianity.

20 Thomas of Celano, *The Remembrance of the Desire of a Soul*, in *Francis of Assisi: Early Documents*, 2:260–62. For discussion of Francis' innovative mysticism, see Cousins, "Francis of Assisi."

21 Thomas of Celano, *The Remembrance of the Desire of a Soul*, in *Francis of Assisi: Early Documents*, 2:374–77. On Francis' attitude toward indulgences, see the documents concerning the *Porziuncola Indulgence*, found in *Francis of Assisi: Early Documents*, 3:807–12.

22 André Vauchez, *Francis of Assisi: The Life and Afterlife of a Medieval Saint*, trans. Michael Cusato (New Haven: Yale University Press, 2012), 133.

23 Ibid., 30.

24 Bonaventure of Bagnoregio, *The Major Legend of Saint Francis*, in *Francis of Assisi: Early Documents*, 2:536.

25 The stableman and riding mount hint at Francis' previous aspirations for knighthood.

26 The icon became property of the Poor Clares when they occupied San Damiano. When the sisters moved to the Basilica of Saint Clare in 1257, the icon went with them. It still resides in the Chapel of the Crucifix.

27 See A.A. MacDonald, H.N.B. Ridderbos, and R.M. Schlusemann, eds., *The Broken Body* (Groningen: Egbert Forsten, 1998).

28 Paul Sabatier, *Life of St. Francis of Assisi*, trans. Louise Seymour Houghton (London: Hodder & Stoughton, 1919), 293.

29 Michael Robson, *The Franciscans in the Middle Ages* (Woodbridge: Boydell Press, 2006), 18, 44; Vauchez, *Francis of Assisi*, 131.

30 Thomas of Celano, *Life of Saint Francis*, in *Francis of Assisi: Early Documents*, 1:263–64.

31 Bonaventure of Bagnoregio, *The Major Legend of Saint Francis*, in *Francis of Assisi: Early Documents*, 2:632–33.

32 Ibid., 2:632.

33 Paroma Chatterjee, "Francis's Secret Stigmata," *Art History* 35, no. 1 (2012): 39.

34 André Vauchez, "The Stigmata of Francis and Its Medieval Detractors," *Greyfriars Review* 13, no. 1 (1999): 61–89. For the later period, see Carolyn Muessig, "The Stigmata Debate in Theology and Art in the Later Middle Ages," in *The Authority of the Word: Reflecting on Image and Text in Northern Europe, 1400–1700*, eds. Celeste Brusati et al. (Leiden: Brill, 2012), 481–504.

35 Vauchez, "The Stigmata of Francis and Its Medieval Detractors," 77–79.

36 Ibid., 83.

37 Ibid., 84–86.

38 Ibid., 66.

39 Arnold Davidson, "Miracles of Bodily Transformation, or How St. Francis Received the Stigmata," *Critical Inquiry* 35, no. 3 (Spring 2009): 451–80.

40 Ibid., 464.

41 Ibid., 496–71.

42 Probably following Thomas of Celano's later *Legend for Use in the Choir*, in which he emends his earlier account to include that Francis "saw above him a crucified Seraph who clearly impressed on him the signs of the crucifixion so that Francis, too, appeared crucified." See *Legend for Use in the Choir*, in *Francis of Assisi: Early Documents*, 1:323.

43 Davidson, "Miracles of Bodily Transformation," 468.

44 See Donal Cooper and Janet Robson, *The Making of Assisi: The Pope, the Franciscans, and the Painting of the Basilica* (New Haven: Yale University Press, 2013), 127.

45 The two brothers are Elias and Rufino. See Thomas of Celano, *Life of Saint Francis*, in *Francis of Assisi: Early Documents*, 2:264, and also, Chatterjee, "Francis's Secret Stigmata," 38–61.

46 Bonaventure of Bagnoregio, *The Major Legend of Saint Francis*, in *Francis of Assisi: Early Documents*, 2:633.

47 Ibid.

48 Davidson, "Miracles of Bodily Transformation," 35–36.

49 Robert Kiely, "Further Considerations of the Holy Stigmata of St. Francis: Where Was Brother Leo?" *Religion and the Arts* 3, no. 1 (1999): 22–28. See also Cooper and Robson, *The Making of Assisi*, 127. One exception is *The Stigmatization of Saint Francis*, a panel originally from Pisa and now in the Louvre. Dated by Julian Gardner to the early fourteenth century and just after Giotto's work in Assisi, the scene lacks some of the traditional elements established by Giotto and includes a few of its own innovations. See Julian Gardner, "The Louvre Stigmatization and the Problem of the Narrative Altarpiece," *Zeitschrift für Kunstgeschichte* 45, no. 3 (1982): 217–47.

50 Kiely, "Further Considerations of the Holy Stigmata of St. Francis," 33–34.

51 On the inducement of such emotions in the viewer, see Jill Bennett, "Stigmata and Sense Memory: St. Francis and the Affective," *Art History* 24, no. 1 (Dec. 2003): 1–16.

52 Davidson, "Miracles of Bodily Transformation," 472–73.

53 Ibid., 473.

54 Ibid.

55 For a discussion of Bellini's and Ghirlandaio's paintings of the stigmatization, see also Oskar Bätschmann, *Giovanni Bellini* (London: Reaktion Books, 2008), 111–13. For discussion on the works by Ghirlandaio, Gozzoli, and Barocci, see Kiely, "Further Considerations of the Holy Stigmata of St. Francis," 20–40.

56 Charles Dempsey, *Inventing the Renaissance Putto* (Chapel Hill: University of North Carolina Press, 2001), 6.

57 Ibid., 26–33.

58 Sally Struthers, *Donatello's Putti: Their Genesis, Importance, and Influence on Quattrocento Sculpture and Painting*, 2 vols., PhD diss., Ohio State University, 1992, 1:3, 1:261–86.

59 Dempsey, *Inventing the Renaissance Putto*, 49.

60 The starred halo represents the miraculous and radiant light that marked the spot of his drowning.

61 Francis de Sales, *Treatise on the Love of God*, trans. Henry Benedict Mackey, O.S.B. (Westport: Greenwood Publishing Group, 1971), 236.

5

St. Francis' Triumph over Temptation

Chapel X

Michael Carroll has argued that the Christocentrism of the Catholic Reformation church, through the preaching orders such as the Franciscans, used dynamic images associated with particular narratives rather than the static miraculous images common and popularly venerated in Italy.[1] At the Sacro Monte di Orta, this technique immerses the viewer in Francis' exemplary actions, with Chapel X constructed to move the pilgrim into affective communion with the moment of Francis' victory over temptation. According to Franciscan tradition, Francis received the Indulgence of the Porziuncola as a unique marker of his special status as a new Christ, manifest in his essential imperviousness to significant temptation. This victory over temptation, the receipt of the Indulgence and, ergo, the chapel itself link the faith of Francis to profound orthodoxy.

The chapel's name, "The Temptation," and its diorama are based on a lesser-known story found in the fourteenth-century Chronicle of the Twenty-four Generals:

> One night around midnight Satan came to blessed Francis as he was at prayer next to his cell and said to him: 'Francis, what are you doing? Do you want to die before your time? Why are you doing such things? Don't you know that sleep is the principal nourishment of the body? You are young, so for you sleep and rest are especially necessary. One time I say to you that you are young, and so another time you can do penance for your sins. Why then do you punish yourself so in vigils and prayers?'

But Francis recognized the devil behind this temptation to relax his penitential practice:

> Then blessed Francis took off his tunic and undershorts and left the hut and passed through the large and dense hedge and entered the wildest and thorn-infested woods that belong to Philip Nurbi, adjoining the church of Saint Mary of the Porziuncola. When blessed Francis was in the middle of the woods, his flesh all stained and bloodied from the thorns, he said: 'It is better for me to acknowledge the passion of my Lord Jesus Christ than to give in to the seduction of the deceiver.'

At that point in the narrative, Francis, pierced and bloodied by an instrument of the Passion, saw the winter thorns transform into rose blossoms as he was suddenly immersed in divine light and surrounded by a host of angels:

Fig. 1. Three Devils plague Francis. Chapel X, Sacro Monte di Orta.

They cried with one voice: 'Blessed Francis, hurry to the Savior and his Mother who await you in the church.' There then appeared to him a straight path as if of decorated silk going up to the church and blessed Francis took from the rose patch twelve red roses and twelve white roses and entered the church.

In the conversation with Jesus and Mary that followed, Francis was granted the Indulgence of the Porziuncola (see discussion of Chapel XI in the Chapter 2, the Catalogue of Chapels), which pardoned the sins of all the faithful who visited the Porziuncola on a certain day each year.[2]

The interior space of the octagonally shaped Chapel X is dominated by a central grouping of terracotta figures surrounded by frescos. In the very center of the diorama, a discreetly nude Francis lies on the ground,[3] surrounded by a chaotic mixture of heavenly beings, assorted wildlife, and the thorn bush reminiscent of Christ's Passion. Organizationally, the scene imitates the medieval commonplace seen in representations of Christ's temptation, which establishes a polarity not between God and the devil but between angels and devils. To Francis' right are a group of demons and to his left are angels, making Francis clearly the object of dispute between the angels and the devil/demons—between divine grace and diabolical temptation.

In the narrative account, only Satan tempts Francis, but in the tableau three demons to Francis' right (the viewers' left) reflect different potentialities of evil (see Fig. 1). First is a talon-footed demon who dangles his finger in his mouth, as he gapes quizzically at Francis. Second is the sophisticated, large, muscular demon, richly dressed and winged like the angels but with horns and elongated fingers that end in claws. He too is in motion, but it is difficult to tell if he is running away in fear or simply advancing off-stage, with an encouraging look back over his shoulder toward Francis as if urging the holy man to follow. His dark skin, a common attribute of demons, symbolizes evil while his graceful physique mimics the beautiful

Fig. 2. Three Angels protect Francis. Chapel X, Sacro Monte di Orta.

angels on the right. Finally, to the far right of Francis, is a small, old, female bat-demon, naked with sagging breasts, who runs away in terror accompanied by her mice.[4] The function of these demons is to recall to the viewer all the instances of Francis' many trials with devils/temptations, not just one example. We can imagine this mixture of demons as perpetrators of the lesser temptations and trials recounted in the various biographical traditions, some of which are depicted in the fresco cycle on the walls around the diorama.

Despite the best efforts of the three demons, however, Francis looks only toward the angels. All four angels attending to Francis are handsome, with colorful wings and varied, elaborate clothing (see Fig. 2). Francis is in many ways one with angels, for in his prologue to the Major Legend of Saint Francis, Bonaventure identifies Francis literally and symbolically as an angel.[5] One young angel who stands behind the reclining saint, ready with a cloak to cover him, invokes the commonly seen motif of the sustaining

Fig. 3. Tobit refuses dinner and defies the Assyrian king in order to bury a fellow Israelite (Tobit 2; 12:13). Chapel X, Sacro Monte di Orta.

angel. When Francis is represented as a suffering saint in post-Tridentine art, an angel typically waits at his head to support him with divine love.[6] The next three angels demonstrate three different ways of explicating Francis' relationship with the surrounding scene. The first looks at Francis, but gestures to the viewers' right toward the path to the Porziuncola; the second directly engages the pilgrim's attention with "eye contact" while directing their gaze, through pointed gestures, to Francis; and the third looks at Francis while gesturing in the opposite direction toward the Porziuncola. These gestures and glances comprise an oracular plot to guide the Pilgrim's gaze from Francis toward the fresco to the viewer's immediate right, a fresco of Christ and his Mother, crowned and enthroned, granting the Indulgence of the Porziuncola. Thus, the designers of Chapel X take a relatively obscure tale about Francis' temptation and transform it into a new way to see Christ in Francis and Francis as intercessor with Christ. In so doing, they deliver a strong Counter-Reformation lesson about the role of the Church in individual salvation.

Italian critic Pier Giorgo Longo has stated that the themes of the dioramas and frescos in the Ortese chapels are not always integrated, but rather are often so distinctly different that it is difficult to make connections among their dissimilar messages. He cites Chapel X as one such example, whose wall images do not coordinate with the sculptural scenes.[7] A closer examination, however, reveals that a deeper agenda does in fact hold the chapel together thematically. While large parts of the ground-level pictures and their cartouches are illegible through decay and graffiti, those surrounding the diorama at eye level and just above elaborate on the diorama with illustrations of other temptations that are mentioned by Francis' biographers. The upper registers of frescos on the walls of Chapel X contain various biblical tales which typologically comment on the events below. Scenes of the demonic temptation of Job and God's testing of the righteous Tobit are next to Christ's confrontation with the

Fig. 4. Lady of the Apocalypse. Chapel X, Sacro Monte di Orta.

devil (see Fig. 3). As recorded in Matthew 4:1–11, Jesus dealt with three temptations: stones to bread, challenging death, and ruling the world. Above these, scenes from Revelation, including the lady of the apocalypse with twelve stars in her crown and the dragon with seven crowned heads, decorate the ceiling (see Fig. 4). Many other motifs are scattered throughout so that altogether at least fifty stories from the Old Testament, the New Testament, Christian hagiography (such as the story of Lucia who is here depicted holding a palm branch, a common symbol of triumph over evil), and the life of Francis are commingled on the walls behind and above the sculptures to create a constant intertextual typological commentary on the action. The walls have a theatrical, highly colored effect reflecting the introduction of the baroque to the Sacro Monte during the middle of the seventeenth century. Thus the fresco cycle is a fairly comprehensive representation of Francis' many brushes with evil, linked with narratives of the Old and New Testaments and of the lives of the early saints depicted on the upper walls and vaults.

As for the illustrations of Francis' temptations, the first eye-level frescoed panel, to

Fig. 5. Francis rejects Frederick II's Concubine. Chapel X, Sacro Monte di Orta.

the left of the door, shows Francis kneeling in prayer in front of the crucifix while being assailed by a variety of vividly colored demons. Its inscription, quoting Mark of Lisbon's *Croniche*, reads "Saint Francis tormented greatly by the demons whom he defeats with help from the Lord."[8] The second panel on the pilgrim's left illustrates a little-known story in which, according to the inscription again from the *Croniche*, Francis kneels on hot coals by the side of a bed as he foils the temptation of King Frederick II's concubine (see Fig. 5).[9] This later addition to Francis' hagiography, which refers to Francis' visit to Emperor Frederick II in 1222 at Bari, does not appear in any thirteenth- or fourteenth-century texts. According to legend, Frederick's banquet entertainment included a sumptuous dance by a beautiful courtesan whose charms Francis easily resisted. This caused Frederick to praise Francis publicly and spend some hours in his company. In the fresco, Francis is able to control his body so well, with the grace of God, that he can equally withstand burning charcoal and its equivalent burn, the sensual heat of a woman.

On the other side of the chapel, the first panel to the viewer's far right is a reproduction of the theme of Chapel XI (the next chapel in the series), the granting of the Indulgence of the Porziuncola to Francis by Jesus and Mary. The fresco to the center right and directly behind the statue of Francis recumbent illustrates a story from Celano's *The Remembrance of the Desire of a Soul* in which the devil tempts Francis with the sin of lust, but:

As soon as the blessed father felt it, he took off his clothes and lashed himself furiously with the cord, saying, "Come on, Brother Ass, that's the way you should stay under the whip! The tunic belongs to religion: no stealing allowed! If you want to leave, leave!"[10]

Earlier in *The Remembrance of the Desire of a Soul*, Celano recounts an incident in which Francis is beaten by devils until he is almost dead. Francis explains to his companion that "Demons are the police of our Lord whom he assigns to punish excess."[11] During this temptation, however, Francis preempts the demon's job and punishes his own flesh. Unfortunately,

> When he saw that the temptation did not leave even after the discipline, though he painted welts all over his limbs black and blue, he opened the cell, went out to the garden, and threw himself naked into the deep snow. Taking snow by the handful he packed it together into balls and made seven piles. Showing them to himself, he began to address his body: "Here, this large one is your wife, and those four over there are your two sons and your two daughters; the other two are your servant and your maid who are needed to serve them. So hurry, he said, get all of them clothes, because they are freezing to death! But if complicated care of them is annoying, then take care to serve one master! At that, the devil went away in confusion."[12]

The choice of this story and its placement within the chapel is important for understanding the overall didactic agenda of not only Chapel X, but also the entire sacred mountain. While the narrative is ostensibly about overcoming the temptation of concupiscence, the numerous unusual details signal that there are in fact multiple agendas in play. As a cautionary tale on lust, it is strikingly lacking in evocations of sexual desire. There are neither female sex objects nor any particular interest in women, negative or positive, operating at the core of the story. Of course, sex was a vexed topic in the Middle Ages, and Francis did preach the problem of female contagion and sexual allure:

> He declared that all conversation with women was unnecessary except for confession, or as often happens, offering very brief words of counsel. And he used to say: "what business does a Lesser Brother have with a woman, except when she religiously makes a request of holy penance or advice about a better life?"[13]

Again, "He ordered avoiding completely the honeyed poison, that is, familiarity with women, by which even holy men are lead astray. He feared that in this the weak spirit would quickly be broken, and the strong spirit often be weakened."[14] However, this particular tale does not have any "honeyed poisons" or even any conversing women. No feminine figure propels the narrative. The lack of a woman here is consistent with the conclusion of Jacques Le Goff that sins such as lust had "little prominence in the thought of Francis" and argued even more emphatically by Jacques Dalarun that there is a decided absence of women, real or otherwise, in Francis' own writings.[15] It seems that carnal temptation was not Francis' great weakness. He was the eternal virgin. According to Bernard of Besse, "He was in every way a mirror of holiness, and also a virgin in the flesh, as he revealed to that very holy man, Brother Leo, and then disclosed to the General Minister. For as the just one is his own first accuser, while Blessed Francis accused himself in public of being the greatest of sinners, in private he never confessed the sin of bodily fornication."[16] Francis' family of snow invokes the motif of sexual temptation from the Desert Fathers and then neutralizes it. In the *Vitae Patrum* a hermit is tempted by lust; in response he makes for himself a mud family which he quickly rejects.[17] The similarity of stories shows how tradition held that Francis absorbed the monastic sensibilities of the hermits but ultimately, in a Christ-like manner, proved himself to be above temptation itself. The tested hermit's substitute mud woman is an obvious substitution for a real woman who is entrapping, gooey, base, of the earth, the antithesis of spirit-bearing man. But Francis nuances woman in a significantly different direction. Here, the snowwoman is the epitome of frigid undesirably. There is no warm, voluptuous, affectionate bedmate here. The snow family and its story represent the temptations of family respectability and the middle-class comforts of children and servants: a carnal need, but not a sexual one. Francis equates "family" with humans who need clothing—the very materialistic object he has so resolutely rejected. Rejecting this mock family enables Francis to embrace the model of family he encourages his brothers to follow, a secular fraternity for which he would be the father and the mother. Francis takes on the feminine to create the snow family in the same way he creates his own fraternal kinship group, but he chooses the superior, exclusively male, model. In driving himself away from the conventional life Satan has offered him, far away from his snowball family, Francis immerses himself in free, unsculpted white snow, a symbol of purity, innocence, and new beginnings. And for Francis this is the perfected family. In this second, winter baptism, Francis reaffirms his identification with Jesus, the bachelor par excellence, surrounded by his family of disciples.

Guidebooks written explicitly for the early pilgrims who visited Sacro Monte di Orta show two different ways to read the chapel, and as such they offer a witness to the many levels on which the didacticism of the pilgrimage site can be experienced.[18] The architects designed simple, immediately intelligible images to reach the illiterate, but they also produced complex, intellectually satisfying didactic programs for the well-educated.[19] *Spiegazione delle sagre capelle fondate sopra Il Monte d'Orta* is an early-seventeenth-century manual that supplies a simple meaning for the chapel: "Francis was born to be the determined enemy of the spirits of hell."[20] Here, emphasis on the universal issues of the psychomachia takes precedence, with a lack of interest in the finer points of a holy man's temptation. Another guide, *Instruzzione al divoto lettore che desidera visitare Il Sacro Monte di S. Francesco d'Orta* provides a more nuanced reading. It takes the biblical Song of Songs 2:2 as its theme: "Come un giglio fra i cardi" ["Like a lily among the thorns"]. While the commentary begins with Francis' contest of wills with demonic powers, it concludes that the meaning of the temptation is found in the cloud of angels and banks of roses which attend Francis to his ultimate legitimization by Jesus and his mother.[21] In this way, pilgrims are guided to understand that the ultimate meaning of Francis' temptation is found in his commitment to the Church as the sole administrator of grace.

According to his biographers, Francis was not really vulnerable to profound temptation, but by entering fully into the trial of testing, he offers a way for his followers to imitate him. And *imitatio Francesci* is an avenue to *imitatio Christi*. In the narrative traditions, Francis' temptations were sometimes vague, sometimes concrete attempts to call him away from his higher mission. But the image-saturated theatrical scenes of Chapel X at Orta universalize all of these temptations for the edification of the audience. The architects designed the chapel with the expectation that if pilgrims were to embrace the example of Francis, they would grow closer to Christ and to His church.

Endnotes

1 Michael P. Carroll, *Veiled Threats: The Logic of Popular Catholicism in Italy* (Baltimore: Johns Hopkins University Press, 1996), 80.

2 Arnald of Sarrant, *Chronicle of the Twenty-four Generals*, in *Francis of Assisi: Early Documents*, 3 vols., eds. Regis Armstrong, O.F.M. Cap., et al. (New York: New City Press, 1999–2001), 3:810–12. Eventually the Indulgence was assigned the first Sunday in August. For more on the Porziuncola Indulgence, see Chapter 2 in this volume and the description of Chapel XI.

3 The story makes no mention of Francis lying on the ground. However, another temptation story, recounted in Celano's *The Remembrance of the Desire of a Soul* and depicted in the fresco immediately behind the diorama, tells of Francis rolling on snowy ground in an attempt to deny the corrupting desires of his flesh (see Thomas of Celano, *The Remembrance of the Desire of a Soul*, in *Francis of Assisi: Early Documents*, 2:325). Francis in repose may be an intentional evocation and echo of this other story, thus providing a figurative way to signify their thematic correlation.

4 David Brakke, "Ethiopian Demons: Male Sexuality, the Black-Skinned Other, and the Monastic Self," *Journal of the History of Sexuality* 10, nos. 3–4 (2001): 501–35. On representations of demons, see also Erzsébet Tatai, "An Iconographical Approach to the Representations of the Devil," in *Christian Demonology and Popular Mythology*, eds. G. Klaniczay and É. Pócs (Budapest: Central European University Press, 2005), 2:54–70; Valerie Edden, "Devils, Sermon Stories, and the Problem of Popular Belief in the Middle Ages," *The Yearbook of English Studies* 22 (1992): 213–25; and Jeffrey Burton Russell, *The Devil: Perceptions of Evil from Antiquity to Primitive Christianity* (Ithaca: Cornell University Press, 1987). Medieval paintings of Christ's temptation depict ministering angels, threatening demons, depictions of the three distinct temptations, and Christ treading upon a beast or dragon.

5 Bonaventure of Bagnoregio, *The Major Legend of Saint Francis*, in *Francis of Assisi: Early Documents*, 2:527.

6 Pamela Askew, "The Angelic Consolation of St. Francis of Assisi in Post-Tridentine Italian Painting," *Journal of the Warburg and Courtauld Institutes* 32 (1969): 290.

7 Pier Giorgio Longo, "Immagini e immaginario di San Francesco al Sacro Monte di Orta," in *Antiche Guide del Sacro Monte di Orta*, ed. Loredana Racchelli (Orta: Ente di Gestione delle Reserve Naturali Speciali del Sacro Monte di Orta, del Monte Mesma e del Colle della Torre di Buccione, 2008), 51.

8 "San Francesco travaliato grandemente da dimonii gli vince con aiuto del Signore," from Mark of Lisbon, *Croniche degli ordini instituiti dal P. San Francesco. Prima parte divisa in dieci libri che contiente la sua vita, la sua morte e i suoi miracoli, composta dal R. P. Fra Marco da Lisbona, traduz. dal portoghese* (Naples, 1680), 105. On the Croniche as an artistic source, see Roberto Cobianchi, "Iconographic and Visual Sources for Bernardo Strozzi's 'Vision of St Dominic'," *The Burlington Magazine* 140, no. 1147 (1998): 670, n. 10.

9 The accompanying cartouche says, "Il santo invitato a peccare da una cortigiana si gitta sopra la bragie ardente di cuoco e restando illeso converte la donna, e vince la tentazione ordita-gli dai cortigiani di Federico secondo imperator." See Mark of Lisbon, *Croniche degli ordini instituiti dal P. San Francesco*, 107–8.

10 Thomas of Celano, *The Remembrance of the Desire of a Soul*, in *Francis of Assisi: Early Documents*, 2:325.

11 Ibid.

12 Ibid., 2:311.

13 Ibid., 2:323.

14 Ibid., 2:321.

15 Jacques Le Goff, *St. Francis of Assisi*, trans. Christine Rhone (London: Routledge, 2004), 126; Jacques Dalarun, *Francis of Assisi and the Feminine*, trans. Paula Pierce and Mary Sutphin (St. Bonaventure: Franciscan Institute, 2006), 17–52, esp. 20–23, 29–30, 39.

16 Bernard of Besse, *A Book of Praises of Saint Francis*, in *Francis of Assisi: Early Documents*, 3:47.

17 Concetto Del Popolo, "Intrecci agiografici: eremiti ed altri," *Rivista di Storia e Letteratura Religiosa* 43 (2007): 123–53, cols. 746–47.

18   In these early guides, the present-day Chapel X is called "Chapel XI" because a Chapel X on the Third Order (the Franciscan lay order) was planned but never built.

19   Dorothy Habel, *Federico Borromeo and the Ambrosiana: Art Patronage and Reform in Seventeenth Century Milan* (Cambridge: Cambridge University Press, 1993), 7.

20   In Italian, "Gli spiriti dell'inferno consideravano Francesco il loro nemico piu determinato che fosse mai nato nel mondo per combatterli strenuamente." See *Spiegazione delle Sagre Capelle Fondate Sopra Il Monte d'Orta, in Antiche Guide del Sacro Monte di Orta*, ed. L. Racchelli (Orta: Ente di Gestione delle Reserve Naturali Speciali del Sacro Monte di Orta, del Monte Mesma e del Colle della Torre di Buccione, 2008), 93.

21   *Instruzzione al divoto lettore che desidera visitare Il Sacro Monte di S. Francesco d'Orta, in Antiche Guide del Sacro Monte di Orta*, ed. L. Racchelli (Orta: Ente di Gestione delle Reserve Naturali Speciali del Sacro Monte di Orta, del Monte Mesma e del Colle della Torre di Buccione, 2008), 125–237.

6

King Carnival in the Yoke of Humility[1]

Chapel XIII

Chapel XIII is typically named "St. Francis Led Naked Through the Streets," or "Besozzo," after the benefactor, the Milanese cavalier Costanzo Besozzo. Besozzo was a well-known figure whose joy in venerating Francis led him to join the Capuchin Order and take the name of Francis. The subject of Chapel XIII is Francis' dismay over his own hypocrisy of eating meat when he was ill. Although the textual basis of the chapel concerns Francis' humility, the central figure of Francis being led by a rope around his neck is in fact embedded in a visual swarm of Carnival celebrants who largely ignore the half-naked saint (see Chapter 2, Catalogue of Chapels, Fig. 47). Except for his four brethren, only a couple of the celebrants heed St. Francis' humiliation.. The chapel is a visual dialectic between Francis' spiritual asceticism and the culture of secular excess as exemplified in seventeenth-century Italian Carnival.

The central penitent, Francis, is led along by four friars. Clustered around Francis and scattered throughout the chapel in a chaotic jumble are groups of two or three people, reacting (or not) in some way to the scene in front of them: some point without looking, some point and look, many are unaware. At the very front, a beggar points to Francis and looks directly at the viewer. To the viewer's right of Francis, family groups seem to predominate. Three families look or gesture toward Francis, and one family even includes a monkey and a dwarf. Beyond them, to the far right, chaos breaks out with a large horse rearing up (while a man tries to control it with leather reins) and three drunken revelers roll on the ground (see Fig. 1). To the viewer's left are several social groups in animated conversation. A crippled beggar, a half clothed man, gamblers, a cross dresser, children, horses, and soldiers make up this varied group (see Fig. 2). Also on the left is "King Carnival" on his horse which rears up while being attacked by a barking dog. All around the chapel walls, various ground level party-goers and women at the windows watch. One man waves a greeting to the viewer from the farthest left corner.

In his *Life of Saint Francis*, Thomas of Celano establishes the connection between eating and humility that continues to be an important theme of Franciscan hagiography, and central to the meaning of this chapel is Francis' complex relationship with food. Francis was fastidiously careful about removing pleasure from eating, as part of his effort not to be indulgent in any kind of physical experience. Celano explains,

> He zealously and carefully safeguarded Lady Holy Poverty. In order to avoid the superfluous, he would not even permit a small plate to remain in the house if,

Fig. 1. Drunken Revelers at Carnival in Assisi. Chapel XIII, Sacro Monte di Orta.

without it, he could avoid dire need. He said it was impossible to satisfy necessity without bowing to pleasure. He rarely or hardly ever ate cooked foods, but if he did, he would sprinkle them with ashes or dampen the flavor of spices with cold water.[2]

Not the food itself, but the lust for it was the sin. As a famous man, Francis was often invited to eat with others. He strove to accommodate himself to custom and also to scripture by seeming to eat. Celano relates that:

Often, when he was wandering through the world to preach the gospel of God, he was called to a dinner given by great princes who venerated him with much fondness. He would taste some meat in order to observe the holy gospel. The rest, which he appeared to eat, he put in his lap, raising his hand to his mouth so that no one could know what he was doing. What shall I say about drinking wine, when he would not allow himself to drink even enough water when he was burning with thirst?[3]

Francis sometimes went beyond this quiet subterfuge in order to create a dramatic exemplum. From Henry d'Avranches (c. 1235):

Francis again gave orders to one of the brothers
That whenever he was wined and dined by people
With high notions, the friar was to heap insults on him
And call him a dealer and mountain man. [bumpkin] Hard though it was
To exactly fulfill these commands, the brother spared him
Not a whit, as he sat among the distinguished.[4]

If there was no one present willing to condemn him, he would do it for himself. According to *The Assisi Compilation*:

Likewise, at another time, he was staying in a hermitage for the Lent of Saint Martin. Because of his illness, the brothers cooked the food they gave him to eat in lard, because oil was very bad for him in his illnesses. When the forty days had ended and he was preaching to a large crowd of people, gathered not far from that hermitage, in the opening words of his sermon he told them: 'You came to me with great devotion and believe me to be a holy man. But I confess to God and to you that during this Lent in that hermitage, I have eaten food flavored with lard'.[5] Despite his personal restrictions, Francis would not allow his followers to practice strict abstinence. In the hagiographic literature, he actively urged them to eat enough to stay healthy, even procuring

Fig. 2. Children, animals, revelers, and King Carnival in Assisi. Chapel XIII, Sacro Monte di Orta.

food for them when needed. He himself would eat to prevent a brother from following his own extreme example: "He had sympathy for all who were ill and when he could not alleviate their pain he offered words of compassion. He would eat on fast days so the weak would not be ashamed of eating, and he was not embarrassed to go through the city's public places to find some meat for a sick brother."[6]

Francis' primary method of teaching was always example rather than preaching; he created the teachable moment for his followers to imitate. But in the case of food, his method is complex and often confusing. He follows his own personal code, he enacts the most stringent of guidelines, he makes his extreme actions known to others, and yet interestingly he does not want to be copied. In this instance, his humility fails him in his desire to be the most abject. Francis did, on occasion, eat meat for two reasons. The first was to follow scriptural admonitions. The disciples were instructed in Luke 10:7 "And in the same house remain, eating and drinking such things as they give: for the laborer is worthy of his hire." He also ate to distance himself from heretical teachings. Fasting itself was not the issue because for medieval Christians as a whole, fasting was a regular practice. Nearly a third of the Christian year was made up of fast days. And, the early Franciscans also had additional fasts:

According to the First Rule, the brothers fasted on Wednesdays and Fridays, and with the permission of blessed Francis, also on Monday and Saturday, and ate meat on other days when eating meat was lawful.[7]

But Timothy 4:1–5 warns:

> The Spirit clearly says that in later times some will abandon the faith and follow deceiving spirits and things taught by demons....They order them to abstain from certain foods, which God created to be received with thanksgiving by those who believe and who know the truth. For everything God created is good, and nothing is to be rejected if it is received with thanksgiving, because it is consecrated by the word of God and prayer.

One of the particular groups seen as disobeying this teaching were the heretical Cathars, who held vegetarianism as one of their distinguishing beliefs. Cathars refused meat and dairy products altogether because they refrained from anything produced through sexual relationships, though Malcolm Barber notes other critics who posit that Cathars abstained from eating meat because of their teaching about the transmigration of souls: the flesh might contain a morsel of soul that would somehow become even more earthbound if ingested and metabolized.[8] Francis presents meat as a necessary evil, a difficult to resist temptation. But in contrast, in a way that is essential to Francis' way of teaching, he also uses the image in a countervalent way, cutting across previous meanings to access another insight which startles the reader. For Christians, the essential meaning of Christ is that he was spirit made flesh, *incarnated* to redeem humankind. This flesh, this *carne*, is in all ways good, accessible in an essential way that offers salvation in the way nothing else can. Christmas, the Feast of the Incarnation, was St. Francis' favorite holiday. Once, when Christmas fell on a Friday, a regular fast day, Brother Morico suggested that the friars should not eat meat and should fast. Francis replied, "You sin, Brother, calling the day on which the Child was born to us a day of fast. It is my wish," he said, "that even the walls should eat meat on such a day, and if they cannot, they should be smeared with meat on the outside."[9] Meat now becomes the ultimate pleasurable gift, a sanctified indulgence, the means of celebration. The word "smear" evokes a careless abundance usually so absent with Francis. Just as the carnal body of Christ is eaten for salvation, all of creation, even inanimate buildings, consume meat to celebrate the Incarnation of the Redeemer. Death and redemption are like Carnival and Lent in their linked opposition. At its core, Francis' minute attention to eating is a part of his lifelong obsession with denying the lust for material satisfaction. His initial forays into Christian service involved divesting cloth from the family business. Vauchez argues that Francis' knowledge of the divine was embodied, perceived through the body itself rather than the heart.[10] And where he once rejected clothing and material comforts in pursuit of denying inappropriate desires of the body, he later came to a vexed relationship with food much like many female medieval religious. While "consumerism" might be a defining characteristic of modernity, consumption of products beyond basic needs has always been a part of being human. The two meanings of *logos*, the word of God and mercantile signifiers, have always been at war. Francis' relationship with materiality in that sense seems very feminine. The specific incident illustrated in Chapel XIII first appears in *The Life of Saint Francis*:

> As normally happens, sometimes the craving to eat something came upon him, but afterwards he would barely allow himself to eat it. Once, because he was ill, he ate a little bit of chicken. When his physical strength returned, he entered the city of Assisi. When he reached the city gate, he commanded the brother

who was with him to tie a cord around his neck and drag him through the whole city as if he were a thief, loudly crying out, "Look! See this glutton who grew fat on the flesh of chickens that he ate without your knowledge." Many people ran to see this grand spectacle, and groaning and weeping, they said: "Woe to us! We are wretches and our whole life is steeped in blood! With excess and drunkenness we feed our hearts and bodies to over flowing!" They were touched in their hearts and were moved to a better way of life by such an example.[11]

Here, the core narrative is presented: because of his guilt over eating meat, he presents himself as a "spectacle" to expose his hypocrisy to the crowds. He presents himself "as if he were a thief" in that he has stolen a bit of chicken that was not his to eat and the trust of the crowds who did not know of his deceit. In his desire for humility, he exaggerates his actions in "glutton" and "grew fat." But unlike the model presented in Acts 2:37 ("Now when they heard this, they were pricked in their heart, and said unto Peter and to the rest of the apostles, Men and brethren, what shall we do?"), where the crowd repents, the inhabitants of the chapel carry on with little self-reproach.

Henri d'Avranches tells essentially the same version, but ratchets up the intensity of Francis' transgression.[12] While Celano presents Francis condemning himself (and leaves it, I think, to the reader to see how unjustified they are), Avranches uses the accusatory tone. His piece of chicken becomes a "blood red feast," and "fat chickens." Francis becomes a "parasite glutton, a glum-looking fraud," He is even compared to the hypocritical faster of Matthew 6:16. Subsequent versions add more details. In *The Assisi Compilation*,[13] the friar is anguished to tether and drag the holy man, when Francis has not recovered yet from malaria. Although Francis confesses that he ate meat and broth flavored with meat, the sympathies of everyone, including the narrator and the crowd are clearly with the innocent Francis. Bonaventure adds that Francis gives a sermon on "the stone where criminals received their punishment,"[14] which is represented in the chapel by a pillar along with a handcuffed Jewish prisoner. Even Bonaventure observes that this kind of humility is hard to imitate: They were well aware of his austerity, and so their hearts were struck with compunction; but they professed that his humility was easier to admire than to imitate. Although this incident seemed to more a portent like that of a prophetic utterance than an example, nevertheless it was a lesson in true humility instructing the follower of Christ that he must condemn the fame of transitory praise.[15] Francis became sensitive to being called a hypocrite after a particularly unfortunate encounter in which only a miracle saved him from being unjustly called a fraud. In Celano's version: Francis is honored by a believer who prepares a fat capon for a feast. A man of demon-like intentions, "a sort of Belial" pretends to beg alms. When Francis gives him a piece of chicken for the love of God, the man hides it away as evidence. He presents it to the crowd the next day to expose Francis' hypocrisy, but God had changed the chicken to fish. After the accuser repents, it miraculously becomes meat again.[16]

Chapel XIII then unambiguously interprets the medieval narrative which shows Francis being led in penance as he makes his body a sermon for humility. But what of all the contrasts surrounding him, the secular, public, unleashed celebration of Carnival? Francis' contrast of the material and spiritual becomes embedded in the very real social climate of the northern Italian experience.

In Cardinal and Milanese Archbishop Carlo Borromeo's work with the reforming Council of Trent, he was instrumental in promoting reforms in Catholic practice, and in the use of didactic literature and art. He passionately supported the traditional idea of seasonal penance and made it one of his favorite preaching themes.[17] He had an equally

Fig. 3. Well-dressed men and women at Carnival in Assisi. Chapel XIII, Sacro Monte di Orta.

fervent desire to blot out what he saw as the secular dissolution of Carnival, the celebration which preceded the forty days of fast. His *Discorso contro il Carnevale* bitterly denounces the inappropriate liberties practiced at Carnival, especially by women. On March 7, 1579 Borromeo "issued an edict attacking the customary carnival entertainments in unusually sharp terms, and prohibiting all jousts, theatrical performances, tournaments, dances, and masquerades during the Sundays and feast days of the Lenten and pre-Lenten season. Organizers and participants were excommunicated, while spectators and assistants automatically incurred the interdict."[18] This attack provoked the Milanese civil authorities and general population into a significant protest which ended with an appeal to the pope, who sided with the Milanese.

Francis' desire for abstemious self-control and humility in the face of human failings makes a fitting vehicle for another attack on Carnival culture, still robust a century after Carlo Borromeo began his anti-Carnival crusade. The crowd in Celano's medieval narrative look at Francis and are very aware that they are being called to repentance. The Carnival revelers within the chapel are also called to reflection (with disappointing results). In addition, the pilgrims who have come to see the chapel create another layer of viewing, as they are offered the chance to evaluate their terracotta peers. The very human viewers have even greater temptations, for they see not only Francis the exemplar but also specific lures of human desires. *Luxuria*, the outward expression of overweening pride, a sin in which the Carnival crowd seems to indulge, wages war with Humility. To further augment the affective experience for the pilgrims, everyone in the carefully rendered crowd reflects contemporary post-Reformation (rather than medieval) Assisi material culture, and thus seems to recreate contemporary Carnival culture.

From the fourteenth century, Milan had a long history of crafting and selling complex textile crafts and armor. Public rhetoric that argued youth and women were indulging themselves in the worst excesses of fashion produced the sumptuary laws promulgated at the very end of the century (1396). In the Late Medieval Period, local Italian governments issued sumptuary laws regulating the "useless," "grave and onerous," and "costly" expense of clothing and ornaments.[19] Milan, for example, had a long history of crafting and selling complex textile crafts and armor. Public rhetoric that argued youth and women were indulging themselves in the worst excesses of fashion produced the sumptuary laws promulgated between the mid thirteenth-early fourteenth centuries.[20] Fashion is thus carefully observed in the chapel. Among the revelers are a number of well-dressed women who reflect the fashions of the late seventeenth century, rather than the imagined world of Francis or that of his world shown in medieval art. Many of the clothing styles of the well dressed men and women in the chapel are reinterpreted, simplified versions of high fashion which at this time was coming from the French Court. One well dressed woman (see Fig. 3) exemplifies the problems in identifying some didadactic specifics—she might illustrate the problem of consumerism, or the appropriate use of resources, or both. She reflects a number of contemporary styles and offers a pleasant model to encourage female viewing. Her hairdo, which is reminiscent of a cockateel's crest, is distinctive. It appears to be a rendition of the "fontage" which had become the most fashionable women's hairstyle in the late seventeenth century. Named after a mistress of the French King Louis XIV, it was condemned as absurd by social critics. This Italian reveler has created her own version, probably by using the newly invented hair crimp and keeping the edifice in place with gum arabic, a popular sticky, resin-like substance imported from Africa. Her dress demonstrates other fashionable details. Lace was increasingly becoming a luxury item, and her lace collar is a fashion statement. Her dress has golden scrolling motifs, woven but probably embroidered considering Milan's fame for gold thread embroideries on silk. The v-shaped neckline, short wings at the shoulders which could hide fasteners for separate sleeves, and tight sleeves with a cuff are all part of the popular design. Altogether, this appears to be a very fashionable, and very costly, outfit.

Many of the men wear short garments, padded shoulders, elaborate hats, slashed and elongated sleeves, and bright colors (see Fig. 3). Military affectations seem to be the most popular costume. A few men are playfully dressed as women, a practice popular during carnival and representing the inverse social mores of the hedonistic festivities. All of this very careful attention to fashionable detail draws in the audience in a powerful way, to

Fig. 4. A well-dressed Black woman among the Revelers at Carnival in Assisi. Chapel XIII, Sacro Monte di Orta.

strengthen the affective identification and encourage the pilgrims' self-examination.

In contrast to the fashionable ladies celebrating in the streets are a group of women portrayed looking at the scene from the windows above (see Fig. 2). It creates a *mis en abyme*, as viewers of the chapel see their own voyeurism reflected back at them. They might be intended to represent "idlers" as Leon Battista Alberti described in his famous book on the family "those lazy and foolish women who spend the whole day sitting idly at the window with their elbows on the sill, and who as a pretext keep something to sew in the hands and never finish it."[21] These women might even have a more lascivious connotation, for both literature and drama of the times show the window as the place for the courtesan to procure her customers. Whether an object lesson for chaste women or evocative of prostitutes, the windows situated on an upper level occupy "a borderline between the safety and privacy of the bedroom and the openness of the traditionally male-dominated piazza,"[22] a place which Carnival gives women access. Interestingly, the chapel does not portray any women dancing, which is surprising since dancing was an acknowledged part of Carnival. Women may well be omitted from the scene given the Borromean condemnation of dance.

Careful observation of the material world, both ordinary and exotic, makes the chapel dense in images. Representations of Black characters appear scattered throughout the chapels, such as II, IX, XIII, and IX. In Chapel XIII, two young Black young servants are represented; one rushes to control a horse and another gives a horrified gasp. A Black woman, well dressed, stands prominently in the sight line behind Francis, and her role is much more ambiguous (see Fig. 4). She stands with another woman and a cross-dressing man. She wears pearls and clothing as luxurious as the woman next to her, so whether she is an attendant or a free woman participating in Carnival is unclear. She's not, however, clearly in an entourage. Thomas Hahn has noted that in the Middle Ages, artists began to represent ethnicity as "a coherently recognizable, reproducible category of identity.... The increasingly visible and realistic appearance of Black Africans, in scores of paintings from the middle of the fourteenth century and afterwards, seems irrefutable evidence of a keener awareness among European artists (and their audiences) with respect to geopolitical diversity and racial difference."[23] For the Renaissance audience, this woman in the Carnival crowd adds an exoticism and interest to once again draw the attention of the pilgrim and to provide a sense of exciting reality.

Francis' biographers write that, in the thirteenth century, when Francis pursued holiness, he did so by ridding himself of the temptations of the physical world. Following Christ's words, he attempted to take up the yoke, the rope of discipline, and make himself a physical sign of self abnigating humility. As a young man, he liked giving feasts and he liked his clothes, and those became two of his most constant sacrifices. Later in life, when he feared his message would be sullied by hypocrisy, he stripped himself of both again: regretting the food and stripping himself of clothing. He does this to edify his followers and bring them along on the path of humility. The story of Francis being paraded through the streets of Assisi was consistently retold in Franciscan sources for four centuries, and when it is once again fashioned for a chapel at Orta, the same Francis is illustrated there. Yet this time, Francis' story was set inside another frame of reference, the Borromean cultural critique of Carnival. In Chapel XIII, the didactic intent of Francis' act is the same: it is a lesson of Humility. But here the secular, material world which must be denied is contemporary and lavishly displayed, and it is also here that the wide, open tracery of the grille and the absence of kneelers encourages the pilgrim to lose themselves among the crowd and become immersed in the chaos. Rather than demand a devotional position and even identity, the pilgrim might abandon, if for a fleeting moment, their purpose. This curious relationship between pilgrim and Carnival crowd, seemingly antithetical to the didactic program of the chapel, and the shrine writ large, may be an ironic manipulation intended to underscore the vulnerability to temptation, especially during the season of Carnival, of even the most devout.

The didactic intent of Francis' act is the same: Humility. The secular, material world which must be denied is contemporary and lavishly displayed.

Endnotes

1. A version of this chapter was previously published: Cynthia Ho, "King Carnival in the Yoke of Humility," *Medieval Perspectives* 30 (2015): 9–29.
2. Thomas of Celano, *Life of Saint Francis*, in *Francis of Assisi: Early Documents*, 3 vols., eds. Regis Armstrong. O.F.M. Cap., et al. (New York: New City Press, 1999–2001), 3:227.
3. Ibid., 3:235.
4. Henri d'Avranches, *The Versified Life of Saint Francis*, in *Francis of Assisi: Early Documents*, 1:478.
5. *The Assisi Compilation*, in *Francis of Assisi: Early Documents*, 2:182.
6. Thomas of Celano, *Remembrance of the Desire of a Soul*, in *Francis of Assisi: Early Documents*, 2:359.
7. Angelo Clareno, *The Book of Chronicles or the Tribulations of the Order of Lesser Ones*, in *Francis of Assisi: Early Documents*, 3:399.
8. Malcolm Barber, *The Cathars: Dualist Heretics in Languedoc in the High Middle Ages* (New York: Routledge, 2014), 95.
9. Thomas of Celano, *Life of Saint Francis*, in *Francis of Assisi: Early Documents*, 3:199.
10. André Vauchez, *Francis of Assisi: The Life and Afterlife of a Medieval Saint*, trans. Michael Cusato (New Haven: Yale University Press, 2012), 254.
11. Thomas of Celano, *The Life of Saint Francis*, in *Francis of Assisi: Early Documents*, 3:237.
12. Henri d'Avranches, *The Versified Life*, in *Francis of Assisi: Early Documents*, 1:478.
13. *The Assisi Compilation*, in *Francis of Assisi: Early Documents*, 2:181–82.
14. Bonaventure of Bagnoregio, *Major Legend of Saint Francis*, in *Francis of Assisi: Early Documents*, 2:570.
15. Ibid.
16. Thomas of Celano, *The Remembrance of the Desire of a Soul*, in *Francis of Assisi: Early Documents*, 2:298.
17. Wietse de Boer, *The Conquest of the Soul: Confession, Discipline, and Public Order in Counter-Reformation Milan* (Leiden: Brill, 2001), 175.
18. Ibid., 248.
19. Catherine M. Kovesi Kellerby, *Sumptuary Law in Italy: 1200–1500*, Oxford Historical Monographs (Oxford: Oxford University Press, 2002), 36.
20. Ibid., 28.
21. Leon Battista Alberti, *The Family in Renaissance Florence*, trans. Renee Neu Watkings (Columbia: University of South Carolina Press, 1969), 222. See also Jane Tylus, "Women at the Windows: 'Commedia dell'arte' and Theatrical Practice in Early Modern Italy," *Theatre Journal* 49, no. 3 (October 1997): 323–42, and Hanna Scolnicov, *Women's Theatrical Space* (Cambridge: Cambridge University Press, 1994), 62.
22. Jane Tylus, "Women at the Windows," 325.
23. Thomas Hahn, "The Difference the Middle Ages Makes: Color and Race Before the Modern World," *Journal of Medieval and Early Modern Studies* 31, no. 1 (Winter 2001): 1–38. See also Adrienne Childs' discussion, "Blacks in the Exotic Tradition to 1800," in *The Black Exotic: Tradition and Ethnography in Nineteenth-Century Orientalist Art*, PhD diss., University of Maryland, 2005, 51–81.

7

Advancing the Council of Trent[1]
Chapels XI and XVIII

At the Sacro Monte di Orta, the Council of Trent's directives on the use of didactic art were mindfully implemented. Affirmation of a new kind of spirituality, answering the needs of the faithful, was firmly situated within the orthodoxies of the Church; St. Francis embodied both of these ideals—affective piety and orthodoxy—and naturally became an appealing role model. Both Cardinal Carlo Borromeo, a significant force in the Council of Trent, and his cousin Federico Borromeo wrote extensively on the correct use of didactic art in the reform of the church.[2] In 1593 authority over the construction at Orta was given to Carlo Bascapè, Bishop of Novara, with the agenda to make sure all of the chapels were attuned to an appropriate and accurate post-Tridentine vision of the life of Saint Francis of Assisi. Chapels XI and XVIII, in particular, offer answers to the Protestant Reformation's critiques of the Church.[3] They illustrate the dual purposes of the chapels and of the complex as a whole: to invite the worship of pilgrims and to present an edifying, didactic diorama of orthodox truths.

Chapel XI concerns the granting of an indulgence to Francis at the Porziuncola, while Chapel XVIII relates a papal visitation to Francis' tomb in Assisi. Both chapels offer carefully measured replicas of places sacred to the life of Francis, which give viewers a way to enter into a vicarious relationship with both the original pilgrimage locations and the special meaning of Orta. The themes of both offer a staunch rebuff to Protestant attacks and underscore the decisions of Trent regarding the legitimacy of indulgences and the intercessory role of saints.

The Indulgence of Porziuncola is the theme of Chapel XI; it culminates a story begun in the previous chapel. In Chapel X, Francis' battle with temptation (Satan) leads him into the woods surrounding the Porziuncola, his flesh scourged by the thorns. Then, as the *Chronicle of the Twenty-four Generals* relates:

> Suddenly there was a great light in the midst of the forest and in that time of frost, rose blossoms appeared right there where blessed Francis was. And a countless host of angels suddenly appeared both in the woods and in the church and cried in one voice, 'Blessed Francis, hurry to the Savior and his Mother who await you in the church.' There then appeared to him a straight path as if of decorated silk going up to the church, and blessed Francis took from the rose patch twelve red roses and twelve white roses.[4]

The terracotta angels of the diorama direct Francis toward a frescoed scene of Christ and Mary enthroned, thus foreshadowing the Porziuncola Indulgence. The story takes up in Chapel XI, when, after Francis has offered a bouquet of roses to Mary, Jesus in turn of-

Fig. 1. The Vestibule and surrounding Frescos of Chapel XI. Sacro Monte di Orta.

fers Francis an unspecified boon. Francis asks for an indulgence, which becomes known as the Indulgence of Porziuncola. Following the Blessed Virgin's suggestion, Jesus picks August 2 for the indulgence.[5]

Thomas McGrath has studied the history of the Porziuncola Indulgence in art, noting that depictions of the event fell out of favour from the fifteenth to mid-sixteenth centuries. By the late sixteenth century, the image experienced a revival. McGrath ties this reintroduction to competition between the Franciscans and the Dominicans; images of the Porziuncola Indulgence "offered support for the legitimacy of the Perdono legend, called attention to Francis' devotion to the Virgin, and alluded to a Franciscan rosary tradition that directly competed with that of the Dominicans."[6] All of those reasons dovetail nicely with the agenda of the Franciscans at Orta, and make the emphasis on the Indulgence in both Chapels X and XI a logical move.

The exterior of Chapel XI is a miniature reproduction of the huge Basilica Santa Maria degli Angeli in Assisi, which now houses within it the little chapel of Porziuncola (see Chapter 27, the Catalogue of Chapels, Fig. 40). The original Porziuncola was a small abandoned church which the Benedictines allowed Francis to use, and which became a center for the early Franciscans. Here, the friars returned each year for their general chapter, St. Clare entered religious life, and, according to tradition, Francis had the mystical encounter related above and lived out his last days. The walls of Chapel XI are covered with narrative frescos representing the stages involved in granting the indulgence (see Fig. 1): Francis prays to the crucifix for the salvation of all sinners; an angel invites him to the church of Porziuncola where Jesus and Mary await him; a version of Pope Innocent III's dreams with several friars physically supporting the Lateran church; Francis petitions Honorious III for the indulgence; Francis, in the presence of an angel, kneels

Fig. 2. The Vestibule and surrounding Frescos of Chapel XI. Sacro Monte di Orta.

before the altar of the Porziuncola and prays for the souls of all sinners; Francis announces the Porziuncola Indulgence before the pope, bishops, and a crowd of onlookers.[7] Within the diorama, Christ and Mary are equally enthroned on a grand scale behind an altar covered with real linen altar cloth (see Fig. 2). Eight angels are arrayed on either side. Of equal size, wearing identical large crowns, mother and son turn to look at each other. Mary holds her hands out in a questioning gesture, while Christ holds a sceptre in one hand and gestures to the kneeling Francis with the other.

While the Porziuncola Indulgence has remained in place until today, albeit with several revisions, the story's sources and authenticity are still disputed. In the 1260s, as the story became current that Francis had wished for a total indulgence for all sins, the rush of pilgrims created a need for the Franciscans to validate its authenticity. They began to collect notarized testimonies about the Pardon of Assisi and brother Francesco Bartholdi made a compilation of them in 1340.[8] All accounts of its creation are second- or third-hand, such as the following testimony:

> I, Brother Benedict of Arezzo...now bear witness that I often heard from one of the companions of blessed Francis...that he was with blessed Francis at Perugia in the presence of the Lord Pope Honorius when he asked for an indulgence of all sins for those persons who, being contrite and having confessed them, come to Saint Mary of Angels, otherwise known as Portiuncula, from the first vespers of the first day of August to the vespers of the following day. Since this indulgence

was so humbly and yet so earnestly sought by the blessed Francis, it was eventually most liberally granted by the Supreme Pontiff, although he made it plain that it was not the custom of the Apostolic See to grant such indulgences."[9]

Another witness relates that Leo told him that "Francis had himself said that he had petitioned the Pope to attain an indulgence for the church of Portiuncula on the anniversary of its consecration." When the Pope asked for how long he wanted this remission to be, they negotiated almost for seven years, but still Francis was not satisfied until he received the remission of all sins "so that no further [temporal] punishment is attached to them." The Pope granted it, but the cardinals were aghast and asked the Pope to limit it to the length of one natural day per year, which he did. Adding authority to the Indulgence, the account of the meeting concludes: "When the blessed Francis left the Pope after the concession of the indulgence, he heard a voice saying to him: 'Francis, know that, just as this indulgence has been given on earth, so it also has been ratified in heaven'."[10]

Seventeenth-century guidebooks for early pilgrims to the Sacro Monte di Orta illustrate the didactic levels of the artistic program. Simple messages reached the masses, but sophisticated readings were also incorporated for the educated.[11] The *Spiegazione Delle Sagre Capelle Fondate Sopra Il Monte D'Orta* states that the chapel, with Francis hurrying on foot to offer to the Redeemer and Mary the Queen of Heaven the *corona delle sue vittorie*, represents the victory of his chastity.[12] *Corona* is multivalent here because the crown is a garland of roses, both a metaphorical crown of chastity and a "rosary" of his devotion. This is surely a clever intertextual reference to the Franciscan Rosary, or "Crown" (sometimes also known as the Seraphic Rosary, or the Rosary of the Seven Joys of Our Lady). Although the origin of the Franciscan Crown is unclear, the rosary, a distinctive seven decades for the Seven Joys of Mary, and its legend seems to have been codified by Luke Wadding in his *Annales Minorum* (1625–54).[13] Certainly, though, the Marian devotion was popularized within the Franciscan order in the fifteenth century, particularly during the rule of the Franciscan Pope Sixtus IV (1471–85), who in 1479 strongly encouraged the rosary as an invaluable instrument of personal and societal conversion.[14] In any case, the importance of the Franciscan Crown was well established by the time Chapels X and XI were constructed in the early to mid-seventeenth century at the Sacro Monte di Orta. As Marian devotion was a special touch point of the Tridentine reform, here at Orta the Franciscan Capuchins were (re)asserting: 1) Mary's important place in Catholic belief and practice, 2) the Franciscan claim to a privileged relationship with the Queen of Heaven, 3) the importance of the rosary as a devotional practice, and 4) the Franciscan claim to a long-standing tradition of the rosary.[15]

The *Spiegazione Delle Sagre Capelle Fondate Sopra Il Monte D'Orta* goes on to say that, as a special acknowledgment of his love, Jesus and Mary granted to Francis the grace of a plenary indulgence for the remission of the temporal punishment of sins that have been subject to the Sacrament of Confession. This remission would be given to all pilgrims who, in a state of grace, visited the Porziuncola. However, they cautioned Francis that this must be "according to the Pope's conditions."[16] According to tradition, then, Pope Honorius III allowed the indulgence on the second day of August each year.[17] A second pilgrim's guide, the *Instruzzione Al Divoto Lettore Che Desidera Visitare Il Sacro Monte Di S. Francesco D'Orta*, reiterates the story of the indulgence and its authenticity: "In 1223, when Pope Honorius III ruled, Francis presented it to him at the Lateran arousing admiration and amazement for his [Francis'] patience and courage."[18]

This chapel teaches the validity of indulgences and their divine, direct, emphatic institution by Christ. It reconstructs the church at Assisi and refers to the indulgence

Fig. 3. Pope Nicholas V and his prelates experience a vision of St. Francis during a visit to the saint's crypt. Chapel XVIII, Sacro Monte di Orta.

available there. But it also reminds pilgrims of their participation in the divine economy at Orta, where indulgences are also granted for visits to the Sacro Monte.[19] A visit to Chapel XI could earn the pilgrim an indulgence of one hundred days per Saturday Mass in the small chapel.[20]

In the story of the Porziuncola Indulgence, Francis, who traded thorns for roses, accomplished a greater *imitatio Christi* than had ever been seen before, for he become a conduit of grace to the believers which equalled that provided by Christ, thus pilgrims accessed Christ through Francis and by imitating Francis. The creators of the chapels hoped that the worshippers would become so integrated into the "realness" of the scenes that their unmediated sensation would become indistinguishable from the mediated one, and all realities would be fused. Thus references reverberate between Francis (a kind of Christ) and Chapel XI (a kind of Porziuncola). Worshippers who could not partici-

pate in the August indulgence could nevertheless achieve the same effect by viewing the chapel. All of this presupposes on the part of the site's designers and sponsors the absolute legitimacy of the mechanism of plenary indulgence. The importance of the Pope, the rosary, and the Blessed Virgin are confirmed within the program as well.

The story of Chapel XVIII is again the story of two chapels, one being the simulacrum of the other.[21] The first is the tomb of St Francis in Assisi. Bernard of Besse relates that Francis died in 1226, at the age of forty-five, and then

> His most holy body was buried at Assisi in the Church of Saint George, where the Monastery of Saint Clare(?) now stands. After a few years a church was built in the saint's honor near the walls of the city and by the authority of Pope Gregory IX who laid the first stone of the founda-

tion. The site of the church is called the Hill of Paradise.[22]

On the lowest level is the crypt, and above were built two superimposed churches. Francis was interred in 1230. It was consecrated a basilica in 1253.[23]

Orta's Chapel XVIII is part of a carefully executed replica (encompassing Chapels XVIII, XIX, and XX) which powerfully portrays the basilica in Assisi. *Spiegazione Delle Sagre Capelle Fondate Sopra Il Monte D'Orta* explains that the church at Orta "is constructed on three floors to resemble the church in Assisi where the body of St Francis reposes. The lower part, which is subterranean, faithfully represents the sepulchre and the deposition of our father Francis."[24] The complex frescos seen inside most of the other chapels are not present here. The chapel interior simply suggests structural backdrops. It holds only four life-sized sculptures—Francis, a pope, a prelate and an assistant (see Fig. 3). Mark of Lisbon relates that Pope Nicholas V (often erroneously identified in the texts and on the UNESCO website as Nicholas III), along with the Cardinal Archbishop of Milan and Andrea da Norcia (Captain of the Guard) visited Assisi in 1449 and descended into the crypt of the basilica to venerate the remains of the Saint.[25] Nicholas is an interesting person, much admired for his love of letters and his friendship with some of the important humanists of his day. Eamon Duffy has called him "the most attractive of the Humanist Popes."[26] He brought peace, ended schisms, and renovated the city of Rome. His Jubilee of 1450 was an enormous success which revitalized pilgrimage and fostered the display of important relics. Essentially, he "confirmed beyond argument the centrality of Rome and the Pope in popular Catholicism."[27] His canonization of St. Bernardino of Siena, the highly controversial Franciscan preacher, cleverly allied the papacy with the current of popular religious feeling.[28]

According to the the 17th-century guidebook *Speigazione Delle Sagre Capelle Fondate Sopra Il Monte D'Orta*, during the pontiff's visit to the tomb of Francis, the saint appeared before him, standing with his hands crossed over his chest, showing the stigmata. A miraculous perfume emanated from the sacred corpse. When he left, Nicholas could not hide his joy and spread the news of his encounter.[29] The explanation of Orta's Chapel XVIII in another 17th-century guidebook, the *Instruzzione Al Divoto Lettore Che Desidera Visitare Il Sacro Monte Di S. Francesco D'Orta*, begins with a quote from the biblical book of Sirach, in order to make the comparison between Francis and Elisha: "In death he performed miracles" (48:14).[30] The introduction emphasizes that like the great prophet of the Old Testament, Francis remained a herald of God and miracle worker even in death. The pilgrim's goal remained viably attainable (at Orta or Assisi) through mediation of the long dead saint.

At the center of the chapel there is an upright statue of the dead Francis, miraculously standing with his eyes turned to heaven, his arms crossed on his breast, in penitential repose. Before Francis is the kneeling figure of Pope Nicholas V. Just as in Mark of Lisbon's account, two additional figures join the Pope to make a group of three. According to the report, the Pope then clipped some of Francis' hair to keep as a relic.[31]

The tomb of Francis at Assisi is a *scurolo*, that is, a place where the relics of the saint were preserved and venerated. Orta strives to be the *scurolo* of that other tomb and to vicariously hold the relics of Francis. The twin tombs of Francis allow an immediate participation in the events of his death; his death was an imitation of the passion of Christ, and thus individuals are called to intense devotion, to imitating Christ through Francis. Chapel XVIII gives a powerful answer to the critiques of veneration of the saints, since it demonstrates the salvific function of the saints and the concomitant importance of the relic as a central object of faith. Added to this is a glorification of the role of popes and the glory of Rome. In the Counter Reformation culture, Nicholas V epitomizes all that is grand and praiseworthy of the papacy.

The Franciscan chapels at Orta tell the life of Francis, but with a distinctive didactic agenda. The Tridentine reform program was aimed at achieving uniformity of practice and belief; it was also intended to affirm and underscore traditional Catholic practice and belief, such as the mediating role of the saints and the cult of relics. Despite his many individualistic gestures, Francis was theologically orthodox, and thus proved an excellent model for upholding, or perhaps reclaiming, the faithful during the religious struggles of the Early Modern period.

Endnotes

1   A version of this chapter was previously published: Cynthia Ho, "Closing the Borders: St. Francis at Orta," in *Identity and Alterity in Hagiography and the Cult of Saints*, eds. Ana Marinković, Trpimir Vedriš, and Ildikó Csepregi (Zagreb: Hagiotheca, 2010), 245–60.

2   For a discussion of the Borromean influence on art, see Wietse de Boer, *The Conquest of the Soul: Confession, Discipline, and Public Order in Counter-Reformation Milan* (Leiden: Brill, 2001), and Cecelia E. Voelker, "Borromeo's Influence on Sacred Art and Architecture," in *San Carlo Borromeo: Catholic Reform and Ecclesiastical Politics in the Second Half of the Sixteenth Century*, eds. John Headley and John Tomaro (Washington, DC: Folger Books, 1988), 172–87.

3   For a study of the many ways the church responded, see Philip Benedict, "The Catholic Response to Protestantism: Church Activity and Popular Piety in Rouen," in *Religion and the People, 800–1700*, ed. James Obelkevich (Chapel Hill: University of North Carolina Press, 1979), 168–90.

4   Arnald of Sarrant, *Chronicle of the Twenty-four Generals*, in *Francis of Assisi: Early Documents*, 3 vols., eds. Regis Armstrong, O.F.M. Cap., et al. (New York: New City Press, 1999–2001), 3:810.

5   Ibid., 3:810–11.

6   Thomas McGrath, "Dominicans, Franciscans, and the Art of Political Rivalry: Two Drawings and a Fresco by Giovanni Battista della Rovere," *Renaissance Studies* 25, no. 2 (2011): 199–200.

7   For an early version of the prophetic dream, see *Legend of the Three Companions*, in *Francis of Assisi: Early Documents*, 2:97–98.

8   Francesco Bartholdi della Rossa, *Tractatus de Indulgentia S. Maria de Portiuncula*, ed. Paul Sabatier (Paris: Fishbacher, 1900). The one-day indulgence on August 2 was later extended to all Franciscan churches, and in 1967, to all Catholic churches.

9   *Documents Concerning the Portiuncula Indulgence (1277–1300)*, in *Francis of Assisi: Early Documents*, 3:809.

10   Ibid., 3:807–8.

11   On the dual purposes of Counter-Reformation art, see Dorothy Habel, *Federico Borromeo and the Ambrosiana: Art Patronage and Reform in Seventeenth Century Milan* (Cambridge: Cambridge University Press, 1993), 7.

12   *Spiegazione Delle Sagre Capelle Fondate Sopra Il Monte D'Orta*, in *Antiche Guide del Sacro Monte di Orta*, ed. Loredana Racchelli (Orta: Ente di Gestione delle Reserve Naturali Speciali del Sacro Monte di Orta, del Monte Mesma e del Colle della Torre di Buccione, 2008), 73–123.

13   For the history of the Franciscan Crown, see Linus O'Dea, O.S.F., "The History of the Crown," in *Mary in the Franciscan Order: Proceedings of the Third National Meeting of Franciscan Teaching Sisterhoods*, eds. Ignatius Brady et al. (St. Bonaventura: Franciscan Institute, 1955), 173–83. On Pope Sixtus IV and his devotion to the rosary, see Thomas P. Campbell, *Tapestry in the Renaissance: Art and Magnificence* (New York: Metropolitan Museum of Art, 2002), 66.

14   In truth, Pope Sixtus IV granted indulgences to any variety of the rosary, even the very popular rosary of the Franciscan's arch rivals the Dominicans, and their Confraternity of the Rosary founded in 1470. Like the Franciscans, the Dominicans too had a storied history of the rosary and each order claimed to be the authentic representative of the tradition. According to Dominican tradition, St. Dominic received the rosary as a divine gift to aid in combatting heresy. For both the Franciscans and the Dominicans, the rosary—popular and easy to use— remained important in spreading and maintaining devotion for the church of the post-Tridentine era. On the other hand, it was this same pope (Sixtus IV) who banned all images of the Dominican nun St. Catherine and her stigmatization. Another significant bone of contention between the two orders was the question of Mary's Immaculate Conception. The rivalry between Franciscans and Dominicans has only abated in modern times. For additional context on the rivalry between the two mendicant orders, see Thomas McGrath, "Dominicans, Franciscans, and the Art of Political Rivalry: Two Drawings and a Fresco by Giovanni Battista della Rovere," *Renaissance Studies* 25, no. 2 (2011): 185–207, and Thomas

M. Izbicki, "The Immaculate Conception and Ecclesiastical Politics from the Council of Basel to the Council of Trent: The Dominicans and their Foes," *Archiv für Reformationsgeschichte* 96 (2005): 145–70.

15 See Nathan Mitchell, *The Mystery of the Rosary: Marian Devotion and the Reinvention of Catholicism* (New York: New York University Press, 2009), 8–15.

16 "In particulare fu concessa la famosa grazia dell' indulgenza data da Dio per l'intercessione della Sua Gloriosa Genitrice a Francesco che pregando per la salvezza delle anime supplicava che tutti i fedeli, che visitassero quel Sacro Tempio il du di Agosto, potessero ricevere la remissione di tutti i peccati, l'assoluzione dalla colpa e dalla pena, secondo le condizioni che il Papa vorrà disporre e confermare per questa Indulgenza Plenaria." See *Spiegazione Delle Sagre Capelle Fondate Sopra Il Monte D'Orta*, 96–97. The pope did indeed ultimately confirm the indulgence, but limited it to August 2 of each year. Note also that the guide states that pilgrims "could receive the remission of all sins, absolution from guilt and punishment," which is a very distinctive claim for an indulgence which usually applies only to remission of temporal punishments for sins already absolved through the Sacrament of Confession. A second guide, the *Instruzzione Al Divoto Lettore Che Desidera Visitare Il Sacro Monte Di S. Francesco D'Orta*, specifies that only those pilgrims who received the sacraments of confession and holy communion are eligible. *Instruzzione al divoto lettore che desidera visitare Il Sacro Monte di S. Francesco d'Orta*, in *Antiche Guide del Sacro Monte di Orta*, 189. All other textual evidence indicates that the Porziuncola Indulgence conforms to the traditional perameters of indulgences, despite the claim of the *Spiegazione Delle Sagre Capelle Fondate Sopra Il Monte D'Orta*.

17 Subsequent modifications of the Porziuncola Indulgence expanded its scope to include any Franciscan church. Moreover, the faithful may earn more than one plenary indulgence at that annual occasion, depending on the number of times that person fulfills the prayerful obligations. See Raphael Mary Huber, *The Portiuncula Indulgence: From Honorius III to Pius XI*, Franciscan Studies 19–20 (New York: J.W. Wagner, 1938).

18 *Instruzzione al divoto lettore che desidera visitare Il Sacro Monte di S. Francesco d'Orta*, 189–90.

19 Annabel Wharton, *Selling Jerusalem: Relics, Replicas, Theme Parks* (Chicago: Chicago University Press, 2006), 141.

20 *Instruzzione al divoto lettore che desidera visitare Il Sacro Monte di S. Francesco d'Orta*, 191.

21 Chapel XVIII is also called the "Cappella Canobiana" because it was paid for by Abbot Amico Canobio, a nobleman from Novara and supervisor, designer, and a principal promoter of the Sacro Monte.

22 Bernard of Besse, *A Book of the Praises of Saint Francis*, in *Francis of Assisi: Early Documents*, 3:67.

23 In 1476, the tomb of the saint was sealed and hidden. Later, in 1818, Pius VII ordered the tomb excavated and exhumed. To make room for pilgrims, a neo-Classical crypt was built; this was replaced by a simpler, neo-Romanesque tomb in 1925–32. In 1939, Francis of Assisi was declared the patron saint of Italy. In 1978, the tomb was reopened for study of the remains. On the history of St. Francis' tomb, see Rosalind Brooke, "The Rediscovery of St Francis' Body," in *The Image of St. Francis: Responses to Sainthood in the Thirteenth Century* (Cambridge: Cambridge University Press, 2006), 454–71.

24 *Spiegazione Delle Sagre Capelle Fondate Sopra Il Monte D'Orta*, 115.

25 Nicholas III (1225–80) was especially well disposed to the Franciscans, since his father was a friend of Francis and belonged to his third order. He stands out in the early Franciscan documents for his support of Francis' Rule. But he definitely was not in Assisi in the fifteenth century. The account of Nicholas V's vision was first published in the *Chronicles* of Mark of Lisbon. See Mark of Lisbon, *Croniche degli ordini instituiti dal P. San Francesco. Prima parte divisa in dieci libri che contiene la sua vita, la sua morte e i suoi miracoli, composta dal R.P. Fra Marco da Lisbona, traduz. dal portoghese* (Naples, 1680), 302.

26 Eamon Duffy, *Saints and Sinners: A History of the Popes* (New Haven: Yale University Press, 2002), 178.

27 Ibid.

28 Ibid.

29 *Spiegazione Delle Sagre Capelle Fondate Sopra Il Monte D'Orta*, 121.

30 *Instruzzione al divoto lettore che desidera visitare II Sacro Monte di S. Francesco d'Orta*, 229. In this guidebook, Chapel XVIII is numbered XXXI in accordance with the original scheme.

31 Mark of Lisbon, *Croniche degli ordini instituiti dal P. San Francesco*, 302. Interestingly, paintings of Pope Nicholas's encounter with Francis became the vogue in the seventeenth century. Three important painters, Antonio Montúfar, Francisco de Zurbarán, and Jacques Blanchard, all rendered the same newly popular story of Pope Nicholas V's vision in the mid-1600s.

Appendix

Biographies of the Designers and Artists of the Sacro Monte di Orta

The information for the biographies that follow comes from a variety of sources (see notes). The identification of dates and artists associated with each specific chapel in the essays are, in the main, sourced from placards at the site created by the Governing Authority of the Sacri Monti, and the guides by Fr. Angelo Manzini, and Elena De Filippis and Fiorella Carcano.[1]

Bascapè (1550–1615), Carlo, Bishop of Novara (1593–1615)

Born in Milan, Bascapè rose through the ranks of the church as a Barnabite. His position as secretary to Carlo Borromeo led to his appointment as Bishop of Novara. His dedication to the post-Tridentine reform and church renewal is manifest in the multiple building projects to which he dedicated himself, including his meticulous concern for the Sacro Monte di Orta, for which he played an integral role in selecting artists and designing the artistic program of the site.[2]

Beretta, Carlo (Il Berettone, d. ca. 1763), Sculptor, Chapel XIV

Beretta's early history is unknown, but according to the *Annali della fabbrica del duomo di Milano, dall'origine fino al presente*, by 1716 he was regularly employed at the Duomo in Milan where he was working on the sculptural program and designing bronze bas-reliefs. At the Sacro Monte di Orta, Beretta created the terracotta statues for Chapel XIV (and Chapel XV according to the *Dizionario Biografico*, though De Filippis and Carcano, and Manzini give credit to Prestinari). Rossana Bossaglia notes that Beretta was well regarded by his peers, though she describes his work as often "superficially sweet" and "unimaginative" yet imbued with "rococo gracefulness."[3]

Bianchi, Federico (ca. 1635–1719),[4] Painter, Chapel XIII

Bianchi was a Milanese scholar and teacher under the patronage of the Duke of Savoy, who conferred a knighthood on the artist.[5] He was active at Orta in 1692, where he, along with **Giovanni Battista Cantalupi** and **Giovanni Grandi**, painted the wall frescos of Chapel XIII, "The Humility of St. Francis." Bianchi also worked at various churches, palaces, and cloisters around Northern Italy. Bossaglia describes the baroque painter's skill as evolving over time from the "awkward and cumbersome" paintings at Orta to the "noble," "airy and graceful" work of his later years.[6] Giuseppe Pacciarotti is kinder when describing most of Bianchi's work as "traditional," noting the "great theatricality" and "powerful expressions" of his frescos at the Sacri Monti.[7]

Busca, Antonio (1625–86), Painter, Chapels XIX and XX

Busca was student of Ercole Procaccini the Younger (1605–1675/1680), a noted baroque artist in his own right and member of the Procaccini family of painters who established the great art academy in Milan.[8] Busca also apprenticed with Carlos Nuvolone (brother of another painter known at the Sacro Monte di Orta, Guiseppe Nuvolone), and was later appointed director of painting at the Ambrosian Academy in Milan. Busca worked with sculptor Dionigi Bussola at both the Sacro Monte di Varese and at the Sacro Monte di Orta. While his frescos could be "pleasant and friendly owing to the clear and bright palette,"[9] Michael Bryan suggests that after a promising start, Busca never lived up to expectations. Hampered by ill-health (a serious case of gout), Busca "sank into a mannerist, and contented himself with frequently repeating the same subjects."[10] This lackluster assessment of Busca's work is at odds with the finely executed architectural framing and vignettes of the walls of Chapel XX, and theatrically and colorfully expansive ceiling of that same chapel.

Bussola, Dionigi (1615–87), Sculptor, Chapels II, VI, VII, X, XVII, XVIII, and XX

Bussola was a Milanese sculptor, working in both clay and bronze, whose style is characterized by Gabriella Ferri Piccaluga as, in the main, "a fusion of classicism and baroque." He taught at the Ambrosian Academy and worked on the Duomo of Milan.[11] But it was with his work for the Sacro Monte of Varallo, of Varese, of Domodossola, and of Orta, Piccaluga believes, that Bussola achieved full baroque theatrically of expression.[12]

Canobio, Amico (1530/32–1592), Patron of the Sacro Monte di Orta (c. 1590–1592)

Amico Canobio, son of a wealthy Novarese family and abbot of the Benedictine-affiliated St. Bartholomew of Vallombrosa monastery in Novara, took charge of the initial promotion and construction of the Sacro Monte. He commissioned and funded three of the first chapels, Chapels XVIII, XIX, and XX—together a simulacrum of the Basilica of Assisi. He left a generous legacy in his will to fund the ongoing work of the Sacro Monte.[13]

Cantalupi, Giambattista (active c. 1772), Painter, Chapels XII and XIII[14]

Very little is known about this artist, except that he specialized in frescos and was employed in the areas around Vercelli and Miasino, both cities near Orta san Giulio. He was at one point a teacher at the Academy of Parma.[15] Luigi Mallè describes Cantalupi's work in Chapel XIII as "refined and sensitive"[16] and believes that his frescos have been undervalued.[17]

Cleto da Castelletto Ticino (1556–1619), Chief Architect of the Sacro Monte di Orta (1594–1619)

There is no information about Father Cleto's early years or his training (if any) in architecture and construction. It seems that he joined the Capuchins around the age of twenty and by 1585 appears in diocesan records as the head of a convent (no longer in existence) in Romagnano Sesia, where his duties would have included overseeing its construction.[18] In 1590, he appears once again in this capacity for the monastery of Verano Brianza. Also in that year Cleto became involved in the construction of the Sacro Monte di Orta, though the records indicate that he did not take charge of the project, a position to which he was elected, until 1594. Over the next couple of decades, and in addition to his duties at Orta, Cleto was involved in multiple construction projects throughout the region [in Milan, Quarona, Fara Novarese, Locarno (across the border in Switzerland), Soriso, Omegna, Auzate, Varallo, Doccio, Cannobio, Ivrea, Faido, Pallanza, and Cerro Maggiore] on behalf of Bishop Carlo Bascapè who, among his other administrative responsibilities, coordinated these projects for the Province of Novara. Cleto's job at the Sacro Monte di Orta was "hands on": he designed the layout of the mountain, including the streets, chapels and trees; he helped determine a fair salary for artists; and Cleto traveled to the nearby area of Vercelli to procure clay for the sculptors. A letter from Bascapè also indicates, with a reference to Cleto's request for Cesare Ripa Perugino's work *Iconologia*, that Cleto was instrumental in selecting the iconographic program for the chapels.[19]

Crespi Castoldi, Anton Maria (1598?–1630), Painter, Chapel VII

Born into a family of painters from the commune of Busto Arsizio in the area of Varese, most of his surviving works are found in and around Como where he lived. Though nothing is known of his training, Crespi Castoldi painted in the style of Milanese artists such as **Morazzone** and the **Fiammenghini** and was noted for his accomplished portraiture. He, along with his wife and children, died in Como of the plague in 1630.[20]

D'Enrico, Giovanni (1560–1644), Sculptor and Painter, Chapels VII, VIII, IX, and XI

Giovanni Romano describes Giovanni d'Enrico as a gifted sculptor, who both modeled and painted terracottas at Varallo, Oropa and Orta. Along with his brothers **Melchiorre** (the Elder, 1570–1641) and Antonio (Tanzio, 1574–1635), Giovanni operated within the large d'Enrico family workshop in the Val Sesia.[21] **Giacomo Ferro** is mentioned as an assistant to Giovanni in the records of the *fabbricia* for Chapel IX.[22] Though Giovanni's work at Orta was prodigious, he is probably best known for the period he directed the construction of Varallo and where he spent most of his professional life.

D'Enrico, Melchiorre (1570–1641), Painter, Chapels VII, VIII, IX, and XI

Though Melchiorre was regionally known as a fresco artist with significant commissions such as the *Jucio Universal* for the façade of the Church of Riva Valdobbia in Vercelli,[23] he is best remembered working alongside his brother Giovanni painting terracotta statues at Varallo and Orta. Romano describes his work as securely within the Mannerist style popular in the sixteenth century and remaining so at the Sacri Monti well into the seventeeth century.[24]

Della Rovere, Giovan Battista (1561–1630?), Painter, Chapels II, III, IV, V and VI

Giovan Battista and his brother **Giovan Mauro** were both called The Fiamminghino (together The Fiamminghini) owing to their family's Flemish origins. Givan Battista was a very well regarded Milanese painter, who worked at both Varallo and Orta as well as the Duomo of Milan, where he was noted for his skill in painting architectural elements and use of perspective. Leonardo Caviglioli makes special note of his adroit use of color, particularly the tonal qualities of pinks, yellows, and bright greens.[25]

Della Rovere, Giavon Mauro (1575–1640), Painter, Chapels II, III, IV, and VI

A Milanese painter who, like his brother **Giovan Battista**, was known as The Fiamminghino. Leonardo Caviglioli attributes to Giavon Mauro's early works a "grandeur and dynamism, compositional safety and refined chromaticism." Michael Bryan also comments on his compositional grandeur, portraiture, landscapes with animals, and battle scenes. With his brother, Giovan Mauro held commissions throughout Northern Italy (Varallo, Orta, Como, Novara, Brescia, Sorico, and Milan) as well as at the Abbey of Clairvaux.[26]

Falconi, Bernardo (active c. 1657–96), Sculptor, Chapel XIII

Falconi was famed for his bronze and marble statuary, his skill being such that he had frequent royal commissions, including those of Carlo Emanuele II, the Duke of Savoy. Falconi is known to have worked in Venice, Parma, Turin, Genoa, Padua, and, in 1692, at Orta (along with **Rusnati**) on the figures and marble columns of Chapel XIII. A year later, he collaborated on the colossal bronze statue of San Carlo Borromeo in Arona. Paola Rossi suggests that his initial classicizing style matured over the years, retaining a "lingering classical taste" while adding "accents of quiet solemnity to large, emphatic monumental forms."[27]

Ferrario, Federico (1714–1802), Painter, Chapel XIV

Little is known about Ferrario, though he was a prolific painter in Milan (not at the Duomo, however), Lodi, Clairvaux, Bergamo, Cremona, Pavia, and Bergamasco. He also served as a director of the Ambrosian Academy in Milan. Though considered a minor artist, his baroque frescos in Chapel XIV at Orta and in the Chapel of St. John at the Church of St. Angelo in Milan are well regarded.[28]

Gianoli, Pietro Francesco (1624–92), Painter, Our Lady of Sorrows Chapel (Chapel II)

Born in the Val Sesia, Gianoli studied in Milan and then Rome, where he a member of the Academy of St. Mark, but nevertheless spent most of his career working extensively throughout Piedmont and Lombardy. He was noted for his portrait and figural work, and the grandeur, sensitivity, expressiveness, and color which characterized his frescoes. Gianoli's paintings can be found in numerous churches and private Milanese homes, but also in multiple chapels at the Sacro Monte di Varallo (some of his work there is preserved, some is not), and in the Lady of Sorrows Chapel adjacent to Chapel II of the Sacro Monte di Orta.[29]

Grandi, Giovanni Battista (1643–1718), Painter, Chapels XIII and XVII

Grandi was a baroque painter born in Varese. He often worked in partnership with his brother **Gerolamo** (1658–1718), and they in turn collaborated with **Giovanni Battista Cantalupi** and **Federico Bianchi** for the painted program of Chapel XIII at Orta.[30] Grandi was then hired to complete the painting of Chapel XVII, begun by **Giuseppe Nuvolone**. Both Gerolamo and Giovanni Battista Grandi worked at the Sacro Monte di Varese (with **Stefano Maria Legnani**) in addition to Orta. Giovanni Battista was quite adept at ornamental and architectural painting, though claims that he was also an architect remain unsubstantiated.[31]

Legnani, Stefano Maria (Legnanino, 1661–1713), Painter, Chapel XVI

Legnanino ("little Legnani" to distinguish him from his father, also a painter) was trained in Bologna and Rome. Legnani's work is baroque with rococo tendencies and characterized by soft forms, clear colors, and a "high level of technical and stylistic skills."[32] He had an excellent reputation and was in constant demand among the elites of Turin and Milanese society. Legnani is also identified as one of the most important Lombard architects of the period.[33] In addition to working at Orta, Legnani contributed to chapels at the Sacro Monte di Varese.

Martinolio, Cristoforo (Il Rocca, active 1620–1648) Painter, Chapel IX

Martinolio, who emulated the style of **il Morazzone**, was born in the Val Sesia. He worked at the Sacro Monte di Varallo on the frescos of Chapel XV alongside his brother, Gerolamo, who executed the stained glass window for that same chapel,[34] as well as on Chapels XXV and XXX.

Mazzucchelli, Pier Francesco (il Morazzone, 1573–1626), Painter, Chapel XI

Il Morazzone was born in Morazzone in the region of Milan, and began painting in Rome during the Catholic Reformation program of Sixtus V, a renewal that supported a flourishing artistic environment. He then moved to Venice to continue his studies, and later returned to Milan where he worked on the Duomo. Commissions, meanwhile, took him to Varese, Arona, Como, Varallo and Orta. He was so prolific that Alessandro Serafini suspects that Morazzone had a workshop of artists to support the demands of all the commissions. Morazzone was an eclectic and versatile artist, whose bold colors accentuated his careful attention to anatomical detail. His work even earned him a knighthood from his patron, the King of Sardinia.[35]

Monti, Giacomo Gilippo (active c. 1615), Painter, Chapels I and XVIII
Very little is known about Monti other than he was a local artist, from Orta, whose paintings for Chapel I did not rise to Bishop Bascapè's standards of either skill or orthodoxy, hence he did not receive another commission on the Sacro Monte. It is now thought, however, that the architectural and ornamental motifs of Chapel XVIII are his work. De Filippis and Carcano note that he painted in the Mannerist style, was a portraitist, and previously worked in the twelfth-century Basilica of San Giulio on the Island of San Giulio in Lake Orta.[36]

Nuvolone, Carlo Francesco (c. 1609–62), Painter, Chapels X and XVII
Some biographers report that Carlo Francesco was a student at the prestigious Ambrosiana Art Academy, though there seems to be no contemporaneous documentation. It does seem, however, that he was at the very least influenced, if not trained, by noted Milanese painter Giulio Cesare Procaccini.[37] Carlo Francesco's work has been described as graceful, elegant, sweet and harmonious. He appeals to traditional forms using his hallmark soft tones in order to capture a grand, narrative sweep of the times. Giuseppe Pacciarotti describes his compositions as equally reflective of seventh-century and late seventeenth-century styles.[38]

Nuvolone, Giuseppe (1619–1703), Painter, Chapels X and XVII
Giuseppe trained under and worked alongside his brother, **Carlo Francesco**, such that it is often difficult to distinguish the work of one from the other—until, that is, the death of Carlo Francesco in 1662. Even then, however, Giuseppe continued their current projects using the sketches and plans of his brother. Nevertheless, Giuseppe is known by his independent projects in Novara, Bergamo, Brescia, Groppello d'Adda, Chiavenna and several royal commissions in Milan. He also apprenticed some fairly successful students, such as Felice Boselli. While Carlo Francesco was known for soft and harmonious compositions in terms of both tone and expression, Giuseppe created dramatic facial expressions that gave each portrait distinctive emphasis and disrupted compositional harmony.[39] He was adept at chiaroscuro, employing it with "intelligence and vigor."[40]

Pini, Antonio (Antonio Pino da Bellagio, active c. 1654), Sculptor, Chapel X
The terracotta sculptures of Chapel X have been traditionally ascribed to **Diogini Bussola**, but compelling research over the last decade or so attributes them instead to Antonio Pini, a regionally well-regarded sculptor and engraver from Bellagio, though nothing is known of his training. The terracottas are attributed to Pini based on dating, as well as recurring compositional and stylistic features in comparison with his other works. His characteristic style is seen in the delicate features of the angels, the bulking anatomical physicality of the demons, and the fabric treatment of the garments.[41]

Prestinari, Cristoforo (1573–1623), Sculptor, Chapels I, II, III, IV, V, VI, XI, XII, and XV
Prestinari is the most prolific of the artists of Orta but least attested in the literature. He was born in Milan and worked as sculptor at the Milan Duomo between 1597–1621, as did his brother Marco Antonio.[42] Together they worked at the Sacro Monte di Varallo and di Crea, and in 1612, Federico Borromeo selected the Prestinari brothers to work at the Sacro Monte di Varese. Chistoforo otherwise worked at Orta between 1604 and 1623, when he died at Orta San Giulio. Francesca Cosi and Alessandra Repossi describe the expression of his nearly life-sized figures as "content and delicate,"[43] and his figure groupings tend toward the symmetrical and harmonious.

Rustinati, Giuseppe (c. 1650–1713), Sculptor, Chapels XIII and XIX
Originally from the area of Como, Rustinati trained in Rome before working on the Sacri Monti of Orta, Varese, and Domodossola.[44] He seems to have apprenticed under **Diogini Bussola** and, shortly after his work on the statues of Chapel XIII at Orta, he was appointed sculptor for the Milan Duomo.[45]

❀

There were numerous other craftsmen who worked at Orta on the frescos, wooden grills, glass windows, iron screens, marble fixtures, and exteriors. Unfortunately, little more than their names are available to us today. Fr. Manzini has the most comprehensive catalogue of these artists. They include: Paola Rivolta (architect); Biulio Bersano (painter); Pietro Canonica (sculptor); Padre Honorato (architect); Milanese artist Giulio Cesare Procaccini (painter); Agostino da Carcegna (glass and wood artisan); Master Zia da Pella (iron smith); Master Pavese (iron smith); Monti di Borgomanero (architect); Riccardo Donnino (painter); Rossi of Novarra (sculptor); Stefano Penaggio (iron smith); Giovanni Ambrogio Penaggio (iron smith); Pietro Arbana (iron smith); Pietro Ponti (iron smith); Nicoloa Pangelino (goldsmith); Giovanni Battista Contini (iron smith); Santini da Lagna (architect); Giovanni Pietro (iron smith); Giacomo Allegrini (iron smith); Giuseppe Malcotto da Borgomanero (iron smith); Bernardo Franzosino D'Antrona (metal crafter).[46]

Endnotes

1 Ente di Gestione dei Sacri Monti Centro di Documentazione dei Sacri Monti, Calvari e Complessi devozionali europei Riserva speciale del Sacro Monte di Crea, whose official site can be found at: http://www.sacrimonti.net/User/index.php?PAGE=Sito_en/sacri_monti_del_piemonte_e_della_lombardia; Fr. Angel Maria Manzini, O.F.M. Cap., *Sacro Monte of Orta* (Orta: Community of the Franciscan Friars, Custodian of the Sacro Monte of Orta, 2006); Elena de Filippis and Fiorella Mattioli Carcano, *Guide to the Sacro Monte of Orta* (Novara: Riserva Naturale Speciale del Sacro Monte di Orta, 1991).

2 See Paolo Prodi, "Bascapè, Carlo," in *Dizionario Biografico degli Italiani* (Rome: The Institute of the Italian Encyclopedia, 2015), http://www.treccani.it/enciclopedia/carlo-bascape_(Dizionario-Biografico)/. See also Fedele Merelli, O.F.M. Cap., "P. Cleto da Castelletto Ticino Cappuccino (d. 1619): Note per una biografia," *Communicare Network: Radio Missione Francescana*, http://www.comunicare.it/ofmcap/archivio/p.cleto/pcleto.html.

3 Rossana Bossaglia, "Beretta, Carlo, detto el Berrettone," *Dizionario Biografico degli Italiani*, http://www.treccani.it/enciclopedia/beretta-carlo-detto-il-berrettone_(Dizionario-Biografico)/; De Filippis and Carcano, *Guide to the Sacro Monte of Orta*, 49; Manzini, *Sacro Monte of Orta*, 50.

4 Giuseppe Pacciarotti, *La Pintura Barroca en Italia*, trans. Beatriz López González (Madrid: AKAL, 2000), 241.

5 Michael Bryan, "Bianchi, Federigo," *Dictionary of Painters and Engravers, Biographical and Critical*, 2 vols., ed. Robert Edmund Graves (London: George Bell and Sons, 1886), 1:124, 1:566.

6 Rossana Bossaglia, "Bianchi, Federico," in *Dizionario Biografico degli Italiani*, http://www.treccani.it/enciclopedia/federico-bianchi_(Dizionario-Biografico)/.

7 Pacciarotti, *La Pintura Barroca en Italia*, 241, 213.

8 Bryan, "Busca, Antonio," in *Dictionary of Painters and Engravers*, 1:204, and Bryan, "Procaccini, Ercole, the Younger," in *Dictionary of Painters and Engravers*, 2:324.

9 Rossana Bossaglia, "Busca, Antonio," in *Dizionario Biografico degli Italiani*, http://www.treccani.it/enciclopedia/federico-bianchi_(Dizionario-Biografico)/.

10 Bryan, "Busca, Antonio," in *Dictionary of Painters and Engravers*, 1:204.

11 For the ledger of his work at the cathedral, see Milan Cathedral, *Annali della fabbrica del duomo di Milano: dall'origine fino al presente*, 6 vols. (Milan: G. Brigola, 1883), 5:222–43.

12 Gabriella Ferri Piccaluga, "Bussola, Dionigi," in *Dizionario Biografico degli Italiani*, http://www.treccani.it/enciclopedia/dionigi-bussola_(Dizionario-Biografico)/.

13 See Geoffrey Symcox, *Jerusalem in the Alps: The Sacro Monte of Varallo and the Sanctuaries of North-West Italy* (Turnhout: Brepols, 2019), 208–10. See also, Christine Göttler, "The Temptation of the Senses at the Sacro Monte di Varallo," in *Religion and the Senses in Early Modern Europe*, eds. Wietse de Boer and Christine Göttler (Leiden: Brill, 2013), 445.

14 There is some disagreement among historians as to whether Giovanni Battista Cantalupi worked on Chapel XIII or not. The confusion may arise from the fact that both Cantalupi and Giovanni Battista Grandi (who did paint in Chapel XIII) share a given name. De Filippis and Carcano do not mention Cantalupi's involvement in the chapel (*Guide to the Sacro Monte di Orta*, 45), as opposed to Luigi Mallè, who includes Cantalupi among the painters of the chapel. See Luigi Mallè, *Figurative Art in Piedmont*, 2 vols., trans. Shelia Freeman et. al. (Turin: Officine Di Villar Perosa S.P.A., 1972), 2:74. Mallè also credits Cantalupi with work on the Church of Saint Nicolo and Saint Francis at the Sacro Monte di Orta (2:237).

15 Cantalupi is mentioned in a biographical dictionary under an entry for the painter Giuseppe Gaudenzio Mazzola, who was also in Parma. See Micaela Mander, "Mazzola, Giuseppe Gaudenzio," *Dizionario Biografico degli Italiani*, http://www.treccani.it/enciclopedia/giuseppe-gaudenzio-mazzola_(Dizionario-Biografico)/.

16 Mallè, *Figurative Art in Piedmont*, 2:74.

17 Ibid., 2:237.

18 The former convent may have been incorporated into the mid-nineteenth-century Villa Caccia, designed by noted architect Alessandro Antonelli (1798–1888). For more on this architect, see Paolo Portoghesi, "Alessandro Antonelli," *Dizionario Biografico degli Italiani*, http://www.treccani.it/enciclopedia/alessandro-antonelli_(Dizionario-Biografico)/.

19 Merelli, "P. Cleto da Castelletto Ticino Cappuccino (d. 1619)."

20 Marco Bona Castellotti, "Crespi Castoldi," *Dizionario Biografico degli Italiani*, http://www.treccani.it/enciclopedia/crespi-castoldi_(Dizionario-Biografico)/.

21 Giovanni Romano, "D'Enrico, Giovanni," *Dizionario Biografico degli Italiani*, http://www.treccani.it/enciclopedia/giovanni-d-enrico/; "D'Enrico [Family]," http://www.treccani.it/enciclopedia/d-enrico_(Dizionario-Biografico)/; and "D'Enrico, Melchiorre," http://www.treccani.it/enciclopedia/melchiorre-d-enrico_(Dizionario-Biografico)/.

22 Romano, "D'Enrico, Giovanni"; De Filippis and Carcano, *Guide to the Sacro Monte of Orta*, 35.

23 Pacciarotti, *La Pintura Barroca en Italia*, 206–7 and Romano, "D'Enrico, Melchiorre."

24 Romano, "D'Enrico, Melchiorre."

25 Leonardo Caviglioli, "Della Rovere, Giovan Battista," *Dizionario Biografico degli Italiani*, http://www.treccani.it/enciclopedia/della-rovere-giovan-battista-detto-il-fiamminghino_(Dizionario-Biografico)/; Pacciarotti, *La Pintura Barroca en Italia*, 201; Bryan, "Rovere, Giovanni Mauro," in *Dictionary of Painters and Engravers*, 63; Milan Cathedral, *Annali della fabbrica del duomo*, 6 vols. (Milan: G. Brigola, 1880), 3:303; 3:328.

26 Leonardo Caviglioli, "Della Rovere, Giovan Mauro," *Dizionario Biografico degli Italiani*, http://www.treccani.it/enciclopedia/della-rovere-giovan-mauro-detto-il-fiamminghino_(Dizionario-Biografico)/; Pacciarotti, *La Pintura Barroca en Italia*, 201; Michael Bryan, "Rovere, Giovanni Mauro," *Dictionary of Painters and Engravers*, 663; Milan Cathedral, *Annali della fabbrica del duomo* (1883), 5:171, 5:180.

27 Paola Rossi, "Falconi, Bernardo," *Dizionario Biografico degli Italiani*, http://www.treccani.it/enciclopedia/bernardo-falconi_(Dizionario-Biografico)/.

28 Amalia Barigozzi Brini, "Ferrario (Farrari), Federico," *Dizionario Biografico degli Italiani*, http://www.treccani.it/enciclopedia/federico-ferrario_(Dizionario-Biografico)/; Anton Willem Adriaan Boschloo, *Academies of Art: Between Renaissance and Romanticism* (The Hague: SDU, 1989), 140, 157.

29 Alessandra Ancilotto, "Gianoli, Pietro Francesco," *Dizionario Biografico degli Italiani*, http://www.treccani.it/enciclopedia/pietro-francesco-gianoli_(Dizionario-Biografico).

30 See the biographical entry for **Cantalupi, Giovanni Battista** above.

31 Sabina Brevaglieri, "Grandi, Giovani Battista," *Dizionario Biografico degli Italiani*, http://www.treccani.it/enciclopedia/giovanni-battista-grandi_(Dizionario-Biografico)/; Pacciarotti, *La Pintura Barroca en Italia*, 213; De Filippis and Carcano, *Guide to the Sacro Monte of Orta*, 45; Manzini, *Sacro Monte of Orta*, 46.

32 Lucia Casellato, "Legnani, Stefano Maria, detto il Legnanino," *Dizionario Biografico degli Italiani*, http://www.treccani.it/enciclopedia/legnani-stefano-maria-detto-il-legnanino_(Dizionario-Biografico)/. See also Michael Bryan, "Legnani, Stefano, called Legnanino," in *Dictionary of Painters and Engravers*, 395.

33 Pacciarotti, *La Pintura Barroca en Italia*, 246.

34 Casalis, Goffredo, *Dizionario Geografico Storico-Statistico-Commerciale degli Stati di S.M. Il Re Di Sardegna*, 28 vols. (Turin: Gaetano Maspero, 1847), 16:486.

35 Alessandro Serafini, "Mazzucchelli, Pier Francesco, detto il Morazzone," *Dizionario Biografico degli Italiani*, http://www.treccani.it/enciclopedia/mazzucchelli-pier-francesco-detto-il-morazzone_(Dizionario-Biografico)/; Michael Bryan, "Morazzone, Pier Francesco Mazzuchelli," in *Dictionary of Painters and Engravers*, 491; Milan Cathedral, *Annali della fabbrica del duomo*, 5:106; Pacciarotti, *La Pintura Barroca en Italia*, 201.

36 De Filippis and Carcano, *Guide to the Sacro Monte of Orta*, 15, 55; See also Giuseppe Pacciarotti, *La Pintura Barroca en Italia*, 201; and Manzini, *Sacro Monte of Orta*, 58.

37 Nancy Ward Neilson, "Two Drawings by Carlo Francesco Nuvolone," *Master Drawings* 23–24, no. 2 (1985–1986): 212–13, 286–87.

38 Michael Bryan, "Nuvolone, Carlo Francesco," in *A Biographical and Critical Dictionary of Painters and Engravers, with a list of Ciphers, Monograms, and Marks*. ed. George Stanley (London: George Bell and Sons, 1878), 521; Pacciarotti, *La Pintura Barroca en Italia*, 211.

39 Francesco Frangi, "Nuvolone, Giuseppe," *Dizionario Biografico degli Italiani*, http://www.treccani.it/enciclopedia/giuseppe-nuvolone_(Dizionario-Biografico)/; Michael Bryan, "Nuvolone, Giuseppe," in *A Biographical and Critical Dictionary of Painters and Engravers*, 100, 521–22.

40 Bryan, "Nuvolone, Giuseppe," 521.

41 Marina Dell'Omo, "Antonio Pino da Bellagio al Sacro Monte di Orta," *Sacri Monti* 2 (2010): 97–103.

42 Milan Cathedral, *Annali della fabbrica del duomo*, 3:323; Milan Cathedral, *Annali della fabbrica del duomo*, 5:16, 5:30, 5:31, 5:52, 5:63, 5:67, 5:72, 5:75, 5:76, 5:80, 5:81, 5:105, 5:108–13, 5:118, 5:122, 5:126, 5:132; Francesca Cosi and Alessandra Repossi, *Da pellegrini sui Sacri Monti* (Milan: Àncora Editrice, 2013), 53. See also Gian Alberto Dell'Acqua, Marilisa Di Giovanni, and Giulio Melzi d'Eril, *Isola San Giulio e Sacro Monte D'Orta* (Turin: Istituto Bancario San Paolo di Torino, 1977), 130, 149.

43 Cosi and Repossi, *Da pellegrini sui Sacri Monti*, 53.

44 Symcox, *Jerusalem in the Alps*, 215.

45 "Rusnati, Giuseppe," *Dizionario Biografico degli Italiani*, http://www.treccani.it/enciclopedia/giuseppe-rusnati/.

46 Manzini, *Sacro Monte di Orta*.

Bibliography

A Book of Exemplary Stories (1280–1310). In *Francis of Assisi: Early Documents*, Vol. 3: *The Prophet*, edited and translated by Regis Armstrong, O.F.M. Cap., et al., 797–801. New York: New City Press, 2001.

Abate, P. Giuseppe. *La Casa Natale di S. Francesco e la Topografia di Assisi nella prima metà del secolo XIII*. Rome: Miscellanea Francescana, 1966.

Ahl, Diane Cole. *Benozzo Gozzoli: Tradition and Innovation in Renaissance Painting*. New Haven: Yale University Press, 1996.

Alber, Erasmus. *The Alcoran of the Franciscans*. London: L. Curtise, 1679.

Alberti, Leon Battista. *The Family in Renaissance Florence*. Translated by Renee Neu Watkings. Columbia: University of South Carolina Press, 1969.

Angelo da Clareno. *The Book of Chronicles or the Tribulations of the Order of Lesser Ones*. In *Francis of Assisi: Early Documents*, Vol. 3: *The Prophet*, edited and translated by Regis Armstrong, O.F.M. Cap., et al., 380–426. New York: New City Press, 2001.

Armstrong, Regis, O.F.M. Cap., ed. *The Legend of Saint Clare*. In *Clare of Assisi, The Lady: Early Documents*. New York: New City Press, 2006.

Armstrong, Regis, O.F.M. Cap., et al., eds. *Francis of Assisi: Early Documents*. 3 vols. New York: New City Press, 1999–2001.

Arnald of Sarrant. *Chronicle of the Twenty-four Generals*. In *Francis of Assisi: Early Documents*, Vol. 3: *The Prophet*, edited and translated by Regis Armstrong, O.F.M. Cap., et al., 810–12. New York: New City Press, 2001.

———. *The Kinship of Saint Francis*. In *Francis of Assisi: Early Documents*, Vol. 3: *The Prophet*, edited and translated by Regis Armstrong, O.F.M. Cap., et al., 678–733. New York: New City Press, 2001.

Askew, Pamela. "The Angelic Consolation of St. Francis of Assisi in Post-Tridentine Italian Painting." *Journal of the Warburg and Courtauld Institutes* 32 (1969): 280–306. DOI: 10.2307/750615.

Aubert, Roger. *The Church in the Industrial Age*. London: Crossroad, 1981.

Auerbach, Erich. *Mimesis: The Representation of Reality in Western Literature*. Translated by Willard Trask. Princeton: Princeton University Press, 2013.

Bagnoli, Martina, ed. *A Feast for the Senses: Art and Experience in Medieval Europe*. New Haven: Yale University Press, 2017.

Bainton, Roland. "Durer and Luther as the Man of Sorrows." *The Art Bulletin* 29, no. 4 (1947): 269–72. DOI: 10.2307/3047145.

Balass, Golda. "Taddeo Zuccaro's Fresco in the Apse-Conch in S. Sabina, Rome." *Assaph: Studies in Art History* 4 (1999): 105–25. https://arts.tau.ac.il/sites/arts.tau.ac.il/files/media_server/Arts/Research/Journals/asaf/art-history/pdf/art_book1999.pdf.

Barber, Malcolm. *The Cathars: Dualist Heretics in Languedoc in the High Middle Ages.* New York: Routledge, 2014.

Barberini, Maria Giulia. "Base or Noble Material? Clay Sculpture in Seventeenth- and Eighteenth-Century Italy." In *Earth and Fire: Italian Terracotta Sculpture from Donatello to Canova,* edited by Bruce Boucher, 44–59. New Haven: Yale University Press, 2001.

Bardone, Ellen, and Sharon Roseman. *Intersecting Journeys: The Anthropology of Pilgrimage and Tourism.* Champaign: University of Illinois Press, 2004.

Barolsky, Paul. "Naturalism and the Visionary Art of the Early Renaissance." In *Giotto and the World of Early Italian Art: An Anthology of Literature,* Vol. 4: *Franciscanism: The Papacy, and Art in the Age of Giotto: Assisi and Rome,* edited by Andrew Ladis, 317–24. Abingdon-on-Thames: Routledge, 1998.

Barthes, Roland. *Camera Lucida: Reflections on Photography.* Translated by Richard Howard. New York: Hill & Wang, 1981.

Bartholomew of Pisa. *De Conformitate Vitae Beati Francisci ad Vitam Domini Jesu Redemptoris nostril* [*Liber conformitatum*]. Milan: Gotardus Ponticus, 1510.

———. *De Conformitate.* Edited by the Fathers of the College of Saint Bonaventure. Analecta Franciscana 4. Quaracchi: Collegium S. Bonaventurae, 1906.

Bätschmann, Oskar. *Giovanni Bellini.* London: Reaktion Books, 2008.

Bell, Margaret F. "Image as Relic: Bodily Vision and Reconstitution of Viewer/Image Relationships at the Sacro Monte di Varallo." *California Italian Studies* 5, no. 1 (2014): 303–31. https://escholarship.org/uc/item/84q9v2k5.

Benedetto, Carola, ed. *Donne e Madonne nei Sacri Monti del Piemonte e della Lombardia.* Savigliano: L'Artictica Savigliano, 2010.

Benedict, Philip. "The Catholic Response to Protestantism: Church Activity and Popular Piety in Rouen." In *Religion and the People, 800–1700,* edited by James Obelkevich, 168–90. Chapel Hill: University of North Carolina Press, 1979.

Bennett, Jill. "Stigmata and Sense Memory: St. Francis and the Affective." *Art History* 24, no. 1 (Dec. 2003): 1–16. DOI: 10.1111/1467-8365.00247.

Benzan, Carla. "Alone at the Summit: Solitude and the Ascetic Imagination at the Sacro Monte of Varallo." In *Solitudo: Spaces, Places, and Times of Solitude in Late Medieval and Early Modern Cultures,* edited by Karl A. E. Enenkel and Christine Göttler, 336–63. Leiden: Brill, 2018.

Bernard of Besse. "A Book of the Praises of Saint Francis." In *Francis of Assisi: Early Documents,* Vol. 3: *The Prophet,* edited and translated by Regis Armstrong, O.F.M. Cap., et al., 31–74. New York: New City Press, 2001.

Bianconi, Piero, et al. *Il Sacro Monte sopra Varese.* Milan: Paolo Zanzi, Gruppo Editoriale Electa, 1981.

Bonaventure of Bagnoregio. *Bonaventure: The Soul's Journey into God, The Tree of Life, The Life of St. Francis.* Translated by Ewert Cousins. The Classics of Western Spirituality, edited by Richard Payne. New York: Paulist Press, 1978.

———. "The Evening Sermon on Saint Francis." In *Francis of Assisi: Early Documents,* Vol. 2: *The Founder,* edited and translated by Regis Armstrong, O.F.M. Cap., et al., 718–30. New York: New City Press, 2000.

———. "The Morning Sermon on St. Francis." In *Francis of Assisi: Early Documents,* Vol. 2: *The Founder,* edited and translated by Regis Armstrong, O.F.M. Cap., et al., 747–58. New York: New City Press, 2000.

———. "The Major Legend of Saint Francis." In *Francis of Assisi: Early Documents,* Vol. 2: *The Founder,* edited and translated by Regis Armstrong, O.F.M. Cap., et al., 525–683. New York: New City Press, 2000.

———. *Works of St. Bonaventure,* Vol. 1: *On the Reduction of the Arts to Theology.* Translated by Zachary Hayes, O.F.M. St.

Bonaventure: Franciscan Institute Publications, 1996.

———. "The Soliloquium: A Dialogue on the Four Spiritual Exercises." In *Works of St. Bonaventure*, Vol. 10: *Writings on the Spiritual Life*, edited by Edward Coughlin, O.F.M., and Robert J. Karris, O.F.M., 215–344. St. Bonaventure: Franciscan Institute Publications, 2006.

Bossaglia, Rossana. "Beretta, Carlo, detto el Berrettone." *Dizionario Biografico degli Italiani*. http://www.treccani.it/enciclopedia/beretta-carlo-detto-il-berrettone_(Dizionario-Biografico)/.

———. "Bianchi, Federico." *Dizionario Biografico degli Italiani*. http://www.treccani.it/enciclopedia/federico-bianchi_(Dizionario-Biografico)/.

———. "Busca, Antonio." *Dizionario Biografico degli Italiani*. http://www.treccani.it/enciclopedia/federico-bianchi_(Dizionario-Biografico)/.

Boucher, Bruce. "Italian Renaissance Terracotta: Artistic Revival or Technological Innovation?" In *Earth and Fire: Italian Terracotta Sculpture from Donatello to Canova*, edited by Bruce Boucher, 1–31. New Haven: Yale University Press, 2001.

Boschloo, Anton Willem Adriaan. *Academies of Art: Between Renaissance and Romanticism*. The Hague: SDU, 1989.

Brakke, David. "Ethiopian Demons: Male Sexuality, the Black-Skinned Other, and the Monastic Self." *Journal of the History of Sexuality* 10, nos. 3–4 (2001): 501–35. DOI: 10.1353/sex.2001.0049.

Brevaglieri, Sabina. "Grandi, Giovani Battista." *Dizionario Biografico degli Italiani*. http://www.treccani.it/enciclopedia/giovanni-battista-grandi_(Dizionario-Biografico)/.

Brini, Amalia Barigozzi. "Ferrario (Farrari), Federico." *Dizionario Biografico degli Italiani*. http://www.treccani.it/enciclopedia/federico-ferrario_(Dizionario-Biografico)/.

Brooke, Rosalind. *The Image of St. Francis: Responses to Sainthood in the Thirteenth Century*. Cambridge: Cambridge University Press, 2006.

Brown, David Allen, and Sylvia Ferino-Pagden. *Bellini, Giorgione, Titian, and the Renaissance of Venetian Painting*. New Haven: Yale University Press, 2007.

Brunette, Pierre. *Francis of Assisi and His Conversions*. Translated by P. Lachance and K. Krug. Chicago: Franciscan Press, 1997.

Bryan, Michael. *Dictionary of Painters and Engravers, Biographical and Critical*. Edited by Robert Edmund Graves. 2 vols. London: George Bell and Sons, 1886.

———. *A Biographical and Critical Dictionary of Painters and Engravers, with a list of Ciphers, Monograms, and Marks*. Edited by George Stanley. London: George Bell and Sons, 1878.

Buchanan Quatercenary Committee. *George Buchanan: Glasgow Quatercentenary Studies, 1906*. Glasgow: James MacLehose and Sons, 1907.

Butler, Samuel. *Ex Voto: An Account of the Sacro Monte or New Jerusalem at Varallo-Sesia*. London: Dodo Press, 1888.

Bynum, Caroline Walker. *Jesus as Mother: Studies in Spirituality of the High Middle Ages*. Berkeley: University of California Press, 1982.

Campagnola, Stanislao da. *L'angelo del sesto sigillo e l'alter Christus Genesi e sviluppo di due temi francescani nei secoli XII–XIV*. Studi e ricerche 1. Rome: Antonianum, 1971.

Campbell, Thomas P. *Tapestry in the Renaissance: Art and Magnificence*. New York: Metropolitan Museum of Art, 2002.

Cannon-Brookes, Peter. *Lombard Paintings c1595–c1630: The Age of Federico Borromeo*. Birmingham: City Museums and Art Gallery, 1974.

Carroll, Michael P. *Veiled Threats: The Logic of Popular Catholicism in Italy*. Baltimore: Johns Hopkins University Press, 1996.

Casalis, Goffredo. *Dizionario Geografico Storico-Statistico-Commerciale degli Stati di S.M. Il Re Di Sardegna*, Vol. 16. Turin: Gaetano Maspero, 1847.

Casellato, Lucia. "Legnani, Stefano Maria, detto il Legnanino." *Dizionario Biografico degli Italiani*. http://www.treccani.it/enciclopedia/legnani-stefano-maria-detto-il-legnanino_(Dizionario-Biografico)/.

Castellotti, Marco Bona. "Crespi Castoldi." *Dizionario Biografico degli Italiani*. http://www.treccani.it/enciclopedia/crespi-castoldi_(Dizionario-Biografico)/.

Cate, Curtis. *Friedrich Nietzsche*. Woodstock: The Overlook Press, 2002.

Caviglioli, Leonardo. "Della Rovere, Giovan Battista." *Dizionario Biografico degli Italiani*. http://www.treccani.it/enciclopedia/della-rovere-giovan-battista-detto-il-fiamminghino_(Dizionario-Biografico)/.

———. "Della Rovere, Giovan Mauro." *Dizionario Biografico degli Italiani*. http://www.treccani.it/enciclopedia/della-rovere-giovan-mauro-detto-il-fiamminghino_(Dizionario-Biografico)/.

Chatterjee, Paroma. "Francis's Secret Stigmata." *Art History* 35, no. 1 (2012): 38–61. DOI: 10.1111/j.1467–8365.2011.00871.x.

Chérancé, Léopold de, O.F.M. Cap. *Saint Francis of Assisi*. Translated by R.F. O'Connor. London: Burns and Oates, 1880.

Childs, Adrienne. *The Black Exotic: Tradition and Ethnography in Nineteenth-Century Orientalist Art*. PhD Diss., University of Maryland, 2005.

Clark, Stuart. *Vanities of the Eye: Vision in Early Modern European Culture*. Oxford: Oxford University Press, 2007.

Cobianchi, Roberto. "Iconographic and Visual Sources for Bernardo Strozzi's 'Vision of St Dominic'." *The Burlington Magazine* 140, no. 1147 (1998): 668–75. http://www.jstor.org/stable/888159.

Cochrane, Eric. "Counter Reformation or Tridentine Reformation? Italy in the Age of Carlo Borromeo." *In San Carlo Borromeo: Catholic Reform and Ecclesiastical Politics in the Second Half of the Sixteenth Century*, edited by John M. Headley and John B. Tomaro, 31–46. Washington, DC: The Folger Shakespeare Library, 1988.

Constable, Giles. *Three Studies in Medieval and Religious and Social Thought*. Cambridge: Cambridge University Press, 1995.

Cook, Mark. "Gaze and Mutual Gaze in Social Encounters." *American Scientist* 65, no. 3 (May–June 1977): 328–33. https://www.jstor.org/stable/27847843.

Cook, William. *Images of St. Francis of Assisi in Painting, Stone and Glass from the Earliest Images to ca. 1320 in Italy: A Catalogue*. Edited by L.S. Olschki. Florence: Olschki, 1999.

Cooper, Donal, and Janet Robson. *The Making of Assisi: The Pope, the Franciscans, and the Painting of the Basilica*. New Haven: Yale University Press, 2013.

Cosi, Francesca, and Alessandra Repossi. *Da pellegrini sui Sacri Monti*. Milan: Àncora Editrice, 2013.

Cousins, Ewert. "Francis of Assisi: Nature, Poverty, and the Humanity of Christ." In *Mystics of the Book: Themes, Topics, and Typologies*, edited by R.A. Herrara, 203–17. New York: Peter Lang, 1993.

Dalarun, Jacques. *Francis of Assisi and the Feminine*. Translated by Paula Pierce and Mary Sutphin. St. Bonaventure: Franciscan Institute, 2006.

Davies, Paul. "The Lighting of Pilgrimage Shrines in Renaissance Italy." In *The Miraculous Image in the Late Middle Ages and Renaissance*, edited by Erik Thunø and Gerhard Wolf, 57–80. Rome: L'Erma di Bretschneider, 2004.

Davidson, Arnold. "Miracles of Bodily Transformation, or How St. Francis Received the Stigmata." *Critical Inquiry* 35, no. 3 (Spring 2009): 451–80. DOI: 10.1086/600094

De Boer, Wietse. *The Conquest of the Soul: Confession, Discipline, and Public Order in Counter-Reformation Milan*. Leiden: Brill, 2001.

De Filippis, Elena, and Fiorella Mattioli Carcano. *Guide to the Sacro Monte of Orta*. Novara: Riserva Naturale Speciale del Sacro Monte di Orta, 1991.

Deitz, Maribel. *Wandering Monks, Virgins, and Pilgrims: Ascetic Travel in the Mediterranean World, AD 300–800*. University Park: The Pennsylvania State University Press, 2005.

Del Popolo, Concetto. "Intrecci agiografici: eremiti ed altri." *Rivista di Storia e Letteratura Religiosa* 43 (2007): 123–53. https://hdl.handle.net/2027/mdp.39015079663913.

Dell'Omo, Marina. "Antonio Pino da Bellagio al Sacro Monte di Orta." *Sacri Monti* 2 (2010): 97–103.

Della Rossa, Francesco Bartholdi. *Tractatus de Indulgentia S. Maria de Portiuncula*. Edited by Paul Sabatier. Paris: Fishbacher, 1900.

Dempsey, Charles. *Inventing the Renaissance Putto*. Chapel Hill: University of North Carolina Press, 2001.

DeSilva, Jennifer Mara. *The Sacralization of Space and Behavior in the Early Modern World*. London: Routledge, 2015.

Ditchfield, Simon. *Liturgy, Sanctity and History in Tridentine Italy*. Cambridge: Cambridge University Press, 2002.

Documents Concerning the Portiuncula Indulgence (1277–1300). In *Francis of Assisi: Early Documents*, Vol. 3: *The Prophet*, edited and translated by Regis Armstrong, O.F.M. Cap., et al., 806–12. New York: New City Press, 2001.

Dronke, Peter. "Tradition and Innovation in Medieval Western Colour-Imagery." In *The Realms of Colour: Lectures Given at the Eranos Conference in Ascona from August 23rd to 31st, 1972*, edited by Adolf Portmann and Rudolf Ritsema, 51–107. Leiden: Brill, 1974.

Duffy, Eamon. *Saints and Sinners: A History of the Popes*. New Haven: Yale University Press, 2002.

Dyas, Dee. *Pilgrimage in Medieval English Literature, 700–1500*. Suffolk: D.S. Brewer, 2001.

Eck, Diana. *Darśan: Seeing the Divine Image in India*. 3rd edition. New York: Columbia University Press, 1998.

Edden, Valerie. "Devils, Sermon Stories, and the Problem of Popular Belief in the Middle Ages." *The Yearbook of English Studies* 22 (1992): 213–25. DOI: 10.2307/3508387.

Eliade, Mircea. *The Sacred and the Profane*. Translated by Willard Trask. New York: Harcourt, Brace, and World, Inc., 1959.

———. *Patterns in Comparative Religion*. Translated by Rosemary Sheed. Lincoln: University of Nebraska, 1996.

Elsner, Jaś. "Between Mimesis and Divine Power: Visuality in the Greco-Roman World." In *Visuality Before and Beyond the Renaissance: Seeing as Others Saw*, edited by Robert Nelson, 45–69. Cambridge: Cambridge University Press, 2000.

Erickson, Carolly. "Bartholomew of Pisa, Francis Exalted: De conformitate." *Mediaeval Studies* 34 (1972): 253–74. DOI: 10.1484/J.MS.2.306113.

Eusebius. *History of the Church: From Christ to Constantine*. Edited by Andrew Louth. Translated by G.A. Williamson. Revised edition. London: Penguin Classics, 1990.

Foucault, Michel. *The Archaeology of Knowledge and the Discourse on Language*. Translated by A.M. Sheridan Smith. New York: Pantheon Books, 1972.

———. *Discipline and Punish: The Birth of the Prison*. Translated by Alan Sheridan. New York: Vintage Books, 1977.

Francis. *Praise Be To You, Laudato Si': On Care for Our Common Home*. Encyclical Series. San Francisco: Ignatius Press, 2015.

Francis of Assisi. *Earlier Rule*. In *Francis of Assisi: Early Documents*, Vol. 1: *The Saint*, edited and translated by Regis Armstrong, O.F.M. Cap., et al., 63–86. New York: New City Press, 1999.

———. *Letter to the Entire Order*. In *Francis of Assisi: Early Documents*, Vol. 1: *The Saint*, edited and translated by Regis Armstrong, O.F.M. Cap., et al., 116–21. New York: New City Press, 1999.

Franco, Bradley R. "The Functions of Early Franciscan Art." In *The World of St. Francis of Assisi: Essays in Honor of William R. Cook*, edited by Bradley R. Franco and Beth Mulvaney, 19–44. Leiden: Brill, 2015.

Frank, Georgia. "The Pilgrim's Gaze in the Age Before Icons." In *Visuality Before and Beyond the Renaissance: Seeing as Others Saw*, edited by Robert Nelson, 98–115. Cambridge: Cambridge University Press, 2000.

———. "'Taste and See': The Eucharist and the Eyes of Faith in the Fourth Century." *Church History* 70, no. 4 (Dec. 2001): 619–43. DOI: 10.2307/3654543.

———. *The Memory of the Eyes: Pilgrims to Living Saints in Christian Late Antiquity*. Berkeley: University of California Press, 2000.

Freedberg, S.J. *Painting in Italy, 1500–1600*. 3rd. edition. New Haven: Yale University Press, 1993.

Gage, John. *Color and Meaning: Art, Science, and Symbolism*. Berkeley: University of California Press, 2000.

Gallegos, Matthew. "Carlo Borromeo and Catholic Tradition Regarding the Design of Catholic Churches." *The Institute for Sacred Architecture* 9 (2004): 14–18. http://www.sacredarchitecture.org/issues/volume_9.

Gregg, Ryan. "The Sacro Monte of Varallo as a Physical Manifestation of the Spiritual Exercises." *Athanor* 22 (2004): 49–55.

Gardner, Julian. "The Louvre Stigmatization and the Problem of the Narrative Altarpiece." *Zeitschrift für Kunstgeschichte* 45, no. 3 (1982): 217–47. DOI: 10.2307/1482157.

Gaston, Robert. W. "Attention in Court: Visual Decorum in Medieval Prayer Theory and Early Italian Art." In *Visions of Holiness: Art and Devotion in Renaissance Italy*, edited by Andrew Ladis and Shelley E. Zuraw, 137–62. Athens: Georgia Museum of Art, 2001.

"Gianoli, Pietro Francesco." In *Dizionario Biografico degli Italiani*. http://www.treccani.it/enciclopedia/pietro-francesco-gianoli_(Dizionario-Biografico).

Gill, Rebecca M. "Galeazzo Alessi and the Redevelopment of the Sacred Mount of Varallo in Tridentine Italy." *AID Monuments. Conoscere, progettare, ricostruire: Galeazzo Alessi Architect-Engineer*, edited by Caludia Conforti and Vittorio Gusella, 101–13. Rome, ARACNE, 2013.

Gillespie, Alex. "Tourist Photography and the Reverse Gaze." *Ethos* 34, no. 3 (Jan. 2008): 343–66. DOI: 10.1525/eth.2006.34.3.343.

Gobry, Ivan. *Saint Francis of Assisi: A Biography*. San Francisco: Ignatius Press, 2006.

Gelber, Hester Goodenough. "A Theater of Virtue: The Exemplary World of St. Francis of Assisi." In *Saints and Virtues*, edited by John Stratton Hawley Berkeley, 15–35. Comparative Studies in Religion and Society. Berkeley: University of California Press, 1987.

Göttler, Christine. "The Temptation of the Senses at the Sacro Monte di Varallo." In *Religion and the Senses in Early Modern Europe*, edited by Wietse de Boer and Christine Göttler, 393–451. Leiden: Brill, 2013.

Habel, Dorothy. *Federico Borromeo and the Ambrosiana: Art Patronage and Reform in Seventeenth Century Milan*. Cambridge: Cambridge University Press, 1993.

Hahn, Thomas. "The Difference the Middle Ages Makes: Color and Race Before the Modern World." *Journal of Medieval and Early Modern Studies* 31, no. 1 (Winter 2001): 1–38. DOI: 10.1215/10829636-31-1-1.

Council of Nicea II. "The Decree of the Holy, Great, Ecumenical Synod, the Second of Nicea," *Medieval Sourcebook: Decree of the Second Council of Nicea, 787*. Edited by Paul Halsall. Fall 1996. http://sourcebooks.fordham.edu/halsall/source/nicea2-dec.asp.

Hammond, J. M. "Saint Francis's Doxological Mysticism in Light of His Prayers." In *Francis of Assisi: History, Hagiography and Hermeneutics in the Early Documents*, edited by J.M. Hammond, 105–52. Hyde Park: New City Press, 2004.

Hanbridge, Paul, O.F.M. Cap., trans. *The Capuchin Reform, A Franciscan Renaissance: A Portrait of Sixteenth- Century Capuchin Life, An English Translation of La bella e santa riforma* by Melchiorre da Pobladura, O.F.M. Cap. Delhi: Media House, 2003.

Head, Randolf. *Jenatasch's Axe: Social Boundaries, Identity, and Myth in the Era of the Thirty Year's War*. Rochester: University of Rochester Press, 2008.

Henri d'Avranches. "The Versified Life of Saint Francis." In *Francis of Assisi: Early Documents*, Vol. 1: *The Saint*, edited and translated by Regis Armstrong, O.F.M. Cap., et al., 428–520. New York: New City Press, 1999.

Ho, Cynthia. "The Visual Piety of the Sacro Monte di Orta." In *Finding Saint Francis in Literature and Art*, edited by Cynthia Ho, Beth Mulvaney, and John K. Downey, 109–28. New York: Palgrave, 2009.

———. "Closing the Borders: St. Francis at Orta." In *Identity and Alterity in Hagiography and the Cult of Saints*, edited by Ana Marinković, Trpimir Vedriš, and Ildikó Csepregi, 245–60. Zagreb: Hagiotheca, 2010.

———. "King Carnival in the Yoke of Humility." *Medieval Perspectives* 30 (2015): 9–29.

Hood, William. "The Sacro Monte of Varallo: Renaissance Art and Popular Religion." In *Monasticism and the Arts*, edited by Timothy Verdon and John Dally, 291–311. Syracuse: Syracuse University Press, 1984.

Hubbard, Charlotte, and Peta Motture. "The Making of Terracotta Sculpture: Techniques and Observations." In *Earth and Fire: Italian Terracotta Sculpture from Donatello to Canova*, edited by Bruce Boucher, 83–95. New Haven: Yale University Press, 2001.

Huber, Raphael Mary. *The Portiuncula Indulgence: From Honorius III to Pius XI*. Franciscan Studies 19–20. New York: J.W. Wagner, 1938.

Ignatius of Loyola. *Ignatius of Loyola: Spiritual Exercises and Selected Works*. Edited by George E. Ganss, S.J. Classics of Western Spirituality. New York: Paulist Press, 1991.

"Instruzzione Al Divoto Lettore Che Desidera Visitare Il Sacro Monte Di S. Francesco D'Orta." In *Antiche Guide del Sacro Monte di Orta*, edited by Loredana Racchelli, 125–237. Orta: Ente di Gestione delle Reserve Naturali Speciali del Sacro Monte di Orta, del Monte Mesma e del Colle della Torre di Buccione, 2008.

Izbicki, Thomas M. "The Immaculate Conception and Ecclesiastical Politics from the Council of Basel to the Council of Trent: The Dominicans and their Foes." *Archiv für Reformationsgeschichte* 96 (2005): 145–70. DOI: 10.14315/arg-2005-0108.

Jacobs, Fredrika. *The Living Image in Renaissance Art*. Cambridge: Cambridge University Press, 2005.

Jaeger, Stephen C. "Charismatic Body–Charismatic Text." *Exemplaria* 9, no. 1 (1997): 117–37. DOI: 10.1179/exm.1997.9.1.117.

Jardine, Lisa. *Worldly Goods: A New History of the Renaissance*. New York: W.W. Norton, 1998.

Jolly, Penny Howell. "Learned Reading, Vernacular Seeing: Jacques Daret's Presentation in the Temple." *The Art Bulletin* 82, no. 3 (2000): 428–52. DOI: 10.1080/00043079.2000.10786944.

Jones, Pamela. "Federico Borromeo as a Patron of Landscapes and Still Lifes: Christian Optimism in Italy ca. 1600." *The Art Bulletin* 70, no. 2 (1988): 261–72. DOI: 10.2307/3051119.

Justice, Phyllis. "A New Fashion in Imitating Christ." In *The Year 1000: Religious and Social Response to the Turning of the First Millennium*, edited by Michael Frassetto, 165–86. 3rd edition. New York: Palgrave Macmillan, 2002.

Katz, Steven T. "The 'Conservative' Character of Mystical Experience." In *Mysticism and Religious Traditions*, edited by Steven T. Katz, 3–60. Oxford: Oxford University Press, 1983.

Kovesi Kellerby, Catherine M. *Sumptuary Law in Italy: 1200–1500*. Oxford Historical Monographs. Oxford: Oxford University Press, 2002.

Kelley, Nicole. "'The Punishment of the Devil Was Apparent in the Torment of the Human Body': Epilepsy in Early Christianity." In *Disability Studies and Biblical Literature*, edited by Candida Moss and Jeremy Schipper, 205–21. London: Palgrave Macmillan, 2016.

Kiely, Robert. "Further Considerations of the Holy Stigmata of St. Francis: Where Was Brother Leo?" *Religion and the Arts* 3, no. 1 (1999): 22–28. DOI: 10.1163/156852999X00024.

Kiser, Lisa. "Animal Economies: The Lives of St. Francis in Their Medieval Contexts." *Isle: Interdisciplinary Studies in Literature and Environment* 11, no. 1 (Winter 2004): 121–38. DOI: 10.1093/isle/11.1.121.

Knox, Giles. "The Unified Church Interior in Baroque Italy: S. Maria Maggiore in Bergamo." *The Art Bulletin* 82, no. 4 (2000): 679–701. DOI: 10.2307/3051417.

Lackey, Douglas. "Giotto in Padua: A New Geography of the Human Soul." *The Journal of Ethics* 9, nos. 3–4 (2005): 551–72. DOI: 10.1007/s10892-005-3527-8.

Ladis, Andrew, ed. *Giotto and the World of Early Italian Art: An Anthology of Literature, Vol. 4: Franciscanism: The Papacy, and Art in the Age of Giotto: Assisi and Rome*. New York: Garland Publishing, Inc. 1998.

Lasansky, D. Medina. "Body Elision: Acting Out the Passion at the Italian Sacri Monti." In *The Body in Early Modern Italy*, edited by Julia L. Hairston and Walter Stephens, 249–73. Baltimore: Johns Hopkins University Press, 2010.

Le Goff, Jacques. *St. Francis of Assisi*. Translated by Christine Rhone. London: Routledge, 2004.

Leatherbarrow, David. *Topographical Stories: Studies in Landscape and Architecture*. Philadelphia: University of Pennsylvania Press, 2004.

Legend of the Three Companions. In *Francis of Assisi: Early Documents, Vol. 2: The Founder*, edited and translated by Regis Armstrong, O.F.M. Cap., et al., 66–110. New York: New City Press, 2000.

Levin, David. *Modernity and the Hegemony of Vision*. Berkeley: University of California Press, 1993.

Logan, Donald F. *A History of the Church in the Middle Ages*. London: Routledge, 2012.

Longo, Pier Giorgo. "Immagini e immaginario di San Francesco al Sacro Monte di Orta." In *Antiche Guide del Sacro Monte di Orta*, edited by Loredana Racchelli, 11–69. Orta: Ente di Gestione delle Reserve Naturali Speciali del Sacro Monte di Orta, del Monte Mesma e del Colle della Torre di Buccione, 2008.

Love, Nicholas. *Mirror of the Blessed Life of Jesus Christ: A Critical Edition*. Edited by Michael G. Sargent. New York: Garland, 1992.

MacDonald, A.A., H.N.B. Ridderbos, and R.M. Schlusemann, eds. *The Broken Body, Passion Devotion in Late-Medieval Culture*. Groningen: Egbert Forsten, 1998.

MacVicar, Thaddeus, O.F.M. Cap. *The Franciscan Spirituals and the Capuchin Reform*. Edited by Charles McCarron, O.F.M. Cap. St. Bonaventure: The Franciscan Institute, 1986.

Mallè, Luigi. *Figurative Art in Piedmont*. 2 vols. Translated by Shelia Freeman et al. Turin: Officine Di Villar Perosa S.P.A., 1972.

Mander, Micaela. "Mazzola, Giuseppe Gaudenzio." In *Dizionario Biografico degli Italiani*. http://www.treccani.it/enciclopedia/giuseppe-gaudenzio-mazzola_(Dizionario-Biografico)/.

Manzini, Fr. Angelo Maria, O.F.M. Cap. *Sacro Monte of Orta*. Orta: Community of the Franciscan Friars, Custodian of the Sacro Monte of Orta, 2006.

Mark of Lisbon. *Croniche de gli Ordini istituiti dal P.S. Francesco: Nella quale si contiene la sua vita, la morte, & I suoi miracoli, e de'suoi discepoli*. 3 vols. Translated by Horatio Diola of Bologna. 1605.

———. *The Chronicle and Institution of the Order of the Seraphicall Father S. Francis Conteyning his Life, his Death, and his Miracles, and of all his Holie Disciples and

Companions. 2 vols. Translated by William Cape (England: John Heigham, 1618).

———. *Croniche degli ordini instituiti dal P. San Francesco. Prima parte divisa in dieci libri che contiente la sua vita, la sua morte e i suoi miracoli, composta dal R.P. Fra Marco da Lisbona, traduz. dal portoghese.* Naples, 1680.

McGrath, Thomas. "Dominicans, Franciscans, and the Art of Political Rivalry: Two Drawings and a Fresco by Giovanni Battista della Rovere." *Renaissance Studies* 25, no. 2 (2011): 185–207. DOI: 10.1111/j.1477-4658.2010.00665.x.

McNamer, Sarah. *Affective Meditation and the Invention of Medieval Compassion.* Philadelphia: University of Pennsylvania Press, 2010.

———. "The Debate on the Origins of the Meditationes vitae Christi: Recent Arguments and Prospects for Future Research." *Archivum Franciscanum Historicum* 111, nos. 1–2 (June 2018): 65–112.

Meditations on the Life of Christ: An Illustrated Manuscript of the Fourteenth Century. Edited and Translated by Isa Ragusa and Rosalie B. Green. Princeton Monographs in Art and Archaeology 35. Princeton: Princeton University Press, 1961.

Merelli, Fedele, O.F.M. Cap. "P. Cleto da Castelletto Ticino Cappuccino (d. 1619): Note per una biografia." *Communicare Network: Radio Missione Francescana.* http://www.comunicare.it/ofmcap/archivio/p.cleto/pcleto.html.

Miladinov, Marina. "Usage of the Sainthood in the Reformation Controversy: Saints and Witnesses of Truth in Matthias Flacius Illyricus." *New Europe College Yearbook* 10 (2002–2003), 15–61. https://hdl.handle.net/2027/inu.30000107488102.

Milan Cathedral. *Annali della fabbrica del duomo di Milano: dall'origine fino al presente.* 6 vols. Milan: G. Brigola, 1880–1883.

Mitchell, Nathan. *The Mystery of the Rosary: Marian Devotion and the Reinvention of Catholicism.* New York: New York University Press, 2009.

Mols, R., S.J. "Borromeo, Charles, St." In *New Catholic Encyclopedia*, Vol. 2, edited by Thomas Carson and Joann Cerrito, 539–41. 2nd edition. Detroit: Thompson Gale, 2002.

Mooney, Catherine. "Imitatio Christi or Imitatio Mariae? Clare of Assisi and her Interpreters." In *Gendered Voices: Medieval Saints and their Interpreters*, edited by Catherine Mooney, 52–77. The Middle Ages Series. Philadelphia: University of Pennsylvania Press, 1999.

Morgan, David. *Visual Piety: A History and Theory of Popular Religious Images.* Berkeley: University of California Press, 1998.

———. *The Sacred Gaze, Religious Visual Culture in Theory and Practice.* Berkeley: University of California Press, 2005.

Neilson, Nancy Ward. "Camillo Procaccini's Etched Transfiguration." *Burlington Magazine* 118, no. 883 (1976): 699–701. https://www.jstor.org/stable/87856.

Muessig, Carolyn. "Signs of Salvation: The Evolution of Stigmatic Spirituality before Francis of Assisi." *Church History* 82, no. 1 (2013): 40–68. DOI: 10.1017/S000964071200251X.

———. "The Stigmata Debate in Theology and Art in the Later Middle Ages." In *The Authority of the Word: Reflecting on Image and Text in Northern Europe, 1400–1700*, edited by Celeste Brusati, et al., 481–504. Vol. 20 of Intersections. Leiden: Brill, 2012. DOI: 10.1163/9789004226432.

Murray, Peter, and Linda Murray. *A Dictionary of Christian Art.* Oxford: Oxford University Press, 2004.

Nagel, Alexander. *The Controversy of Renaissance Art.* Chicago: University of Chicago Press, 2011.

Neilson, Nancy Ward. "Two Drawings by Carlo Francesco Nuvolone." *Master Drawings* 23–24, no. 2 (1985–1986): 212–13, 286–87. https://www.jstor.org/stable/1553767.

Nevet, Dolev. "The Observant Believer as Participant Observer: 'Ready–Mades' avant la lettre at the Sacro Monte, Varallo, Sesia." *Assaph: Studies in Art History* 2

(1996): 175–93. https://arts.tau.ac.il/sites/arts.tau.ac.il/files/media_server/Arts/Research/Journals/asaf/art-history/pdf/art_book1996.pdf.

Nova, Alessandro. "'Popular' Art in Renaissance Italy: Early Response to the Holy Mountain at Varallo." In *Reframing the Renaissance: Visual Culture in Europe and Latin America, 1450–1650*, edited by Claire Farago, 113–26. New Haven: Yale University Press, 1995.

Novarina, Valère, and Marc Bayard. *Sacri Monti Incandescence baroque en Italie du Nord*. Paris: L'Autre Monde, 2012.

O'Dea, Linus, O.S.F. "The History of the Crown." In *Mary in the Franciscan Order: Proceedings of the Third National Meeting of Franciscan Teaching Sisterhoods*, edited by Ignatius Brady et al., 173–83. St. Bonaventura: Franciscan Institute, 1953.

O'Reilly, Sean. "Roman versus Romantic: Classical Roots in the Origins of a Roman Catholic Ecclesiology." *Architectural History* 40 (1997): 222–40. DOI: 10.2307/1568676.

Orsenigo, Cesare. *Life of St. Charles Borromeo*. Translated by Rudolph Kraus. St. Louis: B. Herder, 1943.

Pacciarotti, Giuseppe. *La Pintura Barroca en Italia*. Translated by Beatriz López González. Madrid, Spain: AKAL, 2000.

Pansters, Krijn. "Dreams in Medieval Saints' Lives: Saint Francis of Assisi." *Dreaming* 19, no. 1 (2009): 55–63. DOI: 10.1037/a0015265.

Panzanelli, Roberta. *Pilgrimage in Hyperreality: Images and Imagination in the Early Phase of the "New Jerusalem" at Varallo (1486–1530)*. PhD Diss., UCLA, 1999.

Papale, Alfredo. *Cultura Materiale del XVIII secolo. Le Botteghe di Tessuit di Giovanni Righetti ad Orta e Miasino. Estr. orig. da Boll. Stor. per la Prov. di Novara*, 1, 1979. Novara: Tip. La Cupola Novara, 1979.

Piccaluga, Gabriella Ferri. "Bussola, Dionigi." In *Dizionario Biografico degli Italiani*. http://www.treccani.it/enciclopedia/dionigi-bussola_(Dizionario-Biografico)/.

Portoghesi, Paolo. "Antonelli, Alessandro." *Dizionario Biografico degli Italiani*. http://www.treccani.it/enciclopedia/alessandro-antonelli_(Dizionario-Biografico)/.

Prodi, Paolo. "Bascapè, Carlo." *Dizionario Biografico degli Italiani*. http://www.treccani.it/enciclopedia/carlo-bascape_(Dizionario-Biografico)/.

Racchelli, Loredana, ed. *Antiche Guide del Sacro Monte di Orta*. Orta: Ente di Gestione delle Reserve Naturali Speciali del Sacro Monte di Orta, del Monte Mesma e del Colle della Torre di Buccione, 2008.

Racinet, Auguste. *Le costume historique*. Edited by Françoise Tétart-Vittu. Cologne: Taschen, 2003.

Ranft, Patricia. *How the Doctrine of Incarnation Shaped Western Culture*. Lanham: Rowman and Littlefield, 2012.

Ripa, Cesare. *Baroque and Rococo Pictorial Imagery, The 1758–60 Hertel Edition of Ripa's "Iconologia." Dover Pictorial Archives*. Edited by Edward A. Maser. New York: Doubleday, 1971.

Rivers, Kimberly. *Preaching the Memory of Virtue and Vice: Memory, Images, and Preaching in the Late Middle Ages*. Turnhout: Brepols, 2010.

Robinson, Paschal. "Bartholomew of Pisa." In *The Catholic Encyclopedia*, Vol. 2, edited by Charles Herbermann et al., 317. New York: Robert Appleton Company, 1907.

Robson, Michael. *The Franciscans in the Middle Ages*. Woodbridge: Boydell Press, 2006.

Romano, Giovanni. "D'Enrico [Family]." In *Dizionario Biografico degli Italiani*. http://www.treccani.it/enciclopedia/d-enrico_(Dizionario-Biografico)/.

———. "D'Enrico, Giovanni." In *Dizionario Biografico degli Italiani*. http://www.treccani.it/enciclopedia/giovanni-d-enrico/.

———. "D'Enrico, Melchiorre." *Dizionario Biografico degli Italiani*. http://www.treccani.it/enciclopedia/melchiorre-d-enrico_(Dizionario-Biografico)/.

Ross, Leslie. *Medieval Art: A Topical Dictionary*. Santa Barbara: Greenwood Publishing Group, 1996.

Rossi, Paola. "Falconi, Bernardo." *Dizionario Biografico degli Italiani*. http://www.treccani.it/enciclopedia/bernardo-falconi_(Dizionario-Biografico)/.

"Rusnati, Giuseppe." In *Dizionario Biografico degli Italiani*. http://www.treccani.it/enciclopedia/giuseppe-rusnati/.

Russell, Jeffrey Burton. *The Devil: Perceptions of Evil from Antiquity to Primitive Christianity*. Ithaca: Cornell University Press, 1987.

Sabatier, Paul. *Life of St. Francis of Assisi*. Translated by Louise Seymour Houghton. London: Hodder & Stoughton, 1919.

Sales, Francis de. *Treatise on the Love of God*. Translated by Henry Benedict Mackey, O.S.B. Westport: Greenwood Publishing Group, 1971.

Salter, David. *Holy and Noble Beasts: Encounters with Animals in Medieval Literature*. Rochester: D.S. Brewer, 2001.

Serafini, Alessandro. "Mazzucchelli, Pier Francesco, detto il Morazzone." In *Dizionario Biografico degli Italiani*. http://www.treccani.it/enciclopedia/mazzucchelli-pier-francesco-detto-il-morazzone_(Dizionario-Biografico)/.

Schiller, Gertrud. *Iconography of Christian Art*. 2 vols. London: Lund Humphries, 1972.

Scolnicov, Hanna. *Women's Theatrical Space*. Cambridge: Cambridge University Press, 1994.

"Spiegazione Delle Sagre Capelle Fondate Sopra Il Monte D'Orta." In *Antiche Guide del Sacro Monte di Orta*, edited by Loredana Racchelli, 73–123. Orta: Ente di Gestione delle Riserve Naturali Speciali del Sacro Monte di Orta, del Monte Mesma e del Colle della Torre di Buccione, 2008.

Stallings-Taney, C. Mary. "The Pseudo-Bonaventure 'Meditaciones vite Christi': Opus Integrum." *Franciscan Studies* 55 (1998): 253–80. DOI: 10.1353/frc.1998.0029.

Stanbury, Sarah. "The Virgin's Gaze: Spectacle and Transgression in Middle English Lyrics of the Passion." *PMLA* 106, no. 5 (Oct. 1991): 1083–93. DOI: 10.2307/462681.

Stierle, Karl-Heinz. "Story as Exemplum—Exemplum as Story: On the Pragmatics and Poetics of Narrative Texts." In *New Perspectives in German Literary Criticism*, edited by Richard Amacher and Victor Lange, 75–93. Princeton: Princeton University Press, 1979.

Struthers, Sally. *Donatello's Putti: Their Genesis, Importance, and Influence on Quattrocento Sculpture and Painting*. 2 vols. PhD Diss., Ohio State University, 1992.

Suleiman, Susan Rubin. *Authoritarian Fictions: The Ideological Novel as a Literary Genre*. New York: Columbia University Press, 1983.

Swanson, Robert. "Passion and Practice: The Social and Ecclesiastical Implications of Passion Devotion in the Late Middle Ages." In *The Broken Body: Passion Devotion in Late-Medieval Culture*, edited by A. MacDonald et al., 1–30. Groningen: Egbert Forsten, 1998.

Symcox, Geoffrey. "Varallo and Oropa: Two Sacri Monti and the House of Savoy." In *La Maison de Savoie et les Alpes: emprise, innovation, identifications XVe–XIXe siècle; Actes du 4e Colloque international des Sabaudian Studies 15–17 mai 2014, Grenoble*, edited by Stéphane Gal and Laurent Perrillat, 151–66. Grenoble: Université de Savoie Mont Blanc, 2015.

———. *Jerusalem in the Alps: The Sacro Monte of Varallo and the Sanctuaries of North-Western Italy*. Cursor Mundi 37. Edited by Heather Sottong. Turnhout: Brepols, 2019.

Tatai, Erzsébet. "An Iconographical Approach to the Representations of the Devil." In *Christian Demonology and Popular Mythology*, edited by G. Klaniczay and É. Pócs, vol. 2, 54–70. Budapest: Central European University Press, 2005.

Terry-Fritsch, Allie. "Performing the Renaissance Body and Mind: Somaesthetic Style and Devotional Practice a the Sacro Monte di Varallo." *Open Arts Journal* 4 (Winter 2014–15): 111–32. DOI: 10.5456/issn.2050–3679/2015w07.

"The Assisi Compilation." In *Francis of Assisi: Early Documents*, Vol. 2: *The Founder*, edited and translated by Regis Armstrong, O.F.M. Cap., et al., 118–230. New York: New City Press, 2000.

"The Considerations on the Holy Stigmata." In *The Little Flowers of Saint Francis*, edited and translated by Raphael Brown, 171–218. New York: Image Books/Doubleday, 1958.

Thomas of Celano. *The Life of Saint Francis*. In *Francis of Assisi: Early Documents*, Vol. 1: *The Saint*, edited and translated by Regis Armstrong, O.F.M. Cap., et al., 180–308. New York: New City Press, 1999.

———. *The Legend for Use in the Choir*. In *Francis of Assisi: Early Documents*, Vol. 1: *The Saint*, edited and translated by Regis Armstrong, O.F.M. Cap., et al., 319–26. New York: New City Press, 1999.

———. *The Remembrance of the Desire of a Soul*. In *Francis of Assisi: Early Documents*, Vol. 3: *The Founder*, edited and translated by Regis Armstrong, O.F.M. Cap., et al., 239–93. New York: New City Press, 2000.

———. *Treatise on the Miracles of St. Francis*. In *Francis of Assisi: Early Documents*, Vol. 2: *The Founder*, edited and translated by Regis Armstrong, O.F.M. Cap., et al., 399–468. New York: New City Press, 2000.

Tolan, John. "The Friar and the Sultan: Francis of Assisi's Mission to Egypt." *European Review* 16, no. 1 (2008): 118–21. DOI: 10.1017/S1062798708000124.

———. *Saint Francis and the Sultan: The Curious History of a Christian-Muslim Encounter*. Oxford: Oxford University Press, 2009.

Turner, Victor, and Edith Turner. *Image and Pilgrimage in Christian Culture*. New York: Columbia University Press, 1978.

Tylus, Jane. "Women at the Windows: 'Commedia dell'arte' and Theatrical Practice in Early Modern Italy." *Theatre Journal* 49, no. 3 (October 1997): 323–42. DOI: 10.1353/tj.1997.0072.

Van Os, H. W. "St. Francis of Assisi as a Second Christ in Early Italian Painting." *Simiolus* 7, no. 3 (1974): 115–32. DOI: 10.2307/3780297.

Vannini, Guido, and Riccardo Pacciani. *La Gerusalemme di S. Vivaldo in Valdelsa*. Montaione: Comune di Montaione, 1998.

Vauchez, André. *Sainthood in the Later Middle Ages*. Translated by Jean Birrell. Cambridge: Cambridge University Press, 1997.

Vauchez, André. *Francis of Assisi: The Life and Afterlife of a Medieval Saint*. Translated by Michael Cusato. New Haven: Yale University Press, 2012.

———. "The Stigmata of Francis and Its Medieval Detractors." *Greyfriars Review* 13, no. 1 (1999): 61–89.

Voelker, E. Cecelia. "Borromeo's Influence on Sacred Art and Architecture." In *San Carlo Borromeo: Catholic Reform and Ecclesiastical Politics in the Second Half of the Sixteenth Century*, edited by John Headley and John Tomaro, 172–87. Washington, DC: Folger Books, 1988.

Voragine, Jacobus de. *The Golden Legend, or, Lives of the Saints*. Edited by F.S. Ellis and Translated by William Caxton. 7 vols. London: J.M. Dent, 1922.

Wandel, Lee Palmer. "The Poverty of Christ." In *The Reformation of Charity: The Secular and Religious in Early Modern Poor Relief*, edited by Thomas M. Safley, 15–29. Leiden: Brill, 2003.

Westervelt, Benjamin. "The Prodigal Son at Santa Justina: The Homily in the Borromean Reform of Pastoral Preaching." *The Sixteenth Century Journal* 32, no. 1 (2001): 109–26. DOI: 10.2307/2671397.

Wenzel, Siegfried. *Fasciculus Morum: A Fourteenth Century Preacher's Handbook*. University Park: Pennsylvania State University Press, 1989.

Wharton, Annabel. *Selling Jerusalem: Relics, Replicas, Theme Parks*. Chicago: Chicago University Press, 2006.

Wittkower, Rudolf. *Idea and Image: Studies in the Italian Renaissance*. London: Thames and Hudson, 1978.

Wolf, Kenneth Baxter. *Poverty of Riches*. Oxford: Oxford University Press, 2003.

Wycliffe, John. *Johannes Wyclif Tractatus de ecclesia*. Edited by Johann Loserth. London: Wyclif Society, 1886.

Zanzi, Luigi. *Sacri Monti e Dintorni: Studi sulla cultura religiosa e artistica della Controriforma*, 2nd edition. Milan: Jaca Book, 2005.

Made in the USA
Monee, IL
09 January 2025